TESSA VERNEY WHEELER

Tessa Verney Wheeler

Women and Archaeology
Before World War Two

L. C. CARR

OXFORD
UNIVERSITY PRESS

OXFORD
UNIVERSITY PRESS

Great Clarendon Street, Oxford, OX2 6DP,
United Kingdom

Oxford University Press is a department of the University of Oxford.
It furthers the University's objective of excellence in research, scholarship,
and education by publishing worldwide. Oxford is a registered trade mark of
Oxford University Press in the UK and in certain other countries

British Library Cataloguing in Publication Data

Data available

Library of Congress Cataloguing in Publication Data

Data available

ISBN 978-0-19-964022-5

Printed in Great Britain
on acid-free paper by
MPG Books Group, Bodmin and King's Lynn

With loving gratitude to
Cristina and Simon Carr
Caleb Carr
Martin Henig

'Mrs. Wheeler is as little as he is tall, but I cannot describe her as his complement, because no one would like to say which was his and which was her share of the work.'

Yorkshire Post, 21 October 1930

'A capable woman of affairs, a very hard worker, she retained the dainty airs and graces, and, if need be, the weapons of woman.'

Cyril Fox, 'Tessa Verney Wheeler, F.S.A.' (1936)

'What we really want to find is how the people lived in those days and what they did.'

Tessa Verney Wheeler at Verulamium in 1931

Acknowledgements

One of the delights of this research has been the enthusiasm with which others have greeted it, and these acknowledgements are as a result an unusual combination of the personal and the professional. At the head of the list must come my original D.Phil supervisors, Sir Barry Cunliffe and Professor Chris Gosden. I was fortunate to receive their guidance, and hope they find the results worth their considerable efforts. I am particularly grateful to Professor Cunliffe for his immediate, enthusiastic interest in the project, back when it was still only two sides of A4.

Initial research into the Jacquetta Hawkes archives at the University of Bradford was undertaken thanks to Alison Cullingford. At the National Museum of Wales, Evan Chapman, Kristine Chapman, and Jenny Evans provided patient, liberal assistance. Nigel Young, webmaster of www.caerleon.net, produced a delightful photograph of the 1927 amphitheatre dig team. He also introduced me to Cecil Davies, who I regret very much is no longer present to see the results of our time together. At the Museum of London, Sally Brooks guided me through the London Museum archives, and introduced me to Tessa Verney's distant cousin Peter Kilburn. The staff of the Somerset County Records Office in Taunton were indefatigable in the successful search for the Wedlake archive, and heroic in their efforts to copy the most important sections during the short time I was able to visit. Sally James guided me through the documents at Lydney Park in Gloucestershire, and Rupert Bathurst, the current Viscount Bledisloe, enthusiastically permitted photo use. Claire Thornton, David Thorold, Kate Warren, and the entire staff of the Verulamium Museum were a continued pleasure to associate with. The staff of the Manuscripts Room at the Bodleian Library allowed me to examine the unsorted personal papers of C. F. C. Hawkes and J. N. L. Myres. At the Library of the Society of Antiquaries of London, Bernard Nurse and Adrian James provided calm help over repeated visits; and the Antiquaries, via Jayne Phenton, provided some of the earliest forums for the dissemination and discussion of this work. Peter Woodward and Jon Murden of the Dorset County Museum put the excellent photographs and ephemera of the Maiden Castle archives at my disposal.

Dr Beatrice de Cardi gave this project heartening encouragement from a very early stage. Dr Margaret Drower, herself an eminent biographer of archaeologists, gave a delightful personal account of the Verulamium excavations. Diana Bonakis Webster shared her memories of researching C. F. C. Hawkes in the 1920s and 1930s. The Reverend David Ridgeway, Vicar of St Stephen's Church in St Albans, provided photographs of and information on his predecessor, Harold Cavalier. Professor Sheppard Frere graciously wrote a letter of reminiscence. Grahame Soffe was a friendly conduit for other sources. Dr Kay Prag was helpful in considering Kathleen Kenyon. Mr Peter Kilburn contributed a draft copy of the family genealogy he is in the process of assembling. P. J. Smith of Cambridge read an early draft of the complete thesis. Lisa Westcott, of *Current Archaeology*, published one of the earliest articles growing from this research. The staff of the Records Office at University College London found the few academic records remaining for Tessa Verney, and the UCL archives produced her last surviving student notebooks. Mr Raymond Albert, the caretaker of 2 Cardinal Mansions, allowed me to visit the Wheeler's former flat in that building. Miss Marlena Whiting put her research skills at my disposal and extended Verney Wheeler's bibliography by several key items. Most importantly, the unstinting help of Carol Wheeler Pettman, Tessa Verney Wheeler's granddaughter, was vital to this work. She has been equally generous with her archives, her friendship, and her affection, and I am very grateful to her.

At Oxford, travel funding was provided by the Meyerstein Fund and Exeter College. Further support was provided by English Heritage via a 2007 Presentation of Heritage Research Award, and by the staff of the Oxfordshire Museum Resource Centre (particularly Kirsty Bell and Pam Triggs) via a three-year post as a curatorial assistant. Professor James Basker of Barnard College employed me for four years as a summer teacher, and more importantly gave me good, tough advice on getting a book out of the door.

Professor Margarita Díaz-Andreu of Durham University extended valuable insights and an introduction to Hilary O'Shea of the Oxford University Press, who has worked patiently for several years to help me turn a D.Phil. into a 'real book'. I am extremely grateful to her, and to everyone at the OUP, especially Taryn Campbell, Tessa Eaton, Kathleen Fearn, Kate Hellier, Desirée Kellerman, Hayley Buckley, and Sarah Barrett, who together oversaw the production process. Simon Ford, Stephen Forrest, and Paul Schwarz edited successive drafts of the original thesis and continuously advanced its expansion into this volume. They are good editors, but even better friends. Thank you, Brains Trust! Malin Engdahl Patterson, Tatiana Grigorenko, Eva Jaffe, and Dorothy Sippo are my first and best friends. Thanks for putting up with me, ladies! Paul Schwarz and his partner, Louisa Legge, have been my unflappable home base in London for many years now. I am truly thankful for the affectionate companionship of Gabriela Carr, Cessa Coté, Lynne Davis, Gwen Denny, Abby Dunn, Milena Grabacovic, Dan Harris, Beatrice Kitzinger, Dave and Caroline Legg, Vicky Liakoupolous, Kate Moriarty, Edmund Robinson, Veronica Vasco, Lindsay Weichel, and Elizabeth Weinfeld. Finally, my dear husband, Michael Corey, is in all ways the love of my life. He knows why, and he knows how much.

No note here could be sufficient to thank my parents, Simon and Cristina, my uncle Caleb, and my mentor, Father Martin Henig. The dedication of this volume is some small indication of my gratitude.

Contents

Abbreviations

A full list of archives consulted may be found in the bibliography.

ASSM   Addey and Stanhope School minutes, 1908–1911
CADW   Cadw archives
DCMA   Archives of the Dorset Natural History and Archaeological
        Society at the Dorset County Museum
JHA   Jacquetta Hawkes archives
MOLA   Museum of London archives
NMWA   National Museum of Wales archives
SALA   Society of Antiquaries of London archives
SCRO   Somerset County Records Office
TVW   Tessa Verney Wheeler
UCLA   University College London Records Office archives
VMA   Verulamium excavation archives
WFP   Wheeler family papers

List of Illustrations

1

Introduction

This book attempts to understand the pioneering early twentieth-century archaeologist Tessa Verney Wheeler (1893–1936) through an investigation of her life and career. Married to the swashbuckling and long-lived archaeologist R. E. M. Wheeler (1890–1978), Verney Wheeler died relatively young at 42. She has since vanished into the footnotes of archaeology's history. Despite this apparent dismissal, memories of her practical teaching, technical work, and personality were treasured by the young archaeologists who knew her—people like Margaret Drower, V. E. Seton-Williams, and J. N. L. Myres, who themselves are or were the modern archaeological establishment. Verney Wheeler published extensively in her short career, excavated some of the most interesting and well-known Roman sites in England and Wales, and was personally instrumental in the development and opening of the University of London's Institute of Archaeology, one of the first institutions to formally teach archaeology. Alongside her husband, she was also a popular figure in the contemporary illustrated press, often appearing in articles in the *Daily Mail* and other newspapers. She was both her husband's partner and his equal. Yet she has been primarily forgotten today.

In this work, she is rediscovered and reconsidered. Who was this curiously elusive woman, who developed and published such seminal archaeological work? In her professional life, she pioneered a new way to be a woman archaeologist, and thus effectively an intellectual woman. Like many of her female predecessors, she vanishes into her husband's considerable shadow if she is only superficially studied. It is time to rediscover this woman and give her the recognition she merits. This is more than the story of a woman neglected by history. This is the story of *why* she has been so neglected, when the work she did and the people she influenced are still vitally important. The answer can only lie in her life.

VERNEY WHEELER THE PIONEERING ARCHAEOLOGIST

Verney Wheeler's primary importance to technical archaeology—apart from the actual excavations she took part in and directed—may be divided into three main sections. Although this work approaches her output chronologically, having the three overarching theoretical themes of her legacy already in mind as her various projects are discussed will help the reader to understand the progression of her development more clearly.

Technique

This aspect of Verney Wheeler's legacy is the most obvious. Her contribution to modern archaeological method comes mainly through her development of improved techniques of site recording, particularly in her emphasis on objects and their correct documentation. As can be seen in the site notebooks and archives of various sites, especially later sites like Verulamium and Maiden Castle, Verney Wheeler made this part of excavating her particular province, reflecting an association of women with small finds that continues to this day. Her context sheets are of particular interest to the working archaeologist. This methodical approach also informed her emphasis on the stratigraphic recording of features, best seen in the 'teaching notebooks' from Maiden Castle, where her corrections of students' sections shows the importance she placed upon accuracy and clarity.

Verney Wheeler's work with one specific feature, mosaics, will receive particular examination in relation to the fine floors of the Roman town of Verulamium, which provide a case study of her technical facility. Although these floors featured at other Wheeler sites, Verulamium provides the best documentation and most extensive set of mosaics, making it ideal for specific investigation.

Teaching

Past students remember Verney Wheeler as a stimulating teacher, able to explain not just the techniques necessary to an excavator or restorer but also those needed to interpret the resulting data. The 'teaching notebooks' of Maiden Castle have already been mentioned, and will be returned to in greater detail at the appropriate time. While any Wheeler dig could serve as an example of how to involve students in practical archaeology, the Maiden Castle documentary archive allows us to see an almost unique example of Verney Wheeler 'marking up' student work via the annotations she made in their section notebooks. She must have collected and inspected notebooks on a regular basis, as her husband later advised site directors to do in his 1954 textbook *Archaeology from the Earth*.[1] Former students on the site have also recorded memories of the regular, informal classes she held in her hotel room after the day's work was done, either going over the meaning of what had been accomplished in the day, or demonstrating a specific skill; Beatrice de Cardi recalls learning how to clean and wrap a horse skull for museum storage in this way.[2]

The 'teaching' component reaches its high point in the Institute of Archaeology at University College London, in whose 1934 foundation Verney Wheeler played a major role. It opened physically shortly after her death in 1936. Her role in creating not just the Institute, but also its stopgap predecessor at the London Museum and Society of Antiquaries, is an important one.

On a side note, the strong affection she inspired and continues to inspire in her former students, while secondary to the knowledge she imparted, is nonetheless important to bear in mind as additional evidence of her teaching ability. Her pupils may remember her with love today because she was a charming and nurturing figure in their lives, but the respect that accompanies that love reflects her strict expectations of those she taught, and the equally strict example she set in the quality of her own work. Here, the oral and written memories of former Verney Wheeler students such as Veronica Seton-Williams, J. N. L. Myres, and Beatrice de Cardi are invaluable.

---

[1] Wheeler (1954: 135).
[2] Interview with Beatrice de Cardi, 14 November 2006, London.

Public work: bring archaeology to the masses

Moving from Verney Wheeler's concrete physical work excavating, and her less physical but no less concrete work teaching, we come finally to her work with the public, via museums, lecturing, and the press. This is fully explored in the discussion of the London Museum and that of the Press, but is apparent as a growing force throughout her life.

From her first solo dig at the Caerleon amphitheatre to the excavation she was engaged on at Maiden Castle when she died, very few of her archaeological projects went without press and public scrutiny. Her husband's superb engagement with the newspapers was primarily responsible for this, but Verney Wheeler's own role must be explored as well. Both Wheelers exploited the media as a medium to explain and present their joint work to the public. As they saw it, the importance of archaeologists involving the public in their work lay far beyond mere fundraising. It was also almost a moral responsibility.[3]

As public money supported archaeology more and more, via private donations and government funding, these ideas became the norm. For the Wheelers, finding innovative methods to fund proposed excavations was frequently as much of a challenge as the actual digging. Verney Wheeler's endless lecturing work grew out of this double desire to educate and obtain funding for further work. She spoke to crowds at the London Museum, archaeological and antiquarian societies across the country, schools, reporters, casual tourists, and her own workmen. This aspect of her official life dates back to its very inception in Wales, and may be followed from there almost to the moment of her death. In it, as in so much, the Wheelers were preceded by a penniless and fiercely brilliant mentor in William Flinders Petrie, whose economically run digs became famous for their Spartan nature.[4] His wife, Hilda, was also Verney Wheeler's first great model of how an archaeological spouse might be expected to comport herself, though it was a pattern she quickly surpassed.

---

[3] Wheeler (1955: 76, 231).   [4] Drower (1985: 217).

WOMEN AND ARCHAEOLOGY: ISSUES OF STUDY

The primary goal of this work is not to present a formal defence or history of the abstract concept 'women in archaeology'. It is to illustrate the life and work of one woman, as unique in her career as any of her contemporaries, and to use her as a *point d'appui* for a greater understanding of the female role in British archaeology prior to the Second World War. While the feminist and historical issues surrounding the study of women in archaeology in this period are not the central object of discussion here, an awareness of these concerns will lend depth to our main topic. With that proviso, some basic topics affecting this field should be understood before beginning on a more in-depth study of Tessa Verney Wheeler.

Several theoretical (or feminist) and practical (or historical) questions should be answered at the outset. Most obviously, why study 'women and archaeology' specifically—is it really necessary to create a sub-discipline of archaeological history with that name? It is certainly becoming one at the moment, regardless of need. Biographies of female archaeologists are proliferating, mainly in essay form, and theoretical discussions of current and historical issues of gender in archaeology have become a focus of research. This extends both to discussions of how an archaeologist's gender may affect his or her interpretation of data, and to discussions of how gender may affect an archaeologist's career and professional opportunities.[5]

Marie Louise Stig Sørensen, one of the clearest thinkers in this field, gives a good, simple outline of the main reasons driving the specific study of women in archaeology in her 1998 essay on the subject.[6] She perceives five main needs.

> [1: to] set the record straight: role model and equity research . . . [2: to determine the] distinct female contribution . . . [3:] integration [of

---

[5] A few recent examples: Gero and Conkey (eds.) 1991; Claassen (1994); Díaz-Andreu and Sørensen (1998); Cohen and Joukowsky (2004). These volumes consist of collected essays by mainly female authors. The editors are exclusively female. The exclusion of men from women's studies, and whether that exclusion was or still is necessary, is no less an issue in archaeology than in any other field.

[6] Sørensen (1998).

women] into the discipline ... [4: the] social impact on [the] discipline
and its product ... [5:] characterizing the individual.[7]

The accuracy of this assessment is apparent in our study of Verney
Wheeler, which clearly reflects Sørensen's theory of basic concepts. In
terms of equity research, it is a case of recognizing and crediting her
for the important work she did and techniques she developed. This
recognition of her specific contribution to archaeology may lead in
turn to an appreciation of the unaccredited contribution other, more
anonymous women in her position may have also made during the
same period. Verney Wheeler is an obvious integrator of the discipline on a personal level, but her social impact also comes in the form
of the women and men she trained and sent out to become the great
archaeologists of the next generation. These archaeologists further
integrated the discipline, and continued to open it to a wider female
perspective. Most importantly, Verney Wheeler is a textbook example
of a woman who worked within the limited gender role society
allowed her, creating a fulfilling personal career as an intellectual.
Her accomplishments are impressive by either gender's standards. If
she had been a man, the work she did would have the same value, and
we would still be interested in her career.

The phrase 'textbook example' is not metaphorical. Where there
have been prior mentions of Verney Wheeler in academic studies, she
is usually given as an example (often alongside Hilda Petrie) of a
woman whose career grew out of and into her husband's so successfully that it is now nigh-impossible to separate the two.[8] Previous
attempts to do so are rare and have not been noticeably successful,
perhaps because the level of study and research required has not been
within the feasible remit of the general studies in which they have
appeared.[9] One book's example may represent them all.

> Women in professional partnerships, however supportive the private
> relationship, have rarely been given full credit for their work, either by
> themselves or by the discipline. The tendency for both partners in
> marriages between archaeologists to work in the same field and often
> on the same sites, furthermore, makes it difficult for later biographers to
> unravel their individual contributions, as with Tessa and Mortimer

---

[7] Sørensen (1998: 34–47).
[8] Besides the other examples given here, see also Champion (1998).
[9] E.g. Hudson (1981: 106–7).

Wheeler. In their case there have been declared attempts to 'rescue' Tessa and to show how in fact she was the practicing field archaeologist, and that the management and daily decision-making on famous excavations such as Maiden Castle were in fact mainly done by her [...] but as yet their separate identities as archaeologists have not been properly established.[10]

The question of whether the Wheelers should have separate professional identities is, of course, central to this book.

There is another aspect to studying women archaeologists of the past via biography, touched on by Sørensen as well as by almost everyone embarking on such a work. That is the need for the acknowledgement and celebration—though hopefully not creation—of a heroic female past, for the sake of posthumous equity and also to inspire modern women working or considering careers as archaeologists.

Let's face it, we all need examples, role models and idols, and few female scholars can serve that purpose.[11]

In fairness, L. B. Jorgensen is describing the history of Danish archaeology. British archaeology is rather more fortunate; different cultural developments in the United Kingdom over the past two centuries mean that a larger group of female scholars can serve as potential inspiration to their successors. Many of them are discussed here; apart from Verney Wheeler herself, Margaret Murray and Kathleen Kenyon, among others, will appear in these pages.

The accomplishments of these role models need no artificial enhancement; as in Verney Wheeler's case, publication records, teaching work, and excavation histories can provide enough proof to support a woman's or a man's claim to fame. The gender difference usually lies in the amount of digging required to unearth the material evidence of that proof.

All cultures need heroes to live up to or live down, and academic cultures are no different. Archaeology has traditionally found its founder figures in the great adventurer archaeologists: in Glyn Daniel's classic 1981 history of the subject we find Lane Fox Pitt-Rivers, William Flinders Petrie, and R. E. M. Wheeler prominently featured.[12] Daniel focused on conventionally heroic

---

[10] Sørensen (1998: 50–5)1.
[11] Jorgensen (1998: 221).
[12] Daniel (1981).

males—dashing military men like Pitt-Rivers and Wheeler, and great, unstoppable excavators like Petrie. There was and is an assumption within the industry that 'true' archaeology involves large-scale invasive excavation,[13] as opposed to, say, curatorial or interpretative work. There is a tied assumption that the initial evidence-gathering digging (virile, open-air, physical) is properly the province of men, while the subsequent interpretive work of objects study and conservation (feminine, domestic, delicate) is that of women. Tracy Sweely has made the seductive argument that this phenomenon represents a subconscious reflection of prehistoric tribal divisions between male hunters—mobile, ranging away from the camp to bring back valuable commodities—and female gatherers or caretakers—sedentary, staying in place to process male produce and supervise crops, children, and the home.[14] It is an interesting idea, though of course more useful as a concept than a guide.

When women are mentioned in archaeology's history, it is often as Verney Wheeler and Hilda Petrie are: as the faithful wife-assistant of a Great Man. As is immediately apparent in examining the Wheelers' earliest Welsh sites, this is quite inaccurate in Verney Wheeler's case. She organized, ran, and published digs independently of, as well as with, her husband; and to his credit, any absence of her name in the historical record is not of his making. He, more than anyone, insisted on her importance.[15]

Even if archaeologists do give in to a perhaps pardonable desire as a culture to create a heroic, active past, women need not be automatically excluded.[16] Women like Verney Wheeler and her contemporaries were as personally varied as the men they worked alongside, and the autobiographies of women like Margaret Murray and M. V. Seton-Williams provide as many conventional adventures as most men's.[17] Despite this, it is more honest to expand (not

---

[13] Champion (1998: 177). Tracy Sweely (1994) discusses the difficulties facing modern women excavators, arising out of but not limited to her own experiences.

[14] Sørensen (1998: 43).

[15] Wheeler (1955: 61).

[16] For 'cowboy archaeologists' and the discipline's self-created past, see Gero (1985), Claassen (1996), and Woodall and Perricone (1981).

[17] Margaret Murray famously described her life as one 'without a single adventure' in her autobiography *My First Hundred Years* (1963: 5). She goes on to describe her childhood in India, where she was born in 1863 six years after the Mutiny. The rest of her life was also not quite without incident. The pressure on biographers to discuss their subjects' lives with unremitting gravity is fortunately not shared by the subjects themselves.

redefine) our definition of past archaeologists (male and female) to include the subjects we now generally consider part of modern archaeology—curatorial work, teaching, objects conservation, land-scape archaeology (essentially what many Victorian antiquarians engaged in), ethnography, and anthropology. Gertrude Bell may not have been practising ethnography in early twentieth-century Baghdad exactly as she would in early twenty-first-century Iraq; if nothing else, Baghdad is rather less safe now than in Bell's day. She *was* engaging in an activity that bears as much resemblance to its modern counterpart as Leonard Woolley's early twentieth-century excavations on Hadrian's Wall do to today's; crude, but a step along the path of development.[18]

Tessa Verney Wheeler was a unique individual, but not a unique phenomenon, and must be understood as part of an appreciably large group of women who worked in various fields of archaeology from the discipline's earliest days. There is a tendency to assume that women in the past accomplished relatively little that can be easily quantified, and that what was achieved was the product of a very small group of exceptional women. Easily quantifiable, in this con-text, usually means similar enough to a man's traditional accomplish-ments to be measured against them; even deliberately feminist writers often fall into the trap of celebrating a woman's work because it is similar to a man's. There is no real remedy for this, except to try to view every subject—male or female, married or single—as an indivi-dual within the society of their own day, not our own.

It is more accurate to say that the intellectually powerful women of the past lack modern publicity. Dale Spender examined the problem memorably in problem in 1982, in her deliberately provocative book *Women of Ideas—and What Men Have Done to Them: From Aphra Behn to Adrienne Rich*. Interestingly, these women (Aphra Behn is an excellent example) did not always lack *contemporary* publicity, often to their personal distress. Newspapers of the past were not normally more interested in fairness or equality than today's—but just like today's, they knew novelty sold. The 1930s groundswell of articles centring on Verney Wheeler are later in date, but still typical of the type.

A scholar never quoted is soon forgotten [. . .] A generation later, only a few will have any idea about who the person in question was.[19]

---

[18] For accounts of both see Bell (1894) and Woolley (1953).
[19] Jorgensen (1998: 221).

In short, there were many fewer women in the field at its outset and during its period of major development than there are today, even allowing for the much smaller population of archaeologists of either gender prior to the twentieth century. *But they were there.*

That does not mean it was easy.[20] There were real practical considerations to be taken into account when women went into the field, though these were often inextricably entangled with simple gender bias. Limiting social conventions also had a role. When Leonard Woolley was excavating at Ur in 1926, he received a 'personal and confidential' letter from George Byron Gordon, the director of the University Museum in Philadelphia (one of his sponsors). Gordon wrote that he was concerned to hear 'slight and inconsequential comment' had arisen around the presence of the only woman volunteer in the camp, Mrs Katherine Keeling.

> Perhaps the presence of a lone woman with four men in camp makes a more interesting figure for some [tourists] [. . .] than the outline of the ziggurats [. . .] Perhaps you will wish to give the matter your best consideration.

The implication is that Katherine Keeling's behaviour is at best unladylike, and may endanger the dig's funding. No museum or university, particularly in America, wishes to be seen as underwriting immorality. What immorality entails is defined and redefined to suit every circumstance, by every controlling force. The only common factor in all the definitions is the desire to limit someone's behaviour.

The 1926 case ended on an ironic note. Woolley replied in suitably shocked tones.

> Mrs Keeling is nearly 40 and has been a widow for over 7 years [. . . with] no intention of remarrying! [. . .] Miss Gertrude Bell several times said what a good thing it was that she was with us.

Bell's name, thus invoked, was effective. The museum backed down. Gordon wrote to say that qualified women, whether married or single, were not disqualified from participating in an excavation. The successful appeal to the higher (female) authority of the 'uncrowned

---

[20] For two examples from other parts of Europe, see essays by Margarita Díaz-Andreu on Spanish women in archaeology over the past century and by Elisabeth Arwill-Nordbladh on the Swedish archaeologist and Verney Wheeler contemporary Hanna Rydh. Both the general and the specific study are included in Díaz-Andreu and Sørensen (1998).

Queen of Iraq' is interesting, and shows perfectly how much power she wielded in Near Eastern archaeology regardless of her gender. In any case, in 1927 Woolley solved the problem definitively by convincing Katherine Keeling to reconsider her widowhood—in other words, he married her.[21] Realistically, accommodation, sanitation, and discipline remained primary difficulties for women excavators. The first two were fairly straightforward, and not gender-limited; any man or woman who wanted to excavate certain locations had to perforce accept the rigours of camp life. Men were often surprised by the level of discomfort women could cheerfully endure. Margaret Murray described excavating with Petrie in Egypt in 1904 with characteristic wit, conscious of the curiosity surrounding his famously uncomfortable camps.

> To anyone accustomed only to a comfortable English bedroom the general effect [...] was like the pictures of the bare and poverty-stricken room in which a suicide is about to kill himself. But appearances are deceitful and the rooms were quite comfortable [...] As to sanitation in a place like Abydos the desert is wide and there are many sheltered hollows.[22]

The question of discipline was potentially more serious, in Britain as well as abroad, but intriguingly it never seems to have really slowed any woman down.[23] On Margaret Murray's first day directing Egyptian diggers, the men simply refused to obey her. She asserted her personality and docked their wages for the day; after that, all ran smoothly.[24] Veronica Seton-Williams never experienced any difficulties in her many years digging in Egypt and the Middle East, and Verney Wheeler was famously beloved in England and Wales.[25] As for their other male colleagues, the educated, upper-class men who made up the intellectual part of an archaeological dig were almost universally the product of single-sex public schools, and often still at university. Their relationships with women, prior to marriage or practical employment, were often extremely

---

[21] All quotations from Moorey (1992: 93).
[22] Murray (1963: 117–18).
[23] The relative social status of upper-class directors and lower-class diggers probably came to their aid.
[24] Murray (1963: 118–19).
[25] Seton Williams (1988: 121).

limited, and the archetypes most familiar to them were the distant, powerful mothers and nannies of childhood. When a young historian came across Margaret Murray, she could be easily slotted subconsciously into a pre-existing model. The psychological implications of that association need not be be laboured here; but it is worth a passing thought to wonder if fear of the women of their childhood was also part of the male reluctance to accept female participants on digs.

Outside the dig, another obstacle for women lay in meeting potential colleagues. For British archaeologists, membership in learned groups like the Society of Antiquaries of London was a passport to participation in professional debates and new excavations, as well as one of the only ways to make connections with other archaeologists. Many of these societies were 'old boys' clubs', and barred themselves to women as long as they could—the Society of Antiquaries did so until the Sex Discrimination Act came into force in 1920.[26] In 1928, Verney Wheeler became only the second woman to be elected by a regular vote. Aileen Fox still felt uncomfortable working there as a student in the early 1930s. There were some societies in which women could play a role; Margaret Murray was one of the first women admitted to Section H (Anthropology) of the British Association in 1913, and was a member of the Society of Antiquaries of Scotland from an early date.

Universities, another place to make valuable contacts, were also difficult for women to utilize. Most academic institutions still refused women degrees and even entry. Importantly, this was not true of University College London—one reason many female archaeologists of this period emerged from or otherwise were linked with Gower Street. Verney Wheeler was among their number, and her matriculation at UCL (rather than Girton or Newnham) is an important clue to her later attitudes.

Before leaving this subject, a warning note must be sounded. This biography is not a gender study; it is a study of a woman. Issues surrounding her gender deeply inform discussion of Verney Wheeler but she herself is its ultimate object.[27] This biography

---

[26] Fox (2000: 58).
[27] Hufton (1997: 931). For a multi-party discussion of some current ideas concerning teaching gender and archaeology, see Cheryl Claassen's (1992b) transcription of a workshop that took place at the 1991 Boone Conference.

must be read as the history of a life, not the elaboration of a philosophical issue.[28]

There are other pitfalls in the discussion of past women by modern women, and none greater than a feminist desire to posthumously empower the subject. While this is laudable in intention, it is dangerous and even damaging in practice. Sara Champion's 1998 discussion of women in early British archaeology illustrates how easy it can be to fall into inaccuracies with the best motivations. In her description of Gertrude Bell, she describes her as going to Persia in 1892 after completing her studies at Oxford 'to pursue an administrative career'.[29] Independent in wealth and intellect, Bell would be as unlikely an administrative candidate today as in 1892; what modern socialite would travel to a strange, faraway location because she longed to be an embassy secretary? Such makeweight job-seekers are disguised as cultural attachés, not office workers.

Bell's excuse for going East was more honest. She went to Tehran because she had always wanted to, and her uncle Sir Frank Lascelles had just been appointed Persian ambassador. He took his wife, and she took Bell as her companion. It was a revelation to the young woman, and her first book, *Persian Pictures*, was only the most visible result of an experience that provided a life-changing direction for a restless, powerful intellect. But to consider the 24-year-old Bell of 1892 in the modern terms we would apply to a young woman of today is misleading at best, and to begin on a false premise only undermines any subsequent discussion of her impressive work creating the Iraq Department of Antiquities and National Museum, not to mention her contribution to the creation of the state of Iraq. An interesting study could and should be written comparing the long-term fates of Gertrude Bell's political and archaeological establishments in the Middle East. It could be argued that the latter had a longer and more stable history, at least until the recent conflicts in that region.

It is, in short, important to avoid over-crediting Verney Wheeler, or considering her in a falsely modern light. Her accomplishments, like Bell's, may be trusted to represent her without too much help.

---

[28] More direct, general considerations of gender may be found in Scott (1999) and Shorter (1977). For specific considerations of gendered archaeology, see (among many others) Gilchrist (1998); Conkey and Spector (1998).

[29] Champion (1998: 178).

It will be seen that in the above discussion, British women and British archaeologists have been focused upon to the exclusion of interesting non-British contemporaries of Verney Wheeler like Hanna Rydh (Sweden) and Harriet Boyd Hawes (USA).[30] This geographic restriction has been imposed by Verney Wheeler's career, which took place exclusively in England and Wales and among British archaeologists. While examination of archaeologists in other countries may provide an interesting counterpoint to Verney Wheeler, these women did not directly affect her working life. They are of little immediate use in exploring our main subject.

WOMEN AND ARCHAEOLOGY: VERNEY WHEELER'S CONTRIBUTION

One of the objects of this work is to understand Verney Wheeler in reference to her place in time. She was not an isolated abnormality, but part of a long, evolving tradition of women intellectuals, and specifically women archaeologists. Verney Wheeler's position in this group was that of a quiet revolutionary: a woman who engaged in a relatively new, still primarily masculine intellectual activity, and was extremely good at it; but who (thanks to various factors, not least her own choice) operated somewhat under the radar. She did everything one would expect of an archaeologist then and now: excavated, published, spoke, taught, appeared in newspaper articles, and was a member of learned societies, yet we do not automatically group her with contemporary female colleagues like Dorothy Garrod or Gertrude Caton Thompson. Is this because, unlike the other two women, she was also a traditional wife who literally worked in the same field as her husband?

Women of this period who remain easily visible to the modern researcher were usually unmarried. Margaret Murray, who worked closely with the Petries, is a particularly apposite example. Her long career in teaching and excavating is still celebrated to a far greater extent than Hilda Petrie's, probably because she built her own extensive bibliography rather than contributing to a man's. Had she

---

[30] Arwill-Nordbladh (1998); Fotou and Brown (2004).

married, this would not have been the case. By contrast, by and after Verney Wheeler, women published in their own names and ran their own digs openly, regardless of their marital status. Besides Verney Wheeler herself, we have the example of Cyril Fox's wife, Aileen, whose career not only outlasted his but also extended far wider geographically. The 'professional wife' became simply a married professional.

Through this development, unmarried women continued to work and publish undaunted, many (like Veronica Seton-Williams) after training by Verney Wheeler. While it is far too early for psychological speculation, Verney Wheeler's policy of separating the sexes on her digs is worth bearing in mind. It was simply practical on one level, necessary on another to reassure parents; but did she also have a subconscious desire to prevent young unmarried women from becoming distracted by their ordained social role of potential wife?

As an archaeologist, Verney Wheeler combined the roles of Hilda Petrie (the professional wife) and Margaret Murray (the single scholar). She began as a traditional silent wife in her first Welsh digs, yet within a few years conducted the excavation and solo publication of an entire amphitheatre at Caerleon. An intelligent woman, she was catapulted into archaeology at exactly the right time, when it became socially permissible to be both a professional wife and an independent intellectual. This does not mean her career was not bound up fully with her husband's; it was. What it means is that she should receive appropriate recognition as his colleague rather than his tool.

In terms of the larger history of women and archaeology, Verney Wheeler belongs to the second generation of female archaeologists. The first generation, women like Margaret Murray and Hilda Petrie, essentially used archaeology as a means of liberation from traditional women's roles, or found their contribution hidden by conventional male–female proprieties.[31] The second generation (Verney Wheeler's) found that the new space they were being allotted brought with it some drawbacks. If the first generation were the revolutionaries, the second had to become the normalizers, reassuring the male establishment that women

---

[31] See Root (2004) for a more extensive discussion of this issue from the viewpoint of women's studies.

intellectuals were not a threat. This aspect of Verney Wheeler can be seen writ small in the brown skirt suit she always wore to excavate, no matter what the site conditions, as she was gradually surrounded by female students dressed daringly in shorts and jodhpurs. She had to maintain a comforting, easily recognizable femininity for the sake of male nerves, and not only those of the men who controlled jobs, funding, and publications. A woman giving orders had to consider her staff's fears of intelligent, masculinized women—the terrible 'Girton girl' of bluestocking fame. The work of the male students and workers she taught and directed was often better in quality and easier to induce if they saw their leader as a traditional woman in an untraditional role. For Verney Wheeler, that meant the evergreen role of 'den mother', nurturing her young men both intellectually and socially. It was a genuine, not an assumed identity; as ever throughout her life, Verney Wheeler tended to slip between expectations even as she fulfilled them. She was a gentle, curiously unyielding woman, who used the conventions of her time to answer her own needs even as she cared for those of others.

By the time the next generation of 'jodhpur girls' like Seton-Williams grew up, they found themselves in a world where being a woman intellectual was (though still not as simple as being a male intellectual) not only accepted but respected. Because Verney Wheeler had dug and published and married without becoming desexed or socially more abnormal than any male archaeologist, her students found their own work and selves considered more seriously and with less question. She normalized their intellectual lives and voices, helping create a way to be an intelligent, academic woman. And she did it consciously. Verney Wheeler formally taught and encouraged the women among her students as much as the men. Hilda Petrie did not make a point of teaching, and Margaret Murray made it her career. Verney Wheeler, their joint heir, actively reached out to younger women intellectually.

VERNEY WHEELER'S CURRENT ABSENCE FROM THE RECORD

Why has Verney Wheeler been neglected for so long by historians, if she is so important to the development of both British archaeology and female intellectuals? Apart from general issues of gender, there are three main reasons. Least important, but nonetheless of bearing, was her personality. Although she published independently and was by all accounts an inspiring lecturer and teacher, Verney Wheeler was always happy to leave the limelight to others (especially her husband). The result was that even when credit was properly afforded her, it was often not remembered in the long term. Attached to this natural diffidence was her early death. She was just 43 when a botched operation caused her unexpected demise, in the midst of a major excavation in Dorset. Her husband, whose career her own had been so tightly bound up with, went on to excavate and write for another forty years. It is not surprising that without her actual presence, the work she did with her spouse was generally attributed solely to him. It is pleasant to note, though, that Wheeler himself credited her importance enthusiastically in his autobiography *Still Digging*.

R. E. M. Wheeler was a man of overwhelming personality with a considerable media presence, an archaeologist who has been lauded and criticized for the last eighty years. He is the major reason his wife is not well known, though again, this was certainly not intentional on his part. He simply overshadowed whomever he stood next to. In the case of his wife, he provided a suitable man onto which her accomplishments could be projected by those uncomfortable with or unconscious of female intellectual ability. Glyn Daniel's entertaining and otherwise very useful *A Short History of Archaeology* (1981) is typical of this trend. And—let it be said here and often—Verney Wheeler used her husband professionally as much as he used her. She was shy in company and detested being interviewed, though she shone as a practical teacher and lecturer. She hated the personal publicity associated with their work, even as she recognized its financial and perhaps moral importance. There is a definite point in the Wheelers' joint work, discussed in more detail in the section dealing with their press publicity, in which it becomes apparent that Verney Wheeler has quietly, firmly refused to be the main public face of the work. Again, this modesty suited a more traditional concept of the feminine, but also happened to be what Verney Wheeler herself wanted. Her selective use of those conventions she found useful is extremely interesting.

There is no intent to denigrate R. E. M. Wheeler in any way in this book. His contributions to archaeology are arguable in their specifics but undeniable in their importance. Any attempt to understand his wife's career does not come at the expense of his accomplishments, and he was always her greatest supporter and promoter. There is no posthumous re-appropriation of credit here—merely the proof of something that Wheeler, Verney Wheeler, and their contemporaries all felt was too obvious to ever formally state: that Verney Wheeler was also an archaeologist, and that she was Wheeler's professional partner. The reverse is also true. A discussion of Verney Wheeler's output must necessarily acknowledge her husband's help and support of her work, and he will appear often within these pages—if only as a guest star.

ARCHAEOBIOGRAPHY: METHODOLOGY AND SOURCES

A work of biography differs from a standard work of archaeology or history in several small but essential ways, though the three fields are closely related. This work attempts to approach part of the history of archaeology via the biography of a participant in that history, and as such draws upon sources and techniques from all three disciplines.[32] Such an approach is increasingly common in this field. The 2004 publication of *Breaking Ground: Pioneering Women Archaeologists* by Brown University is the most recent of a series of books examining the roles of specific women in the history of archaeology.[33] Brown has gone on to maintain an academic database of further biographic essays at http://www.brown.edu/Research/Breaking_Ground/. These essays are of particular value as they attempt to understand women archaeologists on their own terms, rather than fit them into a previously determined theory of gender.[34] As a result, their archaeological work remains at the centre of these women's lives, and theory remains in its appropriate role within an individual's biography: as a tool, not a thesis.

---

[32] John Lewis Gaddis provides an excellent consideration of biography as history in his general discussion of historiological issues *The Landscape of History* (Gaddis 2002: 116–28).

[33] Cohen and Joukowsky (2004). See also Díaz-Andreu and Sørensen (1998).

[34] Root (2004: 3).

Archaeobiography, that new-old field currently explored by a variety of excellent scholars, has yet to find a firm definition. For this author's purposes, it must be seen as the methodical, careful extraction of usable data from the waterfall of papers and ephemera that make up a subject's life. Pamela Jane Smith, among others, has commented on the peculiar symmetry existing between this form of understanding a scholar and the techniques used to comprehend an archaeological site. It is perhaps only appropriate that a woman like Verney Wheeler be explored via such a method. Like archaeology, archaeobiography may be applied to more than archaeologists, and partakes of both science and history. At its best, like a good dig, it can produce that indefinable spark of life that makes sites and personalities so vivid long after those that inhabited them have died.

Sources consulted primarily consist of Verney Wheeler's published work; her letters and other materials preserved in various archives; interviews conducted by the author with her former students and colleagues between 2005 and 2008; and the three major works on her husband, his 1954 textbook *Archaeology from the Earth*, his 1955 autobiography *Still Digging*, and Jacquetta Hawkes' 1982 biography *Adventurer In Archaeology*. Published within a year (in Britain) of *Still Digging*, and occasionally using the same language and phrasing to describe ideas and events, *Archaeology from the Earth* forms a more technical counterbalance to Wheeler's racy and charmingly caustic autobiography. The two books are best read together to fully appreciate the influences on Rik Wheeler's own archaeological works and life that led to the occasionally dogmatic pronouncements of his textbook. Verney Wheeler's place in *Archaeology from the Earth* is a point of no small interest and importance, and will be looked at in more depth during the discussion of the Verulamium excavations. Her role in *Still Digging* will soon speak for itself.

Jacquetta Hawkes' first husband, C. F. C. Hawkes, was one of the Wheelers' first serious students as an Oxford undergraduate, and *Adventurer in Archaeology* will be referenced often in the following pages. Although it is an admittedly partisan biography of Wheeler, with whom Hawkes was friends from the late 1930s until to the end of his life, it deals with his faults as well as his virtues in a fairly clear-eyed manner. Hawkes knew Verney Wheeler only slightly, as she came on the scene close to the older woman's death, but she was well acquainted with the couple's circle of friends, and the first third of her biography deals extensively and sympathetically with the Wheelers' marriage. She includes many stories of great interest or scandal, especially those describing Wheeler's serial infidelities. She does *not* always include specific sources for these—perhaps understandable when we consider that many of the people concerned were still alive in 1982 and able to take legal action. Occasionally this makes it difficult to judge whether her account of an incident is wholly accurate. Generally speaking, I have taken her book at face value, after careful examination of the manuscripts and correspondence Hawkes amassed during its writing (now held by the J. B. Priestley Library at the University of Bradford). Christine Finn, Hawkes' biographer, has kindly discussed the personalities and materials involved with me. It is her opinion that Hawkes is a trustworthy chronicler despite her occasional omissions.[35]

Particular thanks must go to the Wheelers' younger granddaughter, Carol Wheeler Pettman, who graciously allowed full access to many unpublished family photographs and papers dating back to Verney Wheeler's teenage years. These papers are collectively identified here as the Wheeler family papers (WFP).

The most immediate historical source for Verney Wheeler's life lies in the extensive documentary archives preserved at the museums she was associated with. This source has also produced the most scope for original research. Papers relating to Verney Wheeler, which include correspondence, draft papers, site notebooks, and ephemera, have been exhaustively examined: every extant document written by or to the subject has been considered carefully in an effort to reconstruct her professional life. While her published work provides an official record of her accomplishments, the diffuse materials of the public and private archives illustrate the process by which she arrived at those accomplishments. They also illuminate previously unknown elements of her professional life—for example, her close relationship and mentoring of V. E. Nash-Williams at Caerleon in the 1920s. Verney Wheeler has always had an anecdotal reputation as a great teacher even off the excavation, and with the examination of these archives, it is possible to understand some of the reasons why.

Fortunately for the author, many of her papers were retained as discrete sets by the institutions where they are held; for example, all the Welsh material is held by the National Museum of Wales at Cardiff.

---

[35] Hawkes (1982); Christine Finn (pers. comm.).

This has lessened the difficulty of what was already an overwhelming task, and I believe that I have examined every potential institutional archive and major private collection for material. Once again, the Wheeler family papers have provided a range of valuable material from all the stages of Verney Wheeler's life. These archives and collections are fully listed in the Bibliography. Personal examinations of the sites excavated by Verney Wheeler, and the museums she worked and taught in, have also been conducted.

The published paper sources for Verney Wheeler's life lie in her bibliography. This has been greatly expanded by this work, and is listed in Appendix 2. As the major publications are discussed in detail during the chapters assigned to the digs they arose from, there is no need to examine the list at this time. A careful examination of archaeological journals and magazines between 1925 and 1936 has produced rich fruit in the form of short articles and book reviews penned by Verney Wheeler. Of these, perhaps the most interesting is an article she wrote on the preservation of mosaics from the *Museums Journal* for 1933.[36]

On the biographical level, interviews with and personal memoirs of the few remaining students and diggers who knew Verney Wheeler personally have proved invaluable. An initial period of research identified three people still alive and willing to engage in an interview: Beatrice de Cardi and Margaret Drower, former Wheeler students, and Cecil Davies, a former digger at the Caerleon amphitheatre. All interviews were conducted by the author, and have provided absolutely biased and absolutely expert primary sources on that most elusive of qualities, personality. Those who knew her have treasured the memory of Verney Wheeler as a woman for many years. Multiple interviews were carried out with Carol Wheeler Pettman. When it was impossible to interview a source, personal memoirs (both published and unpublished) have often been able to fill the gap, as in the cases of William Wedlake and V. E. Seton-Williams. Jacquetta Hawkes's notes on the interviews she conducted for her epic biography of R. E. M. Wheeler have been preserved in Bradford, and these were also combed for information relating to his wife.

Often these sources have conflated Verney Wheeler's professional and personal qualities, remembering her kindness alongside her

---

[36] T. Verney Wheeler (1933). A full discussion of this article will be found in the section of this volume examining Verney Wheeler's mosaic work.

trenching. It will become quickly apparent that this linking is not an awkward one: Verney Wheeler's personal and public life lay so closely together that they were often effectively the same thing. They must both be seriously discussed in order to examine her impact on the generation of British archaeologists who succeeded her; many were her students.

These varying sources have been analysed, first as discrete groups and then as a single unit, in order to determine the developing patterns at work in Verney Wheeler's life. Those patterns are then considered in the light of the changing currents in archaeology during the 1920s and 1930s—currents Verney Wheeler both directed and was affected by. Other influences on her were more generally social, and it is therefore desirable to create a picture of the time Verney Wheeler moved in. Establishing her in a time and place is important—as a bright girl in a London suburb; a conscientious student at University College London; a young wife and mother in the First World War; and an increasingly professional woman after 1918. Her physical and cultural landscape must be comprehended, especially in the chapters dealing with her time in London and Wales. The roughly chronological approach employed here also helps to see her as a developing mind; uninterested or unaware of archaeology in her early years, while learning the working methods she would later apply to the subject that became her passion after the war.

A NOTE ON NAMES

As this biography deals with a woman whose career took place alongside and along with a homonymous professional partner, she cannot be simply identified as Wheeler without constant confusion. Nor is it desirable to infantilize the subject, after the manner of many patronizing studies, by referring to her exclusively by her first name.[37]

---

[37] The 'Janeites' and followers of Charlotte Bronte are particularly irritating in this regard. Surely two of the finest novelists in the English language deserves the professional treatment of their male contemporaries. No one would refer to 'Walter' or 'Charles' in a critical (rather than personal) discussion of Scott or Dickens. Even Henry and William James are usually distinguished by their full, not just their given, names.

When her professional life is discussed, Tessa Verney Wheeler will be referred to as Verney Wheeler. She never formally hyphenated her name, and thus the inclusion of Verney here is not strictly accurate. However, this use of her maiden name is not without precedent; she often signed herself T. V. Wheeler or T. Verney Wheeler.[38] It would have been a construct easily recognised by both Tessa Verney Wheeler and her contemporaries, and therefore its use is sanctioned for the sake of clarity. This will become especially important in citing bibliographic references. R. E. M. Wheeler will be referred to professionally as Wheeler. When discussing their private life and especially marriage, their first or nicknames, Tessa and Rik, will occasionally be used, to signal the change in tone and intent. In this I follow Jacquetta Hawkes, R. E. M. Wheeler's biographer.[39]

Rik Wheeler was nothing if not an overwhelming personality. In any work in which he appears, it is always a struggle to keep him from striding onto centre stage. When writing of his reticent wife, this danger doubles. He will occasionally be allowed unfettered access to the reader. This is appropriate; he was the centre of Verney Wheeler's emotional world, and the other half of the professional partnership they both depended on. However, this is a biography of Tessa Verney Wheeler. She will always be the priority.

---

[38] See the next chapter for a discussion of her family history. Her firm retention of her absent and unknown father Verney's name is of interest from a psychological standpoint.

[39] Rik was one of Robert Eric Mortimer Wheeler's many nicknames, chosen by Hawkes to describe him throughout her biography of him. As Tessa gave it to him it is doubly appropriate in this context. Jacquetta Hawkes 1982: 19.

2

Girlhood (1893–1910)

To begin at the beginning when discussing Tessa Verney Wheeler is much more difficult than stopping at her end. Her death is marked in time by a certificate and by living memory; the hospital where she died remains intact, if grimy and deserted. Her origins are lost in an African frontier town and a gold war.

Anticipating her birth is a little easier, at least maternally speaking. Tessa Verney's mother, Annie Booth Kilburn, was born in either Tipperary, Ireland, or Bishop Auckland near Durham on 30 September 1866, and spent her early life in Bishop Auckland with her grandparents.[1] Tessa Verney called her origins, presumably meaning her mother's, Irish in a 1928 Welsh newspaper interview, though she may have been romancing to appeal to an audience newly aware of political Celticism.

Annie's life seems extraordinarily liberated by the standards of her day. She came from a moderately prosperous industrial family of ironmongers in County Durham.[2] Her father, Nicholas Kilburn, married Annie Booth, a friend of his sisters', in December 1865. She fell victim within a year to one of the leading killers of Victorian women: childbirth. Her daughter was named after her, and then sent to live with her paternal grandparents. Her father remarried and by

---

[1] United Kingdom National Census Records for Durham, 1871 (1891 (RG12/4057) and Deptford, London, 1901 (RG 13/534).

[2] I am indebted to Annie and Tessa's distant cousin Peter Kilburn, of Stanstead, Quebec, for much of the information on Annie Kilburn included here. Mr Kilburn is engaged in an extensive genealogical project, and very kindly shared all the information at his disposal regarding Annie Kilburn. His manuscript genealogy will be further referenced as Kilburn (2008).

1871 had the first of two additional daughters. There is no record of his further contact after her infancy.[3]

Annie Kilburn thus grew up as the littlest member of a large extended family, essentially without parents but not without grandparents, aunts, uncles, and other adults ready to partially fill parental roles. This was not unusual in a period when small children were often sent away to live with more prosperous relations. Her grandfather had retired, and his household lived off his income even after his death in 1882; he could afford to support a child left behind by his son's new responsibilities.

For the first twenty-five years of her life, Annie lived with her father's parents, and her profession in the National Census is listed as 'granddaughter'. This changes only briefly in 1887, when she made what Jacquetta Hawkes accurately calls a 'hasty, very probably runaway' marriage to a man called John Arthur Mather, a coalminer whose father (also John) was a local ship's carpenter.[4] This, perhaps unsurprisingly, swiftly resulted in the birth of a son, yet another John, in the summer of 1888. He was not quite a 'seven-month baby', as the infant causes of shotgun weddings used to be called, but his gestation was short enough to justify nervousness on the part of Annie's family.

The marriage did not last long. Perhaps that was a relief to the Kilburns. The nice distinctions of middle-class Victorians makes it probable that they looked on Annie as marrying 'down' a step socially. This was bad enough in the case of sons—contemporary homes were filled with mothers hoping their sons would escape the snares of the proverbial barmaid—but in a daughter, it was ruinous. As in the medieval period, a gentleman, upon marrying, brought a woman up to his level, at least officially. A gentlewoman, by contrast, descended as she condescended.

Obligingly, John Mather soon died—at least according to Mrs Mather. By the 1891 census, Annie and her child were back at home with her family at 50 North Bondgate, Durham. It was the residence of her widowed grandmother Ann Kilburn, described as 'living on her own means'. Annie's occupation is still described

---

[3] In this and the following three paragraphs, all genealogical information not identified as Kilburn (2008) was taken from the UK National Census for the year in question.

[4] Hawkes (1982: 48); England and Wales Marriage Index, 1887, p. 188.

as 'granddaughter' and her marital status as 'widowed'. Her son was two years old.

Was she really a widow? John Mather was a common name in the Durham area at the time, and there are a great number of deaths recorded that *might* refer to Annie's husband. None lists any specific identifiers. In all honesty, the main reason for caution is that Annie Agnes Kilburn Mather Pearson Verney Davies, to give her all the names she assumed legally, let alone socially, over her lifetime, was an incurable romancer in both the proper and the emotional sense. To call her a compulsive liar puts it too strongly. She had a cunning simplicity in her makeup that made whatever story she told about her life true to herself, as well as to her listeners. And, critically for the welfare of herself and her children, people seem to have honestly liked her.

Briefly reviewing her many name changes is helpful at this point, before going on with her chronological movements; it is otherwise all too easy to get lost in the forest of surnames.

Born Annie Booth Kilburn in 1866, in 1887 she married for the fist time in Durham and became Annie Mather. She then moved to South Africa for a few years. It is unclear what name she emigrated under, but a newspaper notice in 1960 mentions a lost marriage in South Africa around 1893.

> [...] by her first marriage 1887 to JOHN ARTHUR MATHER and by her second marriage probably Johannesburg South Africa about 1893 to WILLIAM HENRY RITSON PEARSON and by her marriage to JOHN VERNEY.[5]

She likely returned to England as Annie Mather, as in the 1901 National Census 241 Lewisham High Road in London is occupied by Annie Mather, her husband, Theophilus Morgan Davies, and her children, John and Tessa Mather. But on her 1910 application for admission to University College London, Tessa called herself Tessa Verney; and on her marriage certificate in May 1914 she listed a deceased Doctor John Verney as her father.[6] To further complicate matters, a 1924 legal deposition survives, made by Annie on a relative's death. There, her name is Annie Booth Pearson, of 225

---

[5] Kilburn (2008: 9).
[6] This information comes from Verney Wheeler's marriage certificate, a copy of which was obtained from the General Register's Office.

Lewisham High Road, London. She was indeed resident there, and still living with Theophilus Davies.

Annie's first name was also open to self-invention; by 1901 she sometimes identified herself as Agnes, seemingly just because she liked the name. (She also spelled it Agnez on occasion, for variety's sake.)[7] The question of her many marriages, and their relation to her daughter, remains open. The Pearson marriage might easily postdate Tessa's birth; there is no indication she married John Verney, or even that he existed, apart from the *Times* notice and her daughter's marriage certificate. Neither piece of evidence is conclusive.

Perhaps Annie Mather, alone or adrift in Johannesburg, fell pregnant by John Verney and made a hasty marriage to William Pearson to save her reputation, or support herself and her children.[8] In that case, she must have told Pearson that her newborn daughter was the child of John Mather, omitting to mention that Mather had died before she came out to Africa. Who, then, was Doctor John Verney? The nearest candidate, and he is not very close, is a Dr Frank Verney who was employed as a district veterinary surgeon by the Natal and Zululand government over the turn of the twentieth century. He only went out to South Africa in 1896. If he was Tessa's father, she would have to be three years younger than she thought, and the product of a whirlwind Jo'burg romance if not something more sordid. Maddeningly, the head of the Natal Department of Agriculture at that time was an A. Pearson. Pearson was a fairly common surname across Anglo-Africa; Verney much less so.[9]

There is another solution to this problem. It is possible John Verney was fictitious, though it is hard to think why Annie would invent him. If Pearson was Tessa's biological father, why was she never recorded under his name? Did Annie even know who her daughter's father was?

What matters most from the perspective of this biography is that at some point between 1901 and 1910, young Tessa made a decision to use the surname Verney. It was at this time that she also became academically active, and she continued to use her self-selected maiden name as an identifier throughout her life. Her husband had it placed

---

[7] Hawkes (1982: 48).
[8] Though she does sound like a woman eminently capable of looking after herself.
[9] Wills and Barrett (1905: 228).

as one of the four words on her suitably simple grave. Psychologically, John Verney meant something to her.

ANNIE IN SOUTH AFRICA

The house in Durham was a crowded one, and Annie was a woman with her eye on the horizon. African emigration was in the air in 1890. The British had gained control of the Dutch Cape Colony (the future South Africa) in 1806, and it was formally ceded to them by the Netherlands in 1814. The desire of the British government to strengthen their imperial control abroad produced, or was at least matched by, a growing belief that emigration was a way to provide for respectable and ambitious members of the community. Colonial emigration was already a familiar method of disposal of the unwanted of English society, whether working-class convicts, dissolute sprigs of the aristocracy, or, more and more, unmarried women. Now, Canada and Africa began to be portrayed as closer alternatives to Australia and New Zealand, without the overtones of forced transportation.

Africa never achieved the level of British emigration associated with other destinations; popular opinion, despite all H. Rider Haggard could do, was that it was rather a second-class colony, without the desert distances of Australia or the manly wilderness of Canada. Nonetheless, the effects of the European 'scramble for Africa' prior to the First World War showed itself in South Africa via a thriving English-speaking community. It reached its apogee in its arch-representative Cecil Rhodes (1853–1902). Rhodes's life embodies the general character of the English South Africans that Annie Mather joined: a group of industrious and clever men and women, sentimental about the England (or Britain) some of them had never seen, faithful to Queen and Empire, and more or less amoral about everything else.

For 'superfluous' women like Annie, whose traditional societal roles as wife and mother were lost or never taken up, emigration to the Imperial colonies was often pitched as an ideal solution. It was also, increasingly, a respectable and even proto-feminist choice, one that might allow a woman equal chances of marriage or independence. The Female Middle-Class Emigration Society was founded in 1862 with the object of helping single and widowed middle-class women travel to the imperial possessions, via loans and detailed information regarding destinations. It was one of the first, and best known (though not largest or most successful), of a wealth of such organizations. All tended to have quite specific remits focusing on vulnerable groups in society, especially at their outset; orphaned children, widowed middle-class women, or single ladies (as socially opposed to women).[10]

For Annie, the most attractive part of emigration was probably the chance of another marriage, if indeed she went to Africa alone. She may well have gone out with a companion, and her motivations are not at all clear. As she was only in Africa for a few years, she must have lost or given up on her reasons for the move.

John junior was still a toddler when his mother left Durham for the Cape. John senior had supposedly died by 1891. Annie's story is considerably muddied by the lack of good records engendered by changes of government and uncertain times in South Africa. The great Witwatersrand gold rush had begun in 1886, and Johannesburg was a frontier boomtown attracting people of all nations.

Many families were emigrating permanently in this period, and while it is not clear if Annie took her son with her, it is likely she did if she intended to make her life abroad.[11] It is also supported by the 1901 census, which shows John junior living with his mother in London. Alternatively, he could have stayed in Durham and then moved back in with her upon her return to England. A number of parents left small children behind them when they left England for Empire, for reasons of health or cost; and as the case of Annie's own father shows, spare children were often placed out among the extended family.

The next definite major event of Annie's life was the birth in Johannesburg on 27 March 1893 of her daughter Tessa. The birth certificate has disappeared, if there ever was one. Tessa's mother ought to have registered her birth with the English authorities, as the child of at least one native-born British citizen, but this does not seem to have been done. Many babies in the period were born at home or in private nursing

---

[10] Hammerton (1979) and Magee and Thompson (2010) both provide excellent overviews of this fascinating subject.

[11] Hawkes (1982: 48).

homes, and notification of birth to the government was left up to the parents or doctor. There was no proper enforcement of this policy in South Africa, and records are patchy or absent.

Ships' records are in a similar state. Every nation had different emigration and immigration notation policies, and these were again enforced fairly irregularly until the twentieth century. There are no ships listing Annie's return to England, under any of her many names. Her children are also missing. The family, like so many others, was a victim of poor recording practices.

Annie found South Africa hard to bear. According to the stories she told her grandson Michael many years later, she had been in Johannesburg when the township had 'hardly a two-storey building'.[12] Contemporary pictures of Johannesburg show this to be a slight exaggeration, but it was a far cry from suburban Durham.[13] The streets were wide, but churned constantly into mud by carriages and carts; the wide span of oxen preferred for veldt work made soup of what they passed over. Like all young frontier towns, builders gave their structures grandiose names regardless of the size or scope of the constructions. False fronts provided fictitious height for many of these, but there were a good number of genuinely large structures.

It was still a far cry from Cape Town, or older settlements of longer date and more aristocratic pretensions. Johannesburg had only been founded in 1886, and from the start was intended as rough accommodation for the miners and prospectors flooding to the nearby gold and diamond workings. It was not a place to bring up a child. South Africa was in the throes of a deeply divisive conflict, as the British imperialists and white Boer farmers struggled violently for control. In 1893, that control was squarely in the latter camp under Paul Kruger, African-born, German in origin, and firmly Boer in outlook, language, and upbringing. He was reluctant to accord the Uitlanders, or white non-Boers, (effectively, the British) too much voice in government, believing correctly that their primary loyalties lay with the Victorian Empire. The Boers were especially suspicious of Johannesburg, knowing it was becoming a focus of the English population. Further international tensions came from Kaiser Wilhelm, who attempted to placate his

---

[12] She later blamed her dislike of black men on the events of that time. Hawkes (1982: 48).
[13] Meredith (2007: plate 7).

English grandmother while supporting the Dutch and German Boers against the English.

Annie must have struggled, living in what was still a frontier shantytown with a baby girl, perhaps a small boy, and a changing series of men. At some point between 1893 to 1901, she returned to England with her daughter. Most probably she was evacuated or fled before the outbreak of the Second Boer War in 1899, in the aftermath of the hysteria surrounding the abortive Jameson Raid. Rhodes, Leander Starr Jameson, and their companions were eager to bring South Africa into the Empire officially, and were sometimes neither scrupulous nor honest in how they went about their goal.

The Raid of 1895–6 is usually taken as the moment when British forces made their first open attempt on the Boers, though it took four more years of escalating tensions and petty back-biting to produce the official declaration of war in October 1899. Johannesburg was, unusually, mainly Uitlander in its makeup. The English organizers of the Raid saw it as a source of support and focus for rebellion. They believed that once their flag was raised, volunteer militias would flock to the aid of their countrymen. Jameson justified his actions in December 1895 with a pleading letter, allegedly from the people of Johannesburg. It was in reality drafted by the conspirators themselves, and left undated so that Jameson could produce it when necessary. In the event, the aspiring rebels were captured by government forces before they reached Johannesburg, and the letter subsequently published. It purports to speak in part on behalf of Annie and baby Tessa, among 'thousands' more.

> Thousands of unarmed men, women and children of our race will be at the mercy of well-armed Boers, while property of enormous value will be in peril [. . .] It is under these circumstances that we call upon you to come to our aid, should a disturbance arise here.

Jameson read it to his men before the Raid, and it was published in the *Times* of London on 1 January 1896. It caused a patriotic fervour in England, and inspired a poem by the Poet Laureate, Alfred Austin. Their quality is the most unintentionally precise criticism of the raid that could be asked for.

> There are girls in the gold-reef city,
> There are mothers and children too!
> And they cry, Hurry up! for pity!

> So what could a brave man do? [...]
> So we forded and galloped forward,
> As hard as our beasts could pelt,
> First eastward, then trending northward,
> Right over the rolling veldt.

The Uitlanders of Johannesburg were unsettled by the Jameson fiasco and angered by the hostile Boer administration, but not as moved as Londoners were by fictitious descriptions of their own suffering. It took four more years for war to fully develop, and at some point during those years Annie and her daughter left South Africa forever.

ANNIE IN LONDON

By 1901 Annie had settled in London, and finally formed a lasting relationship that gave her both personal security and a loving father for her daughter. Theophilus Morgan Davies (he liked to use both his middle and last names as a surname) was a chemist who owned and ran the rather grandly titled La Pharmacie Centrale, first at Coventry Street and then at 34 Leicester Square, as well as managing shops on the ground floors of his various flats on Lewisham High Street.[14]

By all accounts, he was a pleasant, happy-go-lucky man, a good match for Annie. On the other side of the chemist's counter, he pursued mild hobbies, collected celebrity and royal autographs, and was connected with an 'ill-fated' goldmine that produced nothing more valuable than a tie-pin.[15] He and Annie never married, and at this stage her marital status was indeed rather uncertain. But they remained in a committed relationship until his death in 1931, and she used the name Mrs Morgan Davies from at least 1901 until her death. The importance of the relationship to her may be gauged by her insistence after he died that his cufflinks go to her 17-year-old grandson Michael. She kept his watch, out of his 'very few belongings'. In the same letter, Tessa wrote rather sadly to Davies' sister Winnie Bosisio, 'I myself haven't even a photograph of him.'[16] She did keep one or two of his autograph albums as mementos.

[14] TVW to Winnie Bosisio, 16 February 1931. WFP.
[15] TVW to Winnie Bosisio, 2 March 1931. WFP.
[16] TVW to Winnie Bosisio, 2 March 1931. WFP.

The two had no children of their own, but Davies took to Annie's little girl and raised her as his own daughter. The family lived at various locations on the Lewisham High Road in southeast London, on the border between Deptford and Lewisham. Tessa remained devoted to the man she described formally as her guardian, and within the family as the 'Great Man' (with what one assumes was loving satire). She was his sole executrix when he died in January 1931. Given the tangled nature of Morgan Davies' finances by that point, this was a vote of confidence as well as affection. Although Verney Wheeler refers to his 'considerable business' in contemporary letters, Davies was a gambler commercially. He had declared bankruptcy in 1922, and then immediately reformed his shop and company by making his family (including Tessa's mother) the principal stockholders. He then ran the pharmacy into the ground again, bought into several dubious get-rich schemes like the putative gold-mine mentioned above, and died. Fortunately by 1931 Tessa had been running the bankbooks for excavations for several years, another occupation requiring stamina and financial firmness. She wound up La Pharmacie Centrale with brisk efficiency.[17]

John Mather the younger was not as bonded with his mother's partner. He does not seem to have figured largely in his half-sister's life, and vanishes from it during her childhood. There are no enlistment records surviving for him from the First World War, and it seems likely that he had left England by that point; according to family stories, he vanished into South America. Tessa never mentioned him to any third party, and there is no extant correspondence between the siblings.

Neither of Tessa's parents—for so they may effectively be called from this point—were academics or historians. That does not mean they were without an effect on her later career. Both Theophilus Morgan Davies and Annie Kilburn shared aspects of their personalities with the man Tessa eventually chose to marry. When Davies declared bankruptcy in 1922 and then instantly reformed his company by making his family the principal stockholders, his blithe behaviour is reminiscent of the corners Wheeler cut professionally—never illegal, yet sometimes a little too sharp.[18] And in Annie's many relationships,

---

[17] WFP.
[18] For example, in his attraction of the press at Caerleon by describing what he knew was a Roman amphitheatre as 'King Arthur's Round Table'.

and swift movement between men, it is not hard to see a hint of the sexual and emotional rapacity that characterized Rik.

THE EDWARDIAN MENTALITY

Tessa was born in South Africa, but in personal identification, outlook, upbringing, and behaviour she was a pure Edwardian Londoner. We may follow the general trend of social historians and consider this period as extending very roughly from 1894 to 1914; in other words, the exact period of Tessa's childhood and early girlhood.[19] Here the works of E. Nesbit (1858–1924) embody the flavour of a Lewisham childhood. Nesbit was an unconventional young wife and mother in the London suburbs—how unconventional may be judged by the fact that she was very nearly a mother first and a wife second—and set several of her popular books in Lewisham and Deptford in the early twentieth century. Her first successful children's book, *The Story of the Treasure-Seekers* (1899), is set on the Lewisham Road, and the later *Harding's Luck* (1909) in the slums of Deptford. The middle-class Bastable children of the first book must search for treasure because their father's business partner has embezzled the firm's money, forcing them into the ranks of the shabby-genteel in Lewisham. Dickie Harding, of the second, is a crippled slum child raised in the tiny two-up-two-down houses of the London poor. Tessa's childhood was closer to the Bastables than to Dickie, but not quite close enough for comfort.

> Our ancestral home is in the Lewisham Road. It is semi-detached and has a garden, not a large one [. . .] In London, or at any rate Lewisham, nothing happens unless you make it happen; or if it happens it doesn't happen to you, and you don't know the people it does happen to.[20]

> Dickie lived at New Cross. At least the address was New Cross, but really the house where he lived was one of a row of horrid little houses built on [. . .] the old houses of the Deptford merchants [. . .] Miles and miles and miles of them, and not a green thing to be seen except the cabbages in the greengrocers' shops.[21]

---

[19] For examples, see Harris (1993); Rose (1986); Pearsall (1973); Thompson (1975).
[20] Nesbit (1899).
[21] Nesbit (1909).

Annie and Tessa were not living in Lewisham proper, but on what remains the border between shabby-genteel Lewisham and simply shabby Deptford. The great days of London shipbuilding had passed by, and Deptford was slowly declining. The Davies lived on the Lewisham High Road, now Lewisham Way. It climbs steeply north in a curve up Loampit Hill from Lewisham's railway station, a stiff walk by suburban standards. When Tessa was a child, the road—now crowded with buses—was covered with trams bringing people to and from the rail station at its southern and more prestigious end. Theophilus Davies ran a small pharmacy, Davies Morgan & Co., at 241 and then 225 Lewisham High Road. His family lived over the shop, which was located near the crest of the hill. This is the point when it begins to literally run downhill towards Deptford. Contemporary residents were keenly aware socially which part of the road they lived on.

Tessa's Edwardian life on the Lewisham High Road would be superficially familiar to the modern resident. Many of the current neighbourhood houses date from that period, and the prevalent domestic pattern is still of bread-winning clerk husbands travelling in to London every day for work. Wives stayed home, visited, kept house, and raised the children with the help of domestic servants. In the more prosperous houses, there might be a governess for the children, or a combination gardener and boot boy.

The Davies were in a slightly different position, catering to the families whose husbands worked in the City. Tessa grew up in a flat, not a house, in a little row of terraced houses and shops. While Theophilus Davies had premises in London, he also had a small counter in the same building as their home, and he shared 241 Lewisham High Road with a telephone call office until 1912. It is possible that Annie-Agnes kept the counter, perhaps with her daughter's help outside school hours, while Theophilus looked after the more prestigious concerns of the 'town' shop and the home-made concoctions his stepdaughter describes below.

Pharmacists were skilled, accredited workers by the early twentieth century. Prior to the National Health Insurance Act of 1912, they were a vital resource—often the *only* resource—for those too poor to afford a doctor's fees. Reflecting this, government regulation had steadily increased throughout the Victorian period, and by 1868 the Pharmacy Act required that all pharmacists and chemists with professional access to poisons pass an examination administered by the

London-based Royal Pharmaceutical Society. They were then placed on the Society's registers and allowed to practise openly. Most chemists came to the exam after several years of practical apprenticeship, or time at a pharmaceutical college.[22] Patent medicines, flotsam of the Middle Ages, were decried as quack nostrums, though still created and carried by many respectable establishments.

Despite this laudable caution, the drugs normally dispensed were limited by the technology and medicines of the day. They were usually no more than variations on sugar, simple opiate-derivative painkillers, and laxatives, with a good dose of herbal extracts throughout. The trick was in the preparation and the advertising. Chemists could make their fortunes (Jesse Boot did) with the right branded rose cream for the face, or blackcurrant-flavoured syrup of figs for the digestion. Then as now, pharmacies made an effort to provide more than medicine, in the hopes of trading in good times as well as bad. Davies, for example, made and sold hair and skin creams from his own trademarked recipes, and promoted massages given by a neighbouring doctor.

> If someone came in for a drug, very often he would chaff them into realising that what they needed was Carlsburga to take and a massage with Nasciodine—and so he built up a considerable business.[23]

Tessa's childhood was comfortable, rather than luxurious. She could take a bus to her co-educational day school in Deptford (of which more in a moment), or walk if the weather was fine. The Davies flat was not large, but it was big enough, and the family small enough, for Tessa to have her own room; many girls in the neighbourhood would share with other members of a large family, or sleep on a daybed in the kitchen or sitting room. She would be expected to help her mother in the pharmacy and home, attending to the endless repetitive housekeeping tasks that electricity was beginning to mitigate. Some domestic help still came from servants, whether live-in or come-out. The prevalence of extremely cheap unskilled female labour meant that even lower-middle-class families could afford to pay a maid.

---

[22] For more information on this fascinating sideline of practical medicine, see http://www.rpharms.com/museum-pdfs/tracing-people-and-premises-in-pharmacy.pdf. The Society maintains an excellent research service and small museum, as well as a useful website outlining the history of British dispensing.

[23] TVW to Dr C. E. Nicholas, 9 February 1931. WFP.

Whether she was capable or not was a different matter, and many women in Annie's position regretted the time they spent training 'raw' girls in the domestic arts, only to see them vanish to better pay or marriage.

> Then the servants left and there was only one, a General. A great deal of your comfort and happiness depends on having a good General.[24]

It is hard for the modern mind to understand the deeply ingrained place of servants in every level of pre-war society. Vacuum cleaners, refrigerators, gas and electric cookers, water boilers, modern plumbing, and the light bulb have revolutionized the way we carry out our daily tasks, just as mechanization and the assembly line changed the face of factory work. During Tessa's childhood, 'housemaid's knee' was a real injury, the result of the hours servants spent on their knees scrubbing floors and cleaning carpets with hard brushes. In a period when carpets were overlaid with carpets, and windows hung with velvet, dust accumulated on everything, constantly dispersed and constantly reforming. Without refrigeration, food had to be purchased almost daily or preserved via labour-intensive canning and jarring. Fires had to be stoked with heavy coal, brought up steep cellar stairs in buckets. Washing and drying laundry was a perpetual nightmare of labour, and one that was often farmed out to a poorer neighbour's home for a small fee. Many lower-class women supported their families by taking in washing.

Outside the kitchen and some more modern bathrooms, hot water existed only in jugs in bedrooms, also carried up in cans along steep inconvenient staircases. Chamberpots, also in bedrooms, had to be emptied, and perhaps composted for the garden. For a society much more socially stratified than our own, people of all ranks were forced into a much closer association than ourselves with each other's most personal bodily functions. Perhaps the strict separation of classes seemed more vital because of this.

Until the growth of office culture in the twentieth century, there was also a large surplus pool of unmarried or older women for whom the only respectable employment was domestic service. They ranged in character from the 'general' Guster of *Bleak House* (1853), the charity girl prone to fits and living off scraps in the corner of a squalid

---

[24] Nesbit (1899).

lower-class kitchen, to the aristocratic housekeeper Mrs Rouncewell of that same book, who lives in her own luxurious apartment within the great country house she manages. But the situation was changing. Tessa, born at the end of the nineteenth century, grew up expecting to do far more of her own housework than her mother, born at its height. This was particularly true after the First World War, when women began to desert 'service', or request what employers felt were impossibly high working standards. Around the same time, employers began to find that new developments in the technology of the home meant they simply did not require the same amount of help— that there was in fact *less* work to do. Tessa probably grew up with a 'daily' coming in every morning. As an adult, when she had the funds, she spent them on a weekly charwoman. This was partially because of economic necessity and lifestyle choices (the Wheelers could not be called home-bodies), but also reflects that she simply did not have as much housework to do as her mother.

FIRST STEPS IN EDUCATION

Annie was not a deliberate radical in the mould of E. Nesbit or Marie Stopes, despite her rebellion against social expectations. She simply ignored whatever she found inconvenient, whether it was a common-law marriage or her lack of a birth father for her daughter.

Her mother's luck was also Tessa's. Apart from an affectionate stepfather, settling in London placed her well as an intelligent little girl with no money. The state of education in Britain at the time was uneven. A nascent state system was moving rapidly to overtake or amalgamate traditional private schools and (for girls) home governesses. It is interesting to speculate that if Tessa's parents had just a little more money, she might have had a far less effective education at home in a more traditional style. As it was, she went to the Addey and Stanhope School in Deptford. Five months of fees there, or one term, came to about two pounds, and children occasionally went on to the London universities or to Oxbridge.

Originally founded to teach the area's poor, Addey and Stanhope had expanded by Tessa's time to a middle-class clientele, if one that occasionally had trouble meeting the school costs. That was one reason fees were assessed by the term, rather than year. In 1911, children studied a conventional 'three Rs' curriculum, but also learning singing, bookkeeping, shorthand, needlework, cookery, and woodworking.[25] These were considered the basic ingredients necessary for employment, and also for a happy social life and home. The economic and class forces at work within Deptford are betrayed by the school's assumption that employment was not an exclusively male destiny, and by its occasional discreet fees remission for suddenly out-of-work parents.

Addey and Stanhope was one of the first grammar schools in the area to teach co-educationally, and a participant in the new London County Council's scholarship scheme. These awards, which helped children and young people across a very wide spectrum of backgrounds and interests, were intended to fund the ambitions of poor but bright students, whether via trade school, art academy, or university. The only restriction was that the education in question had to take place within the greater London area. Sidney Webb outlined the process and its aims in the *Educational Times* in March 1907, two years after Tessa entered Addey and Stanhope.[26] The scholarships had first been put into action in 1904, so Webb was also reporting on the programme's initial success rate. Note that he avoids using gendered language when speaking of students.

> What the Council did was to set itself effectively to open the existing secondary schools to all clever children, however poor their parents might be [...] by expanding its old scholarship ladder into a broad educational highway. Every year all the boys and girls who by the age eleven to twelve have reached at all a good position in the public elementary schools [...] are nominated by their head teachers [...] To these twelve thousand are added any who choose to apply [...] From this mass of candidates those are chosen for junior county scholarships [...] by brightness of intelligence or any sort of intellectual promise, for five years' secondary schooling [...] These get free admission to any efficient secondary school at their own choice, so far as accommodation permits; together with allowances for maintenance to those who require them.[27]

These gorgeous scholarships were eventually expanded to allow a 'clever child' to pass from primary school through university or

---

[25] Addey and Stanhope School minutes, 1908–11 (ASSM).
[26] Ibid.   [27] Webb (1907).

trade school at no charge to his or her parents. It was an outstanding scheme, designed to help the 'struggling middle-class man [father]' who could not afford to pay school fees. Webb was straightforward in his defence of the programme. It was morally imperative for poor and middle-class children to have as good an education as the rich, and it was also socially and economically sensible. He did not intend the scheme to benefit only the rare genius child or slum savant, who could take advantage of more traditional bursaries aimed at the gifted few. The point of the County Council work was more humane in object: merely to raise more reasonably intelligent children into well-educated, thinking adult citizens.

> And that it is worth while for the community as a whole to foster every child of genius, however lowly born, and to secure to every clever child, even if not a genius, all the mental training he or she is capable of, is, to any economist or statesman, beyond dispute. It is the plain duty of the London County Council, as it is to the real interest of every Londoner.[28]

Tessa was one of those clever children. Fostered by this far-seeing and even radical educational concept, she represented a very different girl student from those across London being taught at pioneering private girls' schools like the North London Collegiate. It is at this moment that she begins to diverge from the usual storyline of an intellectual woman in the early twentieth century. She came from a relatively humble background, and she had to make her way in a mixed-sex environment. This theme in her response to and creation of educational institutions will be explored much more fully in the next chapter, and when discussing the Institute of Archaeology she co-founded in the 1930s. At this time, it is merely important to note the seed being dropped into receptive soil. It is quite absurd to suggest that tiny Tessa read or understood Webb's call to arms in 1907, but as one of the first group of children to benefit from his educational programmes, she must have absorbed at a molecular level the larger ideas and ideals they represented. Education was for anyone fit to undertake it; women as well as men, poor as well as rich. One became educated in order to earn a living, add to the community, and enrich the minds of others as they went about their own working lives. There is an idealism here related to, but distinct from, the educational ideas of reformers like Dorothea Beale and Millicent Fawcett. It is

---

[28] Webb (1907).

middle-class, focused more on earning a living than on intellectual attainments purely for their own sake. It mirrors, in fact, the differing agendas of the new London universities and the old colleges of Oxford and Cambridge. To be an extraordinary intellectual genius would be nice; but to contribute to one's community by educating and being educated was far more generally achievable, and less dependent on the unpredictable leavening of talent.

There is little record of Tessa's progress and behaviour at Addey and Stanhope, which any teacher will recognize as the mark of the reliable middle-row student—one who requires neither special discipline nor outstanding praise. The school council minutes refer to her only a few times.

11th July 1910: 'All the candidates sent in by the School for the Preliminary Certificate passed viz: Tessa Verney (with distinctions in English Literature and Experimental Science) [...]'

September 12, 1910: 'The following results of examinations have recently come to hand [...] Senior Cambridge Examinations [...]Tessa Verney, 3rd class Hons and spoken French.'[29]

This meant that Tessa could enter one of the London Training Colleges without further examination. However, she had different plans for her scholarship funds, and in 1911 matriculated at University College London. During her year between secondary school and university, she seems to have been employed as a pupil-teacher at the Queen Elizabeth Girls Grammar School in Barnet, North London. The University College London archives preserves a Queen Elizabeth homework schedule from 1910, which Tessa thriftily reused for her university work and lecture schedule around 1911.

Pupil-teaching was an established way for male and female students between 13 and 18 to gain classroom experience and an incidental education before passing on to a formal teacher training college. Two pupil-teachers were assigned to a teacher, the idea being they would thus receive an education and a start in a trade that could support them. It was a faintly medieval idea, an old-fashioned holdover from university sizars and subsizars; there are traces of it at Dotheboys Hall in *Nicholas Nickleby* (1839). The system was on its way out in London by 1910, as teacher training became increasing regulated in its own official facilities. The last pupil-teacher

---

[29] ASSM.

in London went on to a formal training college in 1913. Classroom work under a senior remains a part of a teacher's education today.

The year of pupil-teaching gave Tessa a chance to test the education she had gained at Addey and Stanhope in a different setting. It must have also added a little polish and maturity to her manner. She was a shy girl and physically very small. At Addey and Stanhope, she was almost invisible in the records of the school's many plays, sports, clubs, and organized games. By her time at university she was speaking up, joining committees, and making friends easily. That polish must have come from her year in the front of the classroom. Though she was still living at home, and would until she married, the small salary of a trainee would have been welcome as well.[30]

It is unclear why Tessa chose not to stay in teaching, with its secure path to genteel employment. Hawkes is probably right when she hypothesizes that it was Morgan Davies who encouraged his bright stepdaughter to matriculate at University College London; on her college entry form, she listed him, rather than her mother, as her legal guardian.[31] It was a move away from the established safety of continuing secondary teaching, three more years of non-earning for no guaranteed reward. She plunged in suddenly and eagerly, in one of the unexpected lateral moves that would occasionally surprise contemporaries throughout her life. Those who knew her in later years attributed those abrupt shifts to her loyalty to an abruptly shifting husband; but long before she knew Mortimer Wheeler, Tessa Verney knew her own mind, and was quietly determined to follow her own bent.

[30] London Authorities: www.lgfl.net/lgfl/accounts/holnet/upload/lsb/teachers/pupils.htm.
[31] Hawkes (1982: 48); Tessa Verney matriculation forms, UCLA.

3

UCL's Women and Pre-war Feminism: Tessa Verney's Models

The importance of University College London as Tessa Verney's intellectual birthplace cannot be understated. From 1910 onwards, her life remained oriented towards the magnetic north of Gower Street. UCL was the hub upon which all the major events of her personal and professional career turned. Her education, her marriage, her first home as a young wife, the birth of her only child, her teaching career, the Institute of Archaeology she founded, and the hospital in which she died can all be marked in one section of the Bloomsbury map. She may have worked in some of the more obscure parts of the Borders and one of the more fashionable corners of Piccadilly, but her mental equilibrium was set and balanced between 1910 and 1913.

'GODLESS IN GOWER STREET'

Before going into detail about Verney Wheeler's time at University College London, it is important to briefly examine the character and history of the institution she went to in 1910. It is both the location of her education and her badge of membership in a specific group of intellectual women in pre-war England. The women and men who went to University College were in general quite different from the men who took degrees at the old Oxbridge colleges, and the smaller number of women produced by institutions like Newnham. The most immediate difference was the simplest: a co-educational environment. At UCL, women were taught from 1869, could take the same lectures as men from 1878 onwards, and in 1880 the first four women graduates were released into a doubting world.[1]

That was not the only thing that made University College unusual and even suspect in the small world of Victorian and Edwardian universities. It had been founded in 1827, with lectures beginning the following year, and from the outset it departed from the norm. David Taylor astutely calls it 'a child of the Industrial Revolution', and so in truth it was.[2] Its aims and methods grew directly out of the social and political changes forced on England by the events of the eighteenth and nineteenth century, and in particular the needs of a new autodidactic intellectualism. Often self-taught and mechanical or scientific in their inclinations, these men and women reached their flowering in the Lunar Society of Birmingham and in William Hazlitt's *Spirit of the Age* (1825). They were eager for a new society, but in a constructive not destructive sense. Rather than destroy Oxford and Cambridge, with their medieval colleges, preoccupation with maintaining a classical curriculum, and insistence that students prove themselves communicating members of the state Church, the idealists behind UCL swiftly overleapt the old model and evolved it into something new. It is not too much to compare this process to the new manufacturing methods of James Watt and Josiah Wedgwood.

At its founding, the new college was characterized more by its insistence on religious freedom than by any other point. At the time of UCL's founding, Nonconformist Protestants, Catholics, and Jews were still excluded from an English university education, and had been for many years. While pressure was growing to change the situation, and would eventually result in a reform of the Oxbridge rule of admitting only practising Anglicans, there was a growing group of young men unwilling to wait for recognition before they went to university. The usual alternative was Scotland or the Continent, not a practical solution for most.

Students at University College were, from the first lecture, never required to affirm their membership in any religious group. More subtly, teaching at University College was also deliberately restricted from the beginning to secular subjects. Its founders were eager to prevent UCL from becoming embroiled in the endless religious

---

[1] Taylor (1968: 32–3); Sutherland (1990).   [2] Taylor (1968: 9).

factionalism that plagued Cambridge and especially Oxford. Intellectual in-fighting was far more interesting to their minds, and a lasting emphasis was thus laid on scientific subjects. In this, as in so much, University College reflected the hard-science, sometimes outright atheistic side of contemporary intellectual debates.

In a further move away from religion and monasticism, the college was made primarily non-residential. In 1897, around the time baby Tessa returned to London, there was no accommodation available for men; only thirty places were open for women.[3] The object was to cut students' costs and encourage them to treat college as a serious job. But there was a great additional advantage in 'living out' for female students. One of the objections to their inclusion at the traditional residential men's colleges was the impropriety of housing the sexes together, and the difficulty of maintaining strict proprieties in a mixed social group. In the Victorian period this was no small thing. Even women risking their marriagability through education were not devoid of all the contemporaneous feminine sensitivities—or, at the very least, did not wish to advertise it if they were. Since the majority of UCL's early students were Londoners with parents in the area, they saved money and lived at home.

At the college, separately gendered entrances, student societies, and tea rooms (though not lectures or seminars, because of the cost of paying twice for a teacher's time) were still insisted upon by the authorities.[4] This division grew increasingly feeble through the early twentieth century and vanished in due course, but at Tessa's matriculation, worried parents could still be fairly sure that the college would knowingly provide few unchaperoned entertainments for their daughters. Tessa still managed to meet a young man through a mixed-gender student society; but as this led properly to marriage, whether she is proof of the failure or success of the system is debatable.

At the time of its founding, the new London college was nicknamed the 'Cockney College' and heavily satirized in the contemporary press. Thomas Arnold's description, 'that Godless institution in Gower Street', is still used by neighbouring rival King's College (London) today.[5] It was widely believed that the college would attract the working class, the lower middle class, women, atheists, Quakers,

---

[3] Sutherland (1990: 36); Annan (1978: 5).
[4] Sutherland (1990: 39).   [5] Taylor (1968: 11–12).

Jews, freethinking philosophers, and other undesirables. It did. The
results were brilliant.

ACADEMIC WOMEN: THE SPECIAL ROLE OF UCL

For women, 1910 was an interesting year to walk down Gower Street.
There were a number of well-established female Fellows and graduates, who represented a strand of practical feminism as important as,
if less artistic than, that of their neighbour Virginia Woolf. Middle-
class, leftist women like the Egyptologist Margaret Murray were
arguing for the rights of women who worked as hard for University
College as their male colleagues, insisting on amenities as basic as a
pay envelope and a Common Room. UCL had pioneered the teaching
and qualification of women, but in a more esoteric or social sense was
slow to accept female members. As Gillian Sutherland says, despite
many pioneering social ideals, the constituent colleges of the new
University of London (with which UCL was amalgamated upon the
University of London's founding in 1863) were never completely
'untouched by, or in some special way insulated from, the social
conventions of the day'.[6]

There was continuing societal pressure for single-sex colleges, with
several being founded in London during the Victorian period, and a
university exclusively for women was even spoken of at one point. For
many years, the social environment of the Oxbridge colleges was the
preferred method of understanding and defining a university experience. The purpose of the old colleges was not primarily to gain a
liberal education, although they did produce great scholars. It was to
be educated as a member of an elite class of men whose function was
to variously serve the larger community or nation as aspects of its
ruling bodies; military, civil, political, and religious. This was recognized and applauded by the universities themselves, much as the
public schools that fed them famously aimed at fulfilling Thomas
Hughes' ideal in *Tom Brown at Rugby*.

> The object of all schools is not to ram Latin and Greek into boys, but to
> make them good English boys, good future citizens; and by far the most

---

[6] Sutherland (1990: 39).

important part of that work must be done, or not done, out of school hours.[7]

If the goal of school and university was to raise good English men, women must by definition be excluded. University College represented a redefinition of the university process for men as well as women. It is interesting, therefore, to consider how little it is referenced in discussions concerning the higher education of women in the United Kingdom. This may be attributed in large part to the *Three Guineas* phenomenon. Women's colleges like Girton and Newnham might not award degrees or even offer a full curriculum, but in terms of social prestige they were still more respectable than the co-ed or single sex colleges of the University of London. A 'nice' girl might go to Girton and still get married to a 'nice' boy; her bluestocking ambitions could endanger her chances at fulfilling her ultimate social function as the mother of good English boys (as Gertrude Bell's family feared hers might), but not irreparably.

When examining women active academically in Bloomsbury just before the First World War, Virginia Woolf comes swiftly to mind. Her famous call to young women was not to come until more than a decade after Tessa Verney was active at University College; by 1929 and *A Room of One's Own*, Tessa Verney Wheeler was already a Fellow of the Society of Antiquaries of London, a recognized expert at Roman excavation and history, and generally a serious professional who required no further liberation than that she could achieve by her own efforts. Still, it is of value to examine Woolf's ideas about women and university education, as she represents to a great degree the most elite, upper-class view. Whether that applies to University College is a debatable point.

> What one wants, I thought—and why does not some brilliant student at Newnham or Girton supply it?—is a mass of information [about historical women]; at what age did she marry; how many children had she as a rule; what was her house like; had she a room to herself; did she do the cooking; would she be likely to have a servant?[8]

The questions posed to the brilliant students are all good ones, and in point of fact this chapter addresses many of them in Verney Wheeler's case. However, as Olwen Hufton points out, the queries are all

---

[7] T. Hughes, *Tom Brown at Rugby* (1857).   [8] Woolf (1929: 28).

still oriented towards the idea of the woman as child-bearer and homemaker; the possibility of other roles for her in the society of the past is not considered.[9] There is also an inherent assumption in the questions that a woman worth a historian's discussion would have servants, not be one. All these generalizations arose from the specific social expectations of Woolf and her audience. Girton girls who never married and became academics (like Eileen Power) or public figures (like Gertrude Bell) moved in a higher circle generally than their London counterparts. Virginia Woolf's passionate appeal for private space and a private income for clever women takes on a new, less radical appearance when it is seen as the extension to a certain class of women of what their brothers had enjoyed for hundreds of years. This is not the place for a discussion of whether Woolf intended equality for a social group or a whole gender. It is enough to note here that she was as conflicted concerning the matter as a woman of her intelligence might be expected to be, and as casually prejudiced as a member of her class could hardly avoid being. The interested reader is directed to Alison Light's excellent recent book *Mrs Woolf and the Servants*, which discusses both Woolf and the women servants who made her life possible in the most detailed and intriguing terms. Light's book is a rare accomplishment; well-written, penetrating, and sympathetic to all its subjects without over-romanticizing any of them.[10]

Tessa's matriculation at University College, rather than Girton or Somerville, is one indicator of the type of feminist influences she came under during her college years. The more aristocratic Oxford and Cambridge women's colleges represented a more exclusive approach to educating women, best expressed by Woolf (who resented her own more informal education) in her 1928 talks at Newnham and Girton, the lectures that became *A Room of One's Own*. Practical social differences meant that Tessa received her initial academic training in an environment where women learned alongside men, and where middle-class students expected to earn their own living upon graduation.[11] But whatever the contrasts between the various types of college educations available to women in the period, what

---

[9] Hufton (1997: 931).   [10] Light (2007).

[11] Comparative biographic studies of the intellectual climates at Girton and Newnham respectively at this time may be found in recently published lives of the academics Eileen Power and Jane Harrison (Berg 1996; Robinson 2002).

was learned often mattered less than the method of its teaching. Theresa B. Goell, an American archaeologist born in 1901, studied philosophy, social ethics, and housing during her undergraduate years. The applicability of such a BA to her excavations at Nemrud Dagi in Turkey is not obvious, but she described it in this way: 'I think what I learned at Radcliffe was motivation. I might have just as well gone the other way. I might have settled down, gardened, and painted and played Piano.'[12]

For traditionalist critics of the London University, one woman was the personification of their most extreme fears concerning women graduates. She was intelligent, sexually outspoken, unpredictable, socially amoral, partially educated in Germany, and occasionally embarrassing even to her friends. That these were personal rather than gendered characteristics does not seem to have registered with her contemporaries, perhaps because the lady in question made a lifelong effort to present herself in a most gendered way.

Marie Stopes, the flamboyant scientist and campaigner for birth control, began her career at UCL.[13] She graduated with a B.Sc., double honours, and a gold medal in botany in 1902, and went on to take a doctorate in Munich. In 1911, the year Tessa matriculated, Stopes was made a Fellow of UCL. Her 'respectable' career as a paleobotanist and geologist took place partially within its laboratories. Indeed, her UCL lectureship in paleobotany meant she was actually senior in academic rank to her first husband, the Canadian botanist Reginald Ruggles Gate—a contributing factor in the breakdown of their marriage.

By the time of her second marriage to the unfortunate Humphrey Roe in 1918, Stopes had added two new interests to paleobotany: birth control and eugenics. She was one of the first successful British campaigners for safe family planning and the open expression of a woman's sexuality within traditional marriage. Her books and poetry, especially *Married Love* (1918), remain startling today in their freedom and overblown language. Stopes resigned from University College London in 1920, and went on to a long career in her chosen interests. She remains a complex, even offputting figure, but her importance to the nascent women's rights movement and its later focus on reproductive health and sexual freedom is not small.

---

[12] Sanders and Gill (2004: 483).
[13] See Hall (1977) for the excellent biography of Marie Stopes from which this short passage is condensed.

Tessa Verney was not at all like the outgoing and self-advertising Stopes in character. She had no personal or professional relationship with the scientist as a student or an adult. What the presence of Stopes at UCL in 1911 does mean is that Tessa was spending every day of her university career, developing as a thinking person, in a place where an issue as delicate and modern as birth control was a subject of open debate. Stopes could only have happened at the University of London; it is impossible to think of her at Newnham or Somerville. 'Godless', indeed.

TWO PRACTICAL MODELS

Two direct models can be found at UCL for Tessa's professional life, women whom she knew later personally and at least by sight and by reputation as a student. They are Hilda Petrie, the traditional professor's wife, and Margaret Murray, the single, self-supporting academic. Both were active in the same field—Egyptology—and both are remembered mainly as the adjunct of a great man, the redoubtable William Flinders Petrie, the man Mortimer Wheeler saw as his greatest living model in the field.

Of the two, Margaret Murray may in retrospect be the most important. She is the clearest exponent of the hybrid teaching and working methods Tessa would use herself in later years. They certainly knew each other as colleagues in the 1930s. Hilda Petrie also made a reappearance in Tessa's adult life, when the Petries became socially and professionally acquainted with the young Wheelers.

Hilda Petrie

Hilda Urlin Petrie is a half-translated cipher. She has not been individually studied in a conventional publication, but is extensively discussed in Margaret Drower's definitive 1985 biography of Flinders Petrie. From this work, Drower, a former Petrie student, has also developed an independent essay for Brown University's online Breaking Ground project.[14] Both Hilda Petrie and her husband were well

---

[14] Drower (2004a).

known to the Wheelers in later years. Rik Wheeler considered Flinders Petrie one of the finest minds he ever knew, and the only living archaeologist working according to the strict rules he followed himself. The Petries even vacationed with the Wheelers on their Brecon Gaer dig in the 1920s. An interesting letter (reproduced in Chapter 5) survives from Flinders Petrie to Rik Wheeler, in which he discusses the suppression of Tessa Wheeler's work on the site in the published report. He assumes the reason behind it to be 'family propriety'. Later, in the 1930s, Tessa and Margaret Murray were put in the embarrassing position of dealing with Petrie's high-handed methods of requisition. As his known partisans on the British School in Egypt funding committee, they often had to explain away his pre-emptive financial arrangements.

The Petries are often mentioned in the same breath as the Wheelers as a typical archaeological couple of their period. The parallels are interesting though not exact. Hilda Urlin was a generation older than Tessa, born into an English family temporarily settled in Ireland in 1871.[15] She spent most of her childhood from 1875 onwards in England, where her family enjoyed a comfortable upper-class lifestyle with a main residence in Sussex and a winter house in London. She was educated by a governess at the local rectory, in the approved high-Victorian method for schooling girls. Her opinion of this may be judged by her insistence years later than her own daughter attend a co-educational boarding school alongside her brother.

The Urlins had some unusual connections who enlivened their conventional circle, including, in Sussex, Hilda's friend Philippa and her suffragette mother, Dame Millicent Fawcett. Whether the friendship was fostered by geographical convenience or intellectual sympathies is unclear. Either way, Hilda grew up knowing that there was a degree of freedom possible for young women, if they were willing to fight for it. Philippa Fawcett went on to Newnham and the distinction of scoring 'above the Senior Wrangler', or highest, on the Mathematical Tripos of 1890—Cambridge University having taken this linguistic evasion to avoid awarding the coveted title of Senior Wrangler to a woman.

Hilda went to London instead, 'came out', and was duly launched on the search for a husband which was expected to be the business of

---

[15] The majority of this biographical information is drawn from Drower (2004a), unless otherwise referenced.

her late teens and early 20s. Here she began to strike out a little on her own. She might not be at Cambridge, but she did attend lectures at King's College for Women in London. It was the least academic of the women's colleges in the area, and not strictly attached to the University of London. It did draw some teachers from that amorphous entity, but for the most part focused on subjects traditionally considered appropriate for women. Classes were designed to help young women run a home (dressmaking) or a charity (book-keeping), or to serve as a pleasant hobby (botany or painting). In 1910 this was summarized for the unsympathetic Royal Commission on the University of London.

> We wish to attract the girl of the leisured class who, having left school, has both the time and the desire to follow some course of study which may be of practical use to her, whether in home life or in social or philanthropic work.[16]

This was rather different from the aims of most other women's college and co-educational institutions, whose goals were to produce women academics and women workers. The Royal Commission characterized King's as:

> supplying lectures in literary and scientific subjects, or instruction in music and the fine arts for the ladies of Kensington who can devote only their spare time to them, or as finishing courses of study for girls after leaving school.[17]

The girls taking finishing courses included Hilda Urlin. As a result, she developed an amateur interest in geology and drawing, and this combination of talents brought her in 1896 to Professor Flinders Petrie at University College London. She was recommended to him, possibly by a King's teacher, as an accurate facsimile draftswoman. She could not read hieroglyphics (relatively few people could in the period, even among academics), but she was an excellent copyist and transmitted them precisely for those who could.

In this period, before effective colour reproduction and in the infancy of photography, good watercolour and pencil copies of frescos, hieroglyphs, and art were vital to Egyptology. Apart from their value in disseminating information, these beautiful images were often the only records of destroyed or lost artefacts. Scientific subjects other

---

[16] As quoted in Sutherland (1990: 43).   [17] Ibid.

than archaeology required artists too, but women were often only permitted limited recognition or involvement in the resulting research. At the same time Hilda Urlin first met Flinders Petrie, a shy and cloistered Beatrix Potter was making accurate and sensitive drawings of fungal and lichen forms, both in nature and through a microscope. These led her to a small breakthrough in the understanding of mycology, and her authoring of a paper read on her behalf by her uncle at the Linnaean Society in 1897. Potter drifted away from the subject after being coldly rejected as a student at Kew, and as a contributor by the Royal Society. Her story is a testament to the ways in which women were actively and tacitly discouraged from independent work on scientific subjects.[18]

Flinders Petrie found Hilda Urlin to be passionately interested in developing her embryonic knowledge of Egyptology. She was also beautiful and, in her own informal way, intellectually advanced. Their courtship was hampered by his scruples in taking any wife at all, but she reassured him that his relative poverty and intense focus on his subject held no fears for her. They were married in 1897 and left their wedding breakfast early for an archaeological honeymoon on the Nile.

Now Hilda Petrie found herself in her element. She shed her skirts in the privacy of the sand hollows, and threw herself into assisting her husband. How fortunate that helping him, that most appropriate of wifely duties, also meant following her own intellectual bent! And in the desert, she began to unfold her personality. In public, and in publications, she remained until death the dutiful, silent shadow of her great husband, faithful to her high Victorian training. In the East, she expanded into her true self. Her role on digs was made up of what she wanted to do and what she was good at, not dictated by social expectations.

Apart from her skills with pen and pencil, she learned to manage their local diggers and few European assistants with aplomb. With the greatest archaeologist of the day as her constant example, she swiftly became proficient in the thousand technical details of conducting a dig and dealing with the information it produced. Unlike most male archaeologists then and now, Petrie did not expect her to take on the domestic management of his camps. Hilda had no interest in and no

---

[18] Lane (1968: 41–4).

talent for the traditional female role of nurse, cook, and confidante. Tessa Verney Wheeler was the 'mother' and general commissary for all the digs she ran, and Margaret Murray doctored everyone brought to her in the East, but Hilda Petrie firmly avoided such activities. As Margaret Drower remembered, Hilda never 'could boil an egg'.[19] Granted, Petrie's style of digging left precious little domesticity *to* manage. Generations of Petrie students wailed over his Spartan living arrangements, sitting on boxes and eating bland tinned food (occasionally from tins the frugal Petrie had buried, unused, the season before). He was a scrupulous man, and wanted every penny available spent on the work rather than fleeting personal comforts. Even chocolate bars were not just a convenient source of energy; they provided an excellent supply of thin foil perfect for taking copies of shallow reliefs.[20]

Hilda Petrie's work with her husband is interesting psychologically. The greater part of the work she did was outgoing and 'male'— managing the dig workers and physically inspecting dangerous sites and monuments. Her silence in the long-term record, though, is archetypally inwards and 'female'. Even when she managed digs independently, with an all-female research staff, she left it to other women on that staff to publish the results. Compared to Margaret Murray or Tessa Verney Wheeler, her bibliography seems pitifully thin and is mainly composed of introductions to and chapters in the books of others. Why would a woman who was intrepid enough to travel independently by camel in the most dangerous parts of the Sinai be afraid of publicizing the work she did once she arrived at her destination?

The answer, in her husband's own words, was 'family propriety', the phrase he used many years later when wondering why Tessa Verney Wheeler's name was absent from a Welsh site report. To publish

---

[19] Drower (2004a: 11).

[20] *How to Observe in Archaeology*, a 1920 guide for interested amateur travellers, deserves to be better known today; if only for its Petrie-authored sections on Methods and Equipment, and on Egypt. It is freely available online via the Gutenberg project, and includes a good deal of timelessly useful advice. In a few places, Petrie's sly sense of humour shows itself; e.g. regarding travel in the Middle East and Africa: 'It is best to carry money in a little bag or screw of paper, loose in the jacket pocket, if in a risky district. It can then be dropped on any alarm and picked up afterwards.' It is difficult to see how this serves the unfortunate wanderer, apart from getting the mugging over with a little faster.

independently or with her husband was to set herself up, however mildly, in equal competition with him. That might be all right for Margaret Murray, a single suffragette, but it hardly seemed appropriate for a loving helpmate. Hilda Urlin was brought up to support her husband to the fullest extent she could professionally—to an impressive degree in her case. But the key word here is *support*, not challenge. Tessa Wheeler would struggle with this idea herself briefly upon leaving Cardiff in the 1920s, as she began to publish both alone and with her husband. Unlike her predecessor, though, she was able to work around the limitations of personal and spousal expectations and find a more open working partnership with her husband.

Hilda Petrie did take on some specifically female tasks in Egypt. Like a Dickens heroine, and like Tessa, she kept the running accounts and managed the day-to-day money. She also recorded the small finds on her husband's instruction, laying the groundwork for the careful notation critical to the later Wheeler system. Women continue to be more active than men in small objects work today, reflecting a long-surviving idea of what is appropriate to a presumably domestic gender; costume and textile studies, almost totally dominated by women, are examples of this.[21] Fundraising was also Hilda's province, as it became Tessa's, but that is an issue for another chapter. At the moment, it is enough to note that Tessa found at least one potential model for her later life as a married archaeologist working only a few hundred feet away in the Edwards Library—at least outside the excavation season.

Margaret Murray

Unlike Tessa Wheeler and Hilda Petrie, Margaret Murray presents one specific gift to the biographer. She left behind a first-person account of her life and career via her 1964 autobiography, one of her hundreds of bibliographical credits. She represents an important model from which Tessa could draw information about how to be an archaeologist, and how to maintain a female identity in the male world of academia.

Murray was also an important figure at UCL during Tessa's undergraduate years, working on woman's welfare issues at the college

[21] Root (2004).

alongside the first Lady Superintendent and then the Tutor to Women Students. This certainly brought her in contact with a young Tessa Verney, who in the fullness of time became a similar mentor figure to the young women *she* trained.[22]

Murray has been fairly extensively reminisced on, if not re-examined, since her death. Most recently, her former pupil Margaret S. Drower published a biographical essay in the 2004 book *Breaking Ground: Pioneering Women Archaeologists*. Murray's own autobiography was published in 1964 under the mischievous title *My First Hundred Years*.[23]

When Margaret Murray came to University College London in January 1894, she was 31 years old and without any defined path in life. She was born in India to missionary parents and grew up in various Indian and European locations, had never married, and by 1894 had passed the age of ever expecting to.[24] Her peripatetic education had been relatively good. She and her older sister had been primarily taught at home, barring two or three years in a girl's school at Sydenham.[25] They were instructed in arithmetic, geography, and history by their mother, herself a most intelligent and interesting woman. Murray inherited her lifelong interest in women's rights from her mother, Margaret Carr Murray, a strong-minded woman whose medical ambitions had been thwarted. Instead, the elder Murray became a missionary worker in Calcutta of the most enlightened and admirable type, working to improve the living conditions of the veiled wives in the Hindu zenanas through group employment and personal emancipation. Margaret Carr Murray is of particular interest to the modern reader in her emphasis on the importance of Christian behaviour and a Christian heart, rather than the simplistic and heavy-handed cultural imperialism dealt out by many other Victorian missionaries. She may be profitably compared to John Lockwood Kipling, another Victorian whose limited racial viewpoint was leavened by a genuine appreciation of and sensitivity to Indian culture.[26]

Mrs Murray found various tutors to teach her daughters music, drawing, and French.[27] The three women also lived in Bonn for two years at her instigation, leaving Murray with fluent German.[28] This

---

[22] Murray (1963: ch. 9).   [23] Murray (1963).
[24] Drower (1985: 210).   [25] Murray (1963: 74–5).
[26] Ibid. 20–21.   [27] Ibid. 30, 65, 70–71, 74–5; Drower (2004b: 110).
[28] Murray (1963: 71).

range of subjects was unusual for a Victorian girl, but not unique, and while it is impossible to generalize about the quality of at-home education in this period, in Murray's case it was very good. It is also an illustration of how much maternal care affected quality of contemporary female middle-class education. Her mother wanted her daughters, her only children, to be intellectually capable; the move to Bonn was made partially so that they could learn German and be educated in the stern German intellectual tradition.[29] In later years, Marie Stopes would take her doctorate in Munich with the same aims.

Margaret wanted to become a nurse, but like Florence Nightingale only a little earlier faced considerable paternal opposition.[30] Despite the work of Nightingale, it was not quite yet a respectable career for a lady. With her mother's support she entered the Calcutta General Hospital as a lady probationer in 1883, on the condition that she on no account be *paid* for her labour. Her nursing career ended after three months on her father's insistence, but her work at the hospital had a glorious coda when the Anglican nuns who ran it asked her to return during a cholera epidemic. At 21, she ran two hospital wards alone and, when the last nun became ill, was in sole charge of the hospital for two days. She wrote many years later that 'the little medical knowledge that I had absorbed [in that time] came in very useful in an excavating camp', and indeed she became the de facto local doctor when working in remote regions.[31]

A second and less heroic attempt on her part to find 'some sort of training' led to philanthropy and district visiting back in England in 1886; this also petered out. Although her father had changed his mind and given her permission to nurse, London hospital regulations declared her too short, at 4 foot 10 inches.[32] She kept up her genteel community work but found the work unchallenging, even if it was padded out with painting, sewing for the poor, and the endlessly complex cycle of social calls.[33] It was an unsatisfying life for a physically active, intelligent woman.

While visiting her married older sister, Mary, in Madras in 1893, a notice of Flinders Petrie's classes in hieroglyphics at UCL was

[29] Ibid. 20.
[30] Ibid. 79.
[31] Murray (1963: 84–5).
[32] Drower (2004b: 111); Janssen and Janssen (1996: 147).
[33] Murray (1963: 85).

discovered by the two women in the *Times*. Murray herself had never heard of Petrie, but her sister insisted she attend. '*Now that I am married* [italics added] I can't go to these classes myself but you must', her sister remembered her saying.[34] It is a revealing phrase. And in January 1894 Murray duly enrolled and began the class in elementary Egyptian, one of only two in the country at that time. She would go on to lecture and teach at UCL for thirty-seven years, retiring in 1935 as a D.Litt. and with the title Assistant Professor of Egyptology.[35] She had so little money at her departure that her students subscribed among themselves to buy her doctoral robes.

Murray took quickly to Egyptian grammar, despite beginning in the second term of the course after the preliminary explanations of the concept of hieroglyphics had already been concluded. She was aided by her fluency in German, as at the time the only real textbook was in that language. Other students began to turn to her for aid, and after about a year she was interested enough to request (along with other pupils) an advanced as well as elementary class.[36] Although she could have entered a degree programme, Murray preferred a course of independent study. The only degree she ever received from UCL was her honorary D.Litt. in 1931.[37] This can be attributed to gender modesty or to her relatively advanced age on coming to UCL. It is not a vital question. It was a was a time and place when academic degrees were more rare than now, for men as well as women, and in which the paths to university departments were far more varied.[38]

Petrie was not in the department when Murray began, as he made a practice of spending the cold weather excavating in Egypt. He lectured brilliantly on his own work during the autumn and spring terms, so much so that the public were allowed to attend his first lecture of every term free, and he often got ovations from his regular students.[39] In the meantime Egyptology was actually taught in somewhat haphazard fashion. Even Murray, one of his most devoted pupils, recognized Petrie as a wonderful lecturer and a terrible teacher. He had no patience with amateur beginners, or those less intelligent than himself, and couldn't manage a class of students

---

[34] Ibid. 30.
[35] Ibid. 92–3.
[36] Ibid. 95.
[37] Janssen and Janssen (1996: 145).
[38] Murray (1963: 153).
[39] Ibid. 93.

inevitably containing members of both those groups. Those with a real interest and ability found him (as Murray did) a mentor in the best sense. Others were merely put off.

When Petrie came back from excavating in Koptos in 1894, Murray volunteered to help with the publication's illustrations. When she finished, he had another assignment: to research the descent of property in the Old Kingdom for him, using the few books on the subject.

> When this was done—and it took some days for my hieroglyphic knowledge was still very elementary—I was about to hand the whole thing over to him, but he said 'No, you have done all the work, now you must write the article.' I met that shock bravely and wrote the article which I showed to Petrie, he made a few verbal alterations, then sent it with a covering letter to the Editor of the *Proceedings of the Society of Biblical Archaeology* [for 1895]. When the proofs came he showed me how to correct them.[40]

It was her first publication, and she never forgot the pleasure of seeing herself in print. It is interesting to consider how much Petrie's support encouraged her in amassing an impressive list of publications, and to wonder whether his wife Hilda's relative silence exists because of or despite her husband's efforts.

Once Petrie was aware of Murray's teaching abilities, he put her to work in 1898 as the teacher of the elementary Egyptian class. She was a junior lecturer at first, on a salary of £20 a year; due to UCL's peculiar payroll system, her wages had to come out of Petrie's.[41] In 1921 she was promoted to a Lecturer, in 1922 a senior lecturer and Fellow, and finally the Assistant Professor of Egyptology (at which level she retired) in 1924.[42]

This led directly to one of her most important legacies: her organization of the UCL Egyptology degree into a training programme. Under her hand, it began to encompass not just language and art, but also some of the practical principles of archaeological excavation.[43] The degree of her involvement cannot be overestimated; it was on her

---

[40] Ibid. 93.

[41] Ibid. 153.

[42] Drower's (2004a) biography lists Murray's dates slightly differently from Murray's own autobiography; e.g. Drower says she became a Fellow in 1932. I follow Murray's dates here.

[43] Murray (1963: 103).

initiative that a real training course was begun in 1910, consisting of two years of intensive study followed by eleven exams and—if all went well for the student—a College Certificate in Egyptology. She eventually drew in professors from other departments and colleges to teach specialized subjects such as skeletal anatomy and physical anthropology, but always did a great deal of the Egyptological work herself. She had very modern priorities for young archaeologists: anatomy, scale drawing, anthropology and ethnology, mineralogy, objects dating, ancient art, and from 1916, organic chemistry. A student who did well in all these areas would be asked to go out to Egypt with Petrie, in a pattern later repeated by the Wheelers.[44]

The 1923–4 general syllabus for Egyptology was typical: Petrie taking a lecture series on religious life in Egypt in the first term, departing (presumably for Egypt) during the second while Murray taught Egyptian history, and then returning in May to give six lectures on his recent finds, and an evening course on objects dating. Simultaneously, Murray also taught six other courses for regular students, and two Egyptology evening courses.[45]

Petrie often took good students (women as well as men) to Egypt with him to assist on his digs. His theories of seriation and ideas about careful excavation methods were revolutionary, and at that early point he could only be sure of his student's abilities if he trained them himself (a pattern the Wheelers would repeat in the 1920s). Petrie's method of excavation training, and what kind of excavators he preferred to turn out, are both excellently discussed in Margaret Drower's 1985 biography. He was as idiosyncratic as most great innovators.

Murray's first dig was in Egypt, in the winter of 1902–3, when Petrie asked her to join his camp in Abydos. She and his wife, Hilda, were assigned the excavation of a buried stone building behind the main temple of Sethos I (later identified as an Osireion), and Murray was also asked to copy the temple inscriptions and graffiti. As it ranged from hieratic to demotic to Coptic, her combined artistic and linguistic experience made her an excellent choice.[46]

---

[44] Janssen (1992: 11–12). Note that Mortimer Wheeler also advised a young man interested in archaeology to lay his groundwork in geology (Hawkes 1982: 128).

[45] Janssen (1992: 13, fig. 5).

[46] She published *Elementary Egyptian Grammar* in 1905, and *Elementary Coptic Grammar* in 1911. Both became standard textbooks and went through multiple editions (Murray 1963: 207; Drower 2004a: 135).

The Abydos team consisted of five men and four women. Although Petrie was in most respects laudably indifferent to the misogyny of his day, he was not completely immune to it, and Murray found Petrie treated her differently from the three men who were also excavating for the first time. They had a week or two of work under Petrie's direction before beginning solo digs, whereas he merely took Murray over the site she was to work on with his wife and gave her an exhaustive lecture on where and how to begin. She said later that she 'learnt more on that one occasion than from all the books on excavations I have read'.[47] And it can certainly be read as a compliment—Murray, working with Hilda Petrie and already an academic Egyptologist, was not in need of the same direction as a beginner. Her first day of work, however, was an open test of her abilities as a woman. Petrie told her to begin the excavation without his wife, whose guidance Murray had depended on. He sent her off to the Osireion as sole leader, at the head of a large group of Egyptian diggers and basket boys. They refused to take her orders.

> Then I realised it was a try-on, so I stopped, made everybody turn round, and marched the whole lot back to the camp, where I was met by Petrie. I knew by his expression that he must have been quite well aware of what was likely to happen and looked upon it as a test of my ability to manage a gang composed of men only. The men and boys lost a whole day's paid work, and I let it be known that I was really angry. So after that I had no trouble with men or boys (or Petrie). The three male beginners had a week or two working with Petrie; then, and only then, [Charles Trick] Currelly was given a dig of his own; but none of them was submitted to a similar test, and I resented the fact.[48]

The excavation was complicated by the structure's size and depth; there was also a problem with groundwater. It was eventually cleared completely in 1930 by another expedition. Murray published an excellent volume on the Osireion in 1904, with copies of the texts and a discourse on the worship of Osiris that prefigured her later interest in fertility cults and folklore.[49] In her autobiography, Murray's only story about Hilda Petrie is a wonderful one about a nocturnal expedition with another man and woman of the Abydos excavation, to see if a rumour of local hooligans destroying the

---

[47] Murray (1963: 118).
[48] Ibid. 118–19.
[49] Murray (1904).

Osireion was true. The three women joined hands and danced across the dunes from the camp to the dig. They horrified their male companion, who while kind was traditional in his ideas about ladies.[50]

In the winter of 1903–4 Murray went out to Egypt again with one of her camp-mates from Abydos, Miss F. Hansard, and another female archaeologist, Jessie Mothersole. Petrie directed the women to Saqqara, where they made copies of the relief sculptures on the walls of the area's Old Kingdom mastabas. Some had already been roughly excavated by Auguste Mariette many years previously. His old *reis* or foreman Rubi still lived in the area, and sped the work by directing them to the tombs he had previously opened.[51] It was a pleasant and profitable season, resulting in Murray's second book, *Saqqara Mastabas, Part I* (1905).[52]

For some time after 1904, a strong sense of family responsibilities often kept Murray in England. As the unmarried daughter, she was responsible for her paralysed mother's care. Drower gives a vignette of Murray preparing classes at her mother's bedside, the traditional maiden daughter allied to the conscientious modern teacher.[53] Petrie was also reluctant to take her away from UCL, as at that time good teachers were more rare than enthusiastic excavators. When Petrie's co-department head, Dr J. H. Walker, died in 1914, another roadblock was thrown up:

> [O]nly Professor Petrie and I were left to run the department. This meant that if one was away the other had to stay. Petrie in normal times went to Egypt in mid-November and did not return until April or even May, and though always willing to help he could not give any regular training to the students.[54]

She would not excavate again until 1921, sacrificing her ambitions in that direction to the needs of Petrie: not because he was a man and she a woman, but because she truly believed him to be a genius whose work deserved priority.

Of all the indirect influences coming into TessaVerney's life as she entered UCL, Margaret Murray may in retrospect have been the most

---

[50] Murray (1963: 116).

[51] Ibid. 125–9.

[52] The second part of the Saqqara publication, containing a translation of the texts, did not appear until 1937.

[53] Murray (1963: 103); Drower (2004b: 115).

[54] Murray (1963: 103).

important. She is the clearest exponent of the hybrid teaching and working methods Tessa would use herself in later years.

My First Hundred Years also preserves an excellent first-hand account of the place of women at UCL during the time Tessa studied there. When Murray came to Gower Street in 1894, she was one of about seventy-two women then enrolled at UCL in various disciplines. She stayed on, first as a lecturer and then as an Assistant Professor, until 1935. She was also a Fellow of the college during that period.

Murray was an early member of the suffragette movement, but never participated in any of its more militant or violent activities. Drower thinks that this was as usual the result of Murray's diminutive height.[55] She certainly had a temperament that drove her to the most activity possible in any role. It was a time when there could still be considerable argument and hand-wringing in the Women's Common Room over whether the lady members should express an opinion to the all-male College Committee regarding who should be appointed the new Tutor for Women Students—that is, who should be appointed as their own representative *on* the College Committee! Murray was outraged at 'the feeling [among...] a certain type of woman, to be afraid to express an opinion which might offend the men'.[56] It was a type of woman that was rapidly vanishing, largely due to the brisk work Murray and her female colleagues did to improve the lot of the younger women of the college.

Change at UCL was not only accomplished through political activity with the suffrage movement, but also through the kind of solid, everyday improvements that are perhaps more often the brainchildren of women than men.[57] The problems Murray tackled were the practical ones that can be as crippling to a student as more esoteric academic difficulties. One of her favourite accomplishments was the establishment of a self-supporting student canteen, a unisex operation that grew out of a specifically female problem. The young ladies of UCL had nowhere to eat or get a cup of tea during their long days of study; the cafes of Bloomsbury were yet to come. Most, like Tessa, lived with their families out in London's suburbs, and tightly packed

---

[55] Drower (2004b: 117).
[56] Murray (1963: 162).
[57] Murray (1963: ch. 10) has a first-hand account of the association. I have been unable to make any satisfactory personal connection between Verney Wheeler and the suffrage/anti-suffrage movements.

lecture schedules made it impossible for them to go home for their meals. The college refectory was expensive and masculine. Murray and the first two Tutors for Women Students took up the cause of a woman's common room and a real student's canteen, resulting in the establishment of both.[58]

Many young women found a personal mentor in her as well. Veronica Seton-Williams, also a beloved student of Verney Wheeler, remembered the kindness Murray showed to her when she arrived at UCL from Australia as a young woman in the 1930s. The older woman took her on weekend walks through London to nearby sites of interest. Even more thoughtfully, she handed over her evening classes in Egyptology at the City Literary Institute to Seton-Williams, who like her had no private income. Murray earned her living and her invalid mother's though many part-time teaching jobs, in a way curiously reminiscent of many modern academics and 'culture sector' workers. There is still a lingering feeling in the academic establishment that, as all academics must spring from the educated (i.e. upper or moneyed) classes, it would almost an offence to pay them properly for their work. In Murray's day, that belief was openly expressed.[59]

It is probable that Murray was a known presence in Tessa's life during her time at UCL, though she did not take any of the many courses the older woman prescribed for students interested in Egyptology.[60] Murray's work among and for women studying all subjects made her an example to many pupils. She was the opposite of the terrible and stereotyped bluestocking—a humorous, cheerful, and affectionate woman, who occasionally handed out chocolates in her lectures. But she was also a serious scholar, whose abbreviated bibliography easily spans five pages and covers everything from technical archaeological reports on Egypt and Palestine to the articles and books on folklore that occupied her later years.[61]

As a feminist, her suffrage work looms the largest in the modern eye, but Margaret Murray was probably more memorable to a young Tessa Verney as the woman professor who efficiently ran the Egyptology department and simultaneously fought for the rights of women students to have comforts as simple as a cup of tea and a room with

---

[58] Ibid. 158–63.
[59] Seton-Williams (1988: 112); Janssen (1992: 31).
[60] Murray (1963: 103); Janssen (1992: 11–12).
[61] Drower (2004a: 135–40).

chairs to drink it in. She was both an academic and a pastoral role model to her female students, and an example (still relevant today), of a woman who consciously used the position she attained to make the way easier for the women who came after her.

Murray could have provided this role model for Tessa whether or not they met personally between 1911 and 1914. Tessa Verney Wheeler's later life, and especially her work with archaeological students, hints at how much she may have been influenced by the example of this other small, intelligent woman, deliberately choosing her as a model over more traditional women like Hilda Petrie, and more radical figures like Marie Stopes. To be a teacher of the Murray school was to be intellectually rigorous, personally accessible, and practically kind, working within the modern school system rather than attempting to completely remake it—a description that could be made of Murray in 1902, or Verney Wheeler in 1932.

THE STUDY OF HISTORY AT UNIVERSITY COLLEGE

While at college, Tessa Verney specialized in the study of languages and history, especially English history. The most established influence on her in that subject was Professor A. F. Pollard, a popular historian of the day with a special interest in reforming the University of London's inadequate history faculty. He was the professor she mentioned most often in later years. He was also the teacher who was most often mentioned by others in connection with her, as proof that she had serious academic training.

Albert Frederick Pollard was born in 1869 on the Isle of Wright, the son of a pharmaceutical chemist of more social standing than Tessa's 'Great Man'. He followed a traditional path from the minor public school Felsted through to Jesus College, Oxford, and took a First in Modern History there in 1891. In an early intimation of the personal acerbity that would dog his career, though, he was 'advised not to look for an academic career at Oxford', as the modern *Dictionary of National Biography* delicately puts it.[62] He went instead to London, where his new wife, Catherine (the daughter of William

---

[62] Collinson (2004).

Lucy, a prosperous Oxford ironmonger—another peculiar parallel to Tessa's background), had been given a house in the suburb of Putney upon their marriage in 1894. Pollard supported himself until 1901 via an assistant editorship at the *Dictionary of National Biography*, as well as through coaching university pupils and examining them—a precarious livelihood for a man with a young family.[63] The extent of his work may be judged by the number of articles he contributed to the *Dictionary*—500, or the equivalent of one volume. In 1903 he was elected to the chair of constitutional history at University College London, and remained there until 1931, completely reforming the department and study of history at UCL over the period of his tenure. His lasting contribution today is generally considered to be the founding of the Institute of Historical Research in the 1920s, the Historical Association in 1906, and (from 1916 onwards) his successful resurrection of the journal *History* through the latter institution.[64]

Pollard was sufficiently well known outside academia to be mentioned as a former teacher in a 1926 profile of the Wheelers by the *South Wales News*, and Tessa continued to reference him as an influence in later years.[65] He was still in his forties when she went to his lectures, having been appointed at the age of thirty-six. History was in his words a 'Cinderella' when he arrived; humanities in general were rather neglected in favour of the experimental and medical sciences preferred by the founding spirits of the College.[66] At the other English universities, history was also neglected, usually studied carelessly by students who intended to go into the civil service. Serious traditional thinkers kept to the hallowed territory of classics and mathematics, with occasional forays in philosophy or religion, leaving progressive minds to the hard sciences; Marie Stopes, with her interest in paleobotany, is an example.

Pollard was determined to change this, and to make his own classrooms as vigorous and full of new ideas as the laboratories across the quad.[67] Inevitably, over the years his own writings on the Tudor

---

[63] One later shared by the young J. R. R. Tolkien. Male academics who chose to marry and have families in their 20s faced considerable financial hardships unknown to their bachelor colleagues, whose smaller expenses were often further reduced by living in college rooms.

[64] Collinson (2004).

[65] 'Departing Leaders', *South Wales News*, 29 March 1926.

[66] Thompson (1990a: 66); Pollard (1907: 265).

[67] Thompson (1990a: 69).

history in which he specialized have been modified, modernized, and mocked by other scholars. His contribution to the study of history at UCL has remained more constantly appreciated by his successors. As early as 1904, he proclaimed in a University College lecture: 'roughly speaking, there is no such thing at the present moment as a History School in the University of London.'[68] By the time that lecture was published in 1907, he was able to add a footnote:

> This is happily no longer true; there are over half a dozen students doing post-graduate work in Modern History, and some have already produced work of no slight value. One was awarded the Royal Historical Society's Alexander Prize last year (1906).[69]

In other notes made in 1907 on his lecture of 1904, he spoke of the improved provisions since he arrived for ancient and modern language training, especially Greek and 'those two indispensible modern languages, French and German'. He was anxious for his students to compete with their nearest Continental rivals, the well-trained, detail-oriented doctoral candidates of the great German universities, and bemoaned the fact that Germany boasted over 200 academic journals of history to England's one.[70] This worry eventually led him to *History* in 1906, which remains a major international forum for historical studies. He was also apprehensive of transatlantic competition, and made a great attempt to capitalize on it by creating strong links between American and English scholars in similar fields.[71]

If Pollard's published lectures are any guide, he was an amusing and instructive professor, and not difficult to learn from. It is clear from his student's memories that he was at his best in a group of learners, rather than on an individual basis. A larger collection of students helped diffuse his acerbic personality, and his surviving talks glitter with the allusive puns and dry wit of the best English historians. When he remarks in a lecture published in 1904 that medieval scholars had the advantage of a common written and spoken language in Latin, to give one instance, he is unable to avoid adding a piquant aside:

> Intercourse with foreign scholars was robbed of its impediments and perhaps some of its amusement [...] Alien and foreigner were not yet

---

[68] Pollard (1907: 265).
[69] Ibid.
[70] Ibid. 271.
[71] Dickens (1966: xix).

terms of insult and contempt. The literature, on which youth was nourished, was not painted red nor adorned with Union Jacks.[72]

Elsewhere, Pollard called for a wider, better organization of history, especially modern history, and praised the University of London for expanding its definition of modern English history up to the death of Queen Victoria in 1901. He pointed out that the nascent University of Chicago had seven professors of history, and that the best and most recent books on English constitutional history were all written and published in and by American universities. There is a bitter note to his assertion that in his early years as an academic, the most important quality a historian could have was not skill or application, but a private income.

His chief critiques were saved for what he perceived as English neglect of its own naval and military history, the history of London itself, and historical analysis of the recently departed nineteenth century. And he became almost livid when discussing the English neglect of 'original authorities', the primary sources dear to undergraduate compendiums today.

> [There should be] competent instruction in the meaning and use of original sources such as hitherto English scholars have had to pick up for themselves or go to [. . .] Paris to learn. The other day I was asked by a history tutor of twenty years' standing (not at this University), 'Can you tell me what an original authority is?' and a University described a living scholar as an original authority on the history of Ancient Greece! Yet the definition of an original authority is the most elementary axiom of historical research, and the basis of all historical criticism.[73]

Little Tessa Verney, taking notes swiftly in her water-stained black and blue school notebooks, must have heard a variation on those words. At the time, she filed them for use on her exams. Years later, standing in the earth in Wales, they would return with renewed force. If a source written in the past could be considered the best original authority on the history of its time, why not extend that definition to include physical objects that had also survived the centuries? And— heretical thought—was it possible that an object, buried and forgotten, might sometimes preserve a more pure window on the past than an often-copied manuscript?

---

[72] Pollard (1907: 8).
[73] Ibid. 281–2.

4

Education and the War (1910–1918)

There may then have been a thousand students or less all told, of
all faculties and disciplines, within its walls: aspiring chemists,
physicists, biologists, artists, lawyers, philosophers, surgeons, psy-
chologists, historians, and just basic humanists like myself. We all
knew one another and collaborated in a multitude of capacities.[1]

In 1911 University College London was a much smaller institution
than it is today, though its centre was already the familiar portico and
dome of the college quad on Gower Street. As Rik Wheeler describes
it above, UCL was also then a place where scientists and artists were
thrown into one another's company on a daily basis. University
College London was still experimental in character; and as the previous chapter pointed out, one of its most experimental qualities was
that it was not residential. Many of its students lived, like Tessa, in the
distant suburban homes of their parents, and commuted in to classes
and lectures. These began at nine in the morning and went on to six at
night. Students were expected to spend a full working day learning—
the same working day passed by their childhood peers in junior
clerkships and secretarial posts.

London, as ever, was the centre of new ideas about education and
gender. This cultural buzz was partially centred on University College, where men and women constantly debated the issues at hand,
trying to redefine or restore traditional definitions of gender, science,
and art. This atmosphere must have had an impact on Tessa. Though
she did not take part directly at this point, by her very presence she
absorbed and considered these new movements. Her husband found
the atmosphere intoxicating.

---

[1] Wheeler (1955: 30).

ACADEMIC RECORDS

There are few files left under Tessa Verney's name at UCL. Besides her entrance document, there is a small but interesting collection of notebooks and ephemeral letters, and a basic academic record.

> Tessa VERNEY (Mrs Wheeler).
> Date of Birth: 27 March 1893.
> Entered UCL: 1911–12.
> Studied (1911–12)
> Latin & Roman History
> English
> French
> English History
> Studied (1912–13)
> History
> Italian
> Passed Intermediate Arts (Special)
> June 1912.
> Left UCL 1913–14
> Died 15 April 1936[2]

Apart from the UCL materials, eight battered blue and black notebooks were preserved by chance elsewhere, identical in appearance to the hundreds of site notebooks Tessa would fill later in life. These hold some of her class notes from UCL and were kept accidentally by one of her college friends, Kathleen Brunt (later Kathleen Tracey). Her son, Michael Tracey, returned them to Rik Wheeler in 1957.

> I am tremendously grateful to you for so kindly sending Tessa Verney's notebooks. They carry one's mind back a very long way, I am afraid, but I am delighted to have them.[3]

Tracey thought they must date from 1914, which is possible; UCL records show Verney Wheeler leaving between 1913 and 1914. However, as her maiden name appears in the front of all the books, and the only date given is October 1912, an earlier date seems more likely.

---

[2] Tessa Verney personal record, UCLA. T. Verney Wheeler (1934b: 101).
[3] Correspondence between M. V. Tracey and Wheeler, between 1 and 17 October 1957. WFP.

They also deal mainly with history, which indicates Tessa's first two years at UCL. Perhaps in 1914 Kathleen enrolled in classes Tessa had already taken. At any rate, she kept her friend's careful notes on constitutional documents and history, medieval charters, the letters of Catherine de Medici and the memoirs of La Hone. The little books are full of Tessa's clear, round notes from lectures and books; occasionally she even inserts loose-leaf pages from days she must have forgotten her regular notebook. The volumes mainly deal with constitutional history and documents, and specifically the lectures and classes in that subject given by A. F. Pollard. The notes are confidently written, like her later site notebooks; she rarely went back to correct or alter. There are no language notes, but in later years Tessa showed a continued comfort with other languages and countries. In 1934, for example, she reviewed a French book on excavations at Salona for the *Journal of Roman Studies.*[4] In this brief article she seems to mention personally visiting the ruins, which are on the northern edge of Split on the Dalmatian coast. She certainly seems to have absorbed Pollard's despairing plea for his London students to learn modern European languages, to communicate and compete with their Continental colleagues.

History was Tessa's focus at UCL, and these books point towards someone with a particular interest in the logical details of its constitutional, legal, and even military branches. They also show someone smart enough to be a source for other undergraduates. She was, in fact, the person we all wished to sit next to as undergraduates—a careful, painstaking note-taker, who went to *all* the lectures and was happy to share her notebooks. There must have been more young women than Kathleen who depended on Tessa to fill in gaps from lectures they had skipped or misunderstood. The image of her small figure quietly passing her books to friends in the imposing library or the cramped Women's Common Room is a sweet, nostalgic one. It is the first of many such that illustrate the unpretentious and gentle kindness that endeared her to so many of her students and peers.

---

[4] Verney Wheeler (1934b).

YOUNG MEN—AND RIK WHEELER

Outside of the classroom, Tessa Verney's options were limited by her institution's peculiarities regarding extracurricular entertainment. Apart from the fears of unchaperoned male–female contact, it was seen as a needless distraction from the serious business of learning. It was still possible in the Edwardian period, and perhaps even normal, for young men to experience college as a social rather than academic education. University College set its face firmly against making its students too comfortable or too entertained, and rather prided itself on its lack of a social scene. There was no major dramatic society as at Oxford or Cambridge; Tessa and Rik, unlike their son, never performed as undergraduates in a Shakespeare production broadcast nationally by the Home Service. It was felt that students were there to learn, take degrees, argue with their professors and one another, and then go out into the world and work. There was none of the traditional sense of the college as monastery-fortress, protecting callow youth and vulnerable don alike from the pressures of outside forces. If Oxbridge was a botanical greenhouse, designed to shelter valuable and tender specimens, the University of London, and University College especially, was more of a forcing-house for the kitchen garden.

The natural forces of youth were against the college authorities. Student societies arose in all directions. They never produced the high-quality results Oxbridge could, but that was because students at University College were channelling their energy and creativity instead into their 'real' work in the laboratories, libraries, and studios. Play was a refuge, not an object. Often the academic and the social were combined, as in the Greek plays produced by architecture and classics students at the turn of the century. There was no theatre at Gower Street, but the amphitheatre-shaped lecture halls were ideal for their temporary purposes.[5]

So keen was the College to prevent its students drifting into distraction that it had no playing fields before 1897. Athletic teams, and then the nascent student Unions, rented fields until the men and women's Unions individually purchased adjoining grounds in 1905.

[5] Harte and North (1991: 138–9).

By the time the grounds were open in 1908, running costs had reached £7,000. None of that was provided by the official College authorities, and the students resorted to various methods of fundraising. Most notable of these was the large Bazaar and Fête of 1909, which lasted three days and was opened by a minor Royal. The surviving ephemera includes a photograph of a young Mortimer Wheeler appearing, characteristically, as one of Penelope's suitors in a Homeric skit.[6]

It is easy to picture Tessa Verney in 1912, taking a train to UCL from south-east London, making her notes on constitutional history, and making use of the new Women's Common Room. In those days, a third-class return fare between Lewisham and Charing Cross would have cost her about a shilling, and a season ticket less than two pounds. Lewisham rail carriers catered to budget-conscious travellers from a commuter suburb who had to travel into town six days a week.[7]

From Charing Cross it was and is a brisk walk or brief bus ride uphill to UCL's front quadrangle. The slight, dark figure of Tessa Verney must have run often up and down the Library steps. The first surviving photographs of her date from around this time, and show a small woman with a cloud of dark hair and a delightful smile—'charm incarnate', according to Jacquetta Hawkes.[8] (Fig. 1.)

Naturally she was already attracting suitors, most notably an heir to the extremely successful London building firm John Mowlem's.[9] They may have met at a local dance in Lewisham, or have had friends in common, or even become acquainted through school or UCL. It is difficult to determine the exact identity of her swain, which would help pinpoint where they first came in contact. Hawkes identifies him simply as a 'young Mowlem' or 'John Mowlem', though there seem to have been no young Johns among the Mowlems in the Edwardian period. There are still several possible partners for Tessa among the extended members of this prosperous family. The future Sir George Mowlem Burt (1884–1964) was an outside superintendent on firm projects in 1911, having worked his way up through the family firm literally from the shop floor. He seems the most likely candidate chronologically, though he married Olave Charlotte Sortain

[6] Ibid.
[7] Read (1992: 34).
[8] Hawkes (1982: 47).
[9] Port (2004).

Figure 1. Young Tessa around 1914, just before her marriage.

in 1911. If he was the unsuccessful suitor, this means that Tessa and Rik must have met in 1911, almost immediately after her matriculation at UCL, and that Mowlem Burt must have recovered from his broken heart fairly quickly. He did have younger siblings, whose gender I have been unable to determine, and they may provide more contenders for this obscure honour. His uncle John Mowlem Burt also had a son, probably also named John, another heir to an interest in the business. This Mowlem was probably more than ten years older than Tessa, but that would not have been considered a bar. But all competition, of whatever age and name, was about to be swept away.

Robert Eric Mortimer (Rik) Wheeler was born in 1890 in Glasgow but raised from an early age in Bradford. His father, also Robert, was a journalist in Bradford and London for the *Yorkshire Observer*, a fact Jacquetta Hawkes and others made much of in discussing Rik's writing style and public approach.[10] When Robert was sent to take over his paper's London desk in late 1905, his family moved south with him. Fifteen-year-old Rik had been enjoying an excellent classical education at the Bradford Grammar School, and his teachers were confident that in another year he would easily win an enviable Oxford scholarship.[11] He had always been precocious, but once he was no longer a pupil at the Grammar School and could not take advantage of its academic links, an Oxbridge scholarship would probably be out of his reach.

He didn't care. Rik and his father were determined to get to London; the two were touchingly close. His sisters and mother remained behind in the north for the first part of Robert's time in London, and the pair enjoyed a purely masculine adventure. Robert Wheeler was a happy man, a combination of Sancho Panza and Don Quixote, who taught his son from infancy to love poetry, antiquarian remains, long walks and rides, and how to feed himself off the very small game of the English countryside.

We were a solitary pair, bound by bonds tighter than we knew.[12]

His father also impressed on him a disdain of physical weakness and a respect for those who endured suffering without complaint, through both active precepts and his own example. The first part of *Still Digging* is a lyrical tribute to the strength and gentleness of a little boy's friendship with his father. Regarding his mother, with whom he had a troubled relationship and much less personal understanding, Rik has less to say.

My mother was a courageous but rather nerve-ridden woman, to whom my father's inconsequent interest in everything except £ s. d. remained an irritating mystery. She had much to put up with, poor soul.

---

[10] Hawkes (1982: 31–2). Robert Wheeler joined the paper in 1894, when it was still published under its original title of the *Bradford Observer*. It became the *Yorkshire Daily Observer* in 1901, and finally the *Yorkshire Observer* in 1909.

[11] Wheeler (1955: 24); Hawkes (1982: 31–2).

[12] Wheeler (1955: 17).

Mother and son were not sympathetic personalities, and clashed early and often. By the time Rik and Tessa became engaged, she was forced to insist they meet with his family as an official couple at University College. This was not a reflection on her—his family found her charming and entirely suitable, and she became close to Robert. But Rik and his mother had been at odds for some time, as he developed into the aggressively male personality that would prove so popular with the media.[13] He could be a very rough relative, impatient especially with women, and in later years relationships were often strained by his assertion that blood ties were no reason for any closer social connection.

As a young teenager in Edwardian London, Rik served a wonderful apprenticeship to the entire metropolis. He had about two years to prepare himself for the University College entrance examinations, which were restricted to those 16 and over, and fourpence a day to find himself food and entertainment. Occasionally he miscalculated his dining bill, and had to retrench dramatically over the next few days—not the healthiest diet for a growing boy, but one he shared with Arthur Conan Doyle and Charles Dickens at a similar age. In between studying to an almost 'orgiastic' extent, he explored.

> I can still recapture the almost tremulous excitement of those years [...] I walked everywhere, map in hand, from the City to Kensington and as far afield as Hampstead Heath [...] My happiest haunt was a room at the Victoria and Albert Museum into which at that time was crowded an incredible number of precious water-colours that invited unending discovery [...] The British Museum I abjured as I abjure it today.[14]

He had to append a shamefaced note to the last comment before publication, by which point he had become a Trustee of the British Museum.

Years later, Rik remembered his first and clearest vision of London. It was of St Paul's dome at dawn, and his father's office at the *Observer*:

> the first-floor office which was to be my father's, and in a sense mine, for many years, and finally [...] a desk-top on which I rolled up in my coat, my head on a pile of ink-scented newspapers, and sank suddenly into oblivion.[15]

---

[13] Hawkes (1982: 52–3).
[14] Wheeler (1955: 26–7).
[15] Ibid. 25.

His first exposure to first-class archaeological materials and museums was bound up in accompanying his father to other events, as varied as the city itself. He was taken to Salvation Army meetings, concerts, picture exhibits, boxing matches, and whatever his father thought might interest readers back in Yorkshire. Afterwards the pair would return to 'their' office, and Rik might be allowed to help write up the experience for the paper's 'London Letter'.

> On rare and exciting occasions I recognized a few of my reluctant sentences in the next day's paper, and was thereby fully rewarded for my pains.[16]

Special permission was gained for Rik to take his University College entrance exams a few months before his 16th birthday. The result of his age and lifestyle, added to the ordeal of the examination room, was a fever and near-breakdown after the first day of tests. He was still a very young man, really a boy, and was pouring his already consider-able mental and physical appetites into too small a vessel. He retook the exams some months later, and matriculated at 16 to read classical honours.

> It was some time before I fully realized that to take examinations for the purpose of producing physical excitement was like burning down pigsties to produce roast pork.[17]

By 1911, Rik was working towards his MA in history at UCL, where he had already taken a BA. He was a tall, gangly young man, with curly reddish hair and an intense expression. Early artistic ambitions had given way to a rapidly all-consuming interest in the growing field of archaeology, especially in the remains of prehistoric and Roman Britain. This reflected both his excellent classical education at the Bradford Grammar School and an early childhood exploring the wild places and ancient monuments of Yorkshire. He was a humorous, dashing youth, already showing the taste for amorous adventures that would, with archaeology, be the two ruling passions of his life.

In 1912, both Rik and Tessa were young, unattached, and serving on the University College Literary Society Committee, Rik as one of many vice-presidents and Tessa as the sole secretary and treasurer.

---

[16] Ibid. 29.
[17] Ibid. 29–30.

A card listing the pair among the committee members was found in Rik's papers after his death, along with family photographs and a packet of letters he wrote to Tessa during his First World War service in France. That she kept it all her life is entirely in character; that he retained it equally carefully less so. This touch of sentiment in the most unsentimental of men is unexpected and revealing.

It was by no means the last committee on which they would both serve. The dating and careful preservation of this little card by first Tessa and then Rik makes it seem likely that it marks the moment they met. What can be definitely said is that in 1913, Rik was awarded one of the one of the earliest archaeological scholarships, the new Franks Studentship. It was jointly administered by UCL and the Society of Antiquaries of London, a nice prognosis of his and Tessa's past and future intellectual homes. While it only meant £50 annually for two years in 1913, Sir Arthur Evans of Crete (then on the selection committee) quietly doubled it.[18] As Rik's prospects were thus bright enough for a fiancée, he and Tessa marked the occasion by becoming formally engaged.

LEAVING UCL: MARRIAGE

It is difficult for the modern Western mind to fully appreciate what marriage meant to Edwardian women. Agatha Miller, who was born six years prior to Tessa and also married in 1914, outlined it with energetic nostalgia in her autobiography. She is better known today as Agatha Christie.

> I only contemplated one thing [as a young woman]—a happy marriage. About that I had complete self-assurance—as all my friends did. We were conscious of the happiness that awaited us; we looked forward to love, to being looked after, cherished and admired, and we intended to get our own way in the things which mattered to us while at the same time putting our husband's life, career and success before all, as was our proud duty [. . .]The real excitement of being a girl—of being, that is, a

---

[18] Wheeler 34–6. Evans generously continued to unobtrusively double the amount for other recipients, until the studentship faltered in 1926 and ceased permanently in 1929. Evans (1956: 397).

woman in embryo—was that life was such a wonderful gamble. *You didn't know what was going to happen to you.* That was what made being a woman so exciting. No worry about what you should be or do— Biology would decide. You were waiting for The Man, and when the man came, he would change your entire life [...] 'Perhaps I shall marry someone in the Diplomatic Service . . . I think I should like that; to go abroad and see all sorts of places . . .' Or: 'I don't think I would like to marry a sailor; you would have to spend such a lot of time in seaside lodgings.' Or: 'Perhaps I'll marry someone who builds bridges, or an explorer.' The whole world was open to you—not open to your *choice*, but open to what Fate *brought* you. You might marry *anyone*; you might, of course, marry a drunkard or be very unhappy, but that only heightened the feeling of excitement.'[19]

Agatha Miller was appreciably higher up the social and financial scale than Tessa Verney, but what she says is sound in principle and a useful general guide for the aspirations of girls in this period. In it we can find the germ of why Tessa gave up Mr Mowlem, despite the suburban security he offered, and elected to spend her life in far more economically precarious circumstances. Quite apart from his dashing personal attractions, Rik offered a level of intellectual companionship and opportunity that a more socially conscious marriage could not have. The Wheelers were never well off, and often (especially in Wales, in the early years of their marriage) actually quite poor. They managed to live in a bohemian way that made the most of their slender resources, eating bread and cheese for dinner and occasionally living in spare offices at the National Museum in Cardiff. Through all the succeeding years of marriage, through Rik's increasing infidelities, through financial upsets, hard work, illness, personal disappointment, and growing professional recognition, there is never an indication that Tessa regretted her choice of husband. As ever, she quietly followed her own inclinations, with the pliable strength of a steel coil; sometimes stretched in new directions, but always returning in the end firmly to its own shape.

In 1914 Rik was appointed a Junior Investigator on the Royal Commission on Historical Monuments. As he put it, on 21 May of that year, 'Tessa and I celebrated the occasion by getting married'.[20] It was a quiet registry wedding in Lambeth, with no religious overtones:

[19] Christie (1977: II.i).
[20] Wheeler (1955: 36).

both principals were amiably agnostic. The ceremony was performed by the Registrar, John Burwick, and the Superintendent Registrar, a Mr Wilmot.

Rik's father, Robert, is listed on the certificate as a witness, but his mother was not present. Nor was she informed of the ceremony until it was finished.[21] According to a copy of the marriage certificate provided by the General Register Office, the other two witnesses were J. Carfax Martin and H. Beresford Kemmis. Beresford Kemmis was a translator who brought out several English versions of French plays in the 1930s. Carfax Martin remains unidentified.

While no one from Tessa's family is listed on the certificate, there is no reason to think they were not there.[22] Jacquetta Hawkes thought—or rather projected—that Annie-Agnes, after her own matrimonial adventures, must have regretted the loss of the 'greater security and grandeur' that a wedding with 'young Mowlem' would have brought. There is no reason to think that the opposite might not as easily be true. Agnes Davies, formerly Annie Kilburn-Mather-Verney-Pearson, set an interesting example: a woman who had her cake and ate it too, socially speaking. Her own life had shown her daughter the possibilities in an unconventionally conventional life and marriage.

At this point, Tessa left University College. She passed her Inter-mediate Arts exams in 1912, enrolled for the 1913–14 academic year (the last year of her degree), and then left before her final exams. Fear of the examination does not seem likely. She had a precise intelligence best shown in the references of her published work and private letters, and always tested fairly well. It seems strange that she left university with relatively little left to do to gain her BA, and it is difficult to determine her reasons. Even if she had accomplished the great social goal of the Edwardian girl in finding a husband, surely she could have finished the few months left in her course before marrying, or after the wedding. So much had been invested in her education, not just by herself but by her stepfather and the London Council. It is possible, from the date of her son's birth, that she may have been in a hurry to wed; and that her condition dictated her departure from education. It would have been a little odd for a young, pregnant, married woman to

[21] Hawkes (1982: 52).
[22] Ibid. 53.

be studying formally, and Tessa may have also had reservations about the effect on her baby's health *in utero*.

Tessa's training at University College was often referenced by others as proof of her serious mind, though she rarely spoke of it directly. The waters are muddied still further by her strong role many years later in founding the Institute of Archaeology and standardizing the academic teaching of her subject. Given her comfort in closely associating the Institute of Archaeology from its start with University College, it is unlikely that she left because of some negative feelings towards Gower Street. Why, then, did she leave without her degree? It suggests that she did not value the BA. Yet in later years she was absolutely instrumental in creating taught archaeology degrees in London. Did she learn to appreciate the useful prestige of a degree in her early years of museum work? Or was a degree course simply the easiest framework for her to teach within? She may have felt that completing the work of the degree was more important than gradu- ating. Or perhaps she didn't consider it at all at the time. She was very young, in love with a charming husband, and pregnant for the first time. What more could she want?

It is best to consider Tessa as still professionally and personally junior to her husband when she left UCL. While her time there was of great importance in forming the bedrock of her intellectual approach, she had yet to develop completely as an independent mind. This would come after the First World War, when her early experiences of archaeological work in Wales acted as a catalyst on all she had absorbed as a student. In only a few years, she passed from a silent participant *in* to an active leader *on* excavations. Not at all coinciden- tally, she would simultaneously bloom as a personality—much as Hilda Petrie did in Egypt decades earlier.

One thing must be kept in mind constantly when thinking of 'the Wheelers'. Tessa was not a put-upon wife, a stereotypical angel sacrificed to his own needs by a selfish husband. She might be quieter than her husband, but in her own way she was just as determined and unconventional. This often escaped the notice of colleagues, and even close friends. Rik was so very loud and outgoing, always dominating any space he inhabited. Within his whirlwind of energy, Tessa calmly got on with her work. Over their years working together, she used his larger-than-life personality as a shield while she almost ruthlessly developed her own interests. It suited her to have her husband shoulder the more public aspects of their work, and it came to him so easily. The Wheelers had a true symbiotic relationship, shoring up each other's weaknesses and feeding off each other's strengths. There were many frictions in their marriage, but as far as their professional work went, they used one another in equal measure. It wasn't perfect psychologically or practically, but the relationship worked from its first day to its last.

THE GREAT WAR: DEATH AND TAXES

In the aftermath of the wedding, the young couple moved in with Rik's parents at Rollescourt Avenue, Herne Hill. Their only child, Michael, was born just under nine months later, in January 1915. Tessa must have fallen pregnant almost immediately after the wedding, or perhaps even slightly before. Premarital relations might be socially frowned upon, but still regularly occurred at all class levels; Agatha Miller knew several young girls who worked around the strictures laid upon them for their own physical amusement.[23] It would be a grave mistake to consider girls of the Edwardian years as sexually free in the way modern young Western women are permitted or even expected to be. But personality and position will always allow some individuals to find hidden methods of self-expression within and without contemporary mores, despite the harshest social strictures; and to engage in sexual play with a fiancé was not considered nearly as morally reprehensible as it would be with a casual boyfriend. Still, having a child outside marriage was quite beyond the pale, because (unlike premarital sex) it could not be hidden simply by leaving it altogether out of social converse.[24]

An interesting side issue is whether Tessa and Rik practised birth control, or whether their small family was a statistical anomaly. It is not surprising that there is no information on this subject in either's writings, but it would not be at all out of character if they had. While Marie Stopes would not open her first birth control clinic until 1921

---

[23] Christie (1977: IV.i).

[24] For a recent overview of this subject, S. Szreter and K. Fisher's 2010 book *Sex Before The Sexual Revolution: Intimate Life in England 1918–1963* is highly recommended. As the title indicates, it deals mainly with a slightly later point in time than that discussed in this chapter, but it is wide-ranging and provides an excellent starting point.

(and that was aimed at poor women of the slums), the discussion of birth control, sensible parenting, and a more open attitude towards sexuality was part of Rik and Tessa's world. The primary barrier methods for preventing pregnancy were becoming cheaper as new technologies and materials (mainly improved forms of rubber) made condoms and diaphragms easier to mass-produce. As a result, middle- and lower-class women were beginning to take advantage of family planning techniques previously only available to the wealthy.

Such care had a great deal to recommend it. Most young women could remember the harrowing deaths of female relatives in childbirth; Tessa's own grandmother had died at 23 of complications associated with her only baby's birth. Puerperal fever, along with third-degree burns from cooking fires, was a leading cause of death among women all over the world. However, in developed countries the new technologies of birth control and electricity were beginning to make an impact on both causes of mortality. There were less immediate benefits too. Even if women survived their first baby, the constant cycle of pregnancy and childbirth was physically debilitating. There was also the difficulty of feeding and housing an ever-increasing number of children, especially as better medical care made it more likely all would survive into adulthood. The social and economic maths was heartless, its truth borne out by the upper-class women who had been clandestinely limiting their own childbearing for many years.[25]

By the time Michael was born, Rik was already serving as an instructing officer in the University of London Officers' Training Corps: like most patriotic young men, he had joined up almost immediately upon the declaration of war in August 1914. Most of his war service was spent as a training officer in the Royal Field Artillery, going from camp to camp in England and Scotland. Tessa and baby Michael were often able to follow him, and a series of charming photographs resulted. With England tensing for war, many couples were marrying in a hurry before the groom was posted elsewhere, trying to cram in a family life that many would never return to. (Fig. 2.)

These snapshots come to an end in 1917, when Rik was finally sent to France and there took part in the horrible battle of Passchendaele.

[25] Hall (2004); see also Hall (2001) and Jones (2001) for general discussions of the sexual and reproductive activity of British women in the 20th century, as well as Szreter and Fisher (2010).

Figure 2. Rik, Tessa, and baby Michael on manoeuvres in England during the War.

He used it in later years as his yardstick for absolute physical misery. Like many aesthetically sensitive men of the time, he prided himself on his toughness; but the little boy who grew up scrambling with his father in the Dales was revolted, physically and psychologically, by the ghastly deaths suffered by the horses and men about him.[26]

[26] Wheeler (1955: 59).

In the meantime, back in England, Tessa joined the 'white blouse revolution': the young women who streamed into clerical positions previously held by men, as other women took no-longer-gender-restricted jobs on farms or in factories as part of the war effort. Tessa was one of the first women to be an assistant surveyor of income tax, and was based in Basingstoke. The job reflected a math-ematical ability that would aid her as the treasurer and chief financial wizard of many excavations. It was relatively unusual for women to take over clerical posts at the start of the conflict, and many men were doubtful that the feminine mind was to be trusted with finance or hard mathematics. By the time Tessa began working, the government no longer had the luxury of doubting anyone's abilities, especially those of a middle-class, educated woman who could understand the bewildering wartime tax codes.[27]

It must have also pushed her into a more independent frame of mind, as she fended for herself among strangers. Many women looked back on their war service as a time of enormous personal liberation, physically and mentally, and of freedom in other respects too.[28] It is likely that baby Michael was left behind in London with one of his grandmothers. Married women who took over these jobs generally were only able to do so because they could take advantage of familial childcare; even then it was often prohibitively difficult. There was no state solution as yet for women workers with young families.[29]

Despite the distance, husband and wife corresponded volumi-nously, and Tessa kept Rik supplied with little luxuries that made life in the trenches easier. She sent large parcels filled with sweets for himself and his men, the particular boots and jodhpurs he liked, and photographs of herself and Michael. He wrote her constantly, and she treasured those letters for the rest of her life. Most moving and most valued was a letter that should never have been sent, but which found its way by accident to Tessa: written by Rik the night of 20 August 1918, just before the final 'big push' of the war. Its envelope reads: 'To be delivered *only in event of death*.' It is his farewell to Tessa, in case all goes wrong, a mixture of love, longing, and practical

---

[27] Braybon and Summerfield (1987: 41). A legal and financial (rather than social) consideration of the wartime tax codes can be found in Martin Daunton's *Just Taxes* (2002).

[28] Braybon and Summerfield (1987) provide a full account of this phenomenon in both World Wars.

[29] Ibid. 101.

considerations. As it was never needed, the reader can also observe without being heartless that it is an extreme example of the 'white feather' patriotism of the period, high-handed in its idealism and much influenced by Kipling. The schoolboyish closure hints at the valiant qualities Rik prized in Tessa. She was always a brave woman.

> I need not say that life is very sweet to you and me, Tess—so sweet that I dare not think too much of it lest I should cling to it rather than to duty. I lie awake at night and dream of you, and when I sleep you are my dreams. So much happiness sometimes makes one feel it cannot last.
>
> With all that, however, you and I, wife of mine, have to face the common-sense aspect of things, and it is common sense that that is going to pull us through this. 'Killed in Action' is the only epitaph a man can have nowadays, and the only tribute that I ask you to pay to this epitaph is that you read it dry-eyed [. . .] I ask it of you as a last gift, that you do not weep and that you never wear mourning. Our love is too great for tears and crepe. Out love cannot die. So chins up!
>
> For the sake of our boy, I know that you will face life cheerfully and with common sense.
>
> Shake hands, Tess.[30]

Rik did not die in France. He acquitted himself very respectably and discovered in himself a talent for and (in a positive sense) an enjoyment of war. There was a mention of Major R. E. M. Wheeler in Haig's dispatches of 8 November 1918, and a Military Cross whose initials would appear henceforth whenever Rik listed his academic credentials. He also took serendipitous advantage of the long postwar period his unit spent near Cologne to research Romano-Rhenish pottery at the local museums, remembering the Franks Studentship that would now become active again. He used what he found to get his Ph.D on returning to Britain; as he put it in a later interview, 'when I came out of the army, I had my thesis in my pocket'.[31]

He had something else in his head. Like many veterans of the Great War, Wheeler came back with the persistent, haunting knowledge that his very survival put him in a minority; his healthy condition an even smaller one. The scar was barely visible on his immediate return; he had escaped shell-shock, gassing, and the other new physical horrors of modern warfare. But there was a psychological cost to pay in survivor's guilt, one he was not yet ready to face. That would

---

[30] Wheeler to T. V. Wheeler, 20 August 1918. WFP.
[31] Hawkes (1982: 74).

come later, in the London Museum and the foundation of the great Institute of Archaeology in the 1930s.

At the moment, Rik found himself at a loose end. He and Tessa moved into a little flat (now demolished) at 16 Taviton Street, near their familiar base of University College; Rik immediately decorated it with murals of embattled aeroplanes.[32] They were rediscovering one another a little after their years apart, in the first house they ever lived in alone as a family. Michael was now four, and the question of how to support them all preoccupied Rik. He returned to his position with the Commission for Historic Monuments, but it had barely paid enough even before the war raised prices. His small 1917 excavation of one of Colchester's Roman gates was entertaining but not profitable in any other way, as was a proposed examination of Pleshey in Essex.[33] It is not likely Tessa took much of a role in these, although the *South Wales News*, which reported extensively on the Wheelers during their Welsh years, once wrote that '[the Wheelers] were about to start excavating in Essex [. . .] when the war broke out'.[34] This probably reflects a general understanding, clearest in later newspaper articles, that the Wheelers had always worked together. An attempt to get a pay rise out of the Commission was met with offensive derision by its representative Gerald Duckworth, who asked Rik 'if he knew there had been a war'.[35] Things began to look a little difficult.

Then their luck changed. Rik, allegedly in a white rage after his meeting with Duckworth, applied for a job as Keeper of Archaeology at the National Museum of Wales in Cardiff and lecturer at the University of South Wales. It carried a better salary, independence, and the chance to really explore his chosen subject. The downside was its location in Cardiff, a city Wheeler had only visited once (for his interview at the Museum) and which he automatically disliked. Of course, after that start, he got the post; and by 1920, the Wheelers were on the way west.[36]

---

[32] Ibid. 77.

[33] Wheeler (1955: 64–5).

[34] *South Wales News*, 20 March 1926. A similar sentence appears, in an article about Verulamium, in the *Belfast Telegraph* of 21 August 1930 probably the result of some mild journalistic plagiarism.

[35] Unlike Rik, he had seen no active service. This is of course the same Duckworth who allegedly abused his half-sisters Virginia and Vanessa Stephen. It is no pleasure to learn that he was as unpleasant in small matters as he was gross in great ones.

[36] Hawkes thinks that Duckworth may have pulled strings to get a 'caged lion' out of his wheelhouse. Certainly he provided a glowing recommendation for the post. Hawkes (1982: 79).

5

Wales (1920–1927)

The job that took the Wheelers to Wales for six years carried the official title 'Keeper of Archaeology in the National Museum of Wales and Lecturer in Archaeology in the University College of South Wales and Monmouthshire'. Expanding its remit over time with Wheeler's promotion to the museum's directorship, it ultimately took Verney Wheeler to Caerleon and her first publications.[1]

A middle-class woman in that time and place would be expected to take a strong personal interest in her husband's work, to the extent of reducing it considerably through her own efforts and even effectively making it her own career. The social conditioning of the period pressured women to express their ambitions through their husbands, but it could also (more positively) give them a congenial creative or organizational outlet. A husband's occupation determined his wife's vocation, in a pattern still seen today in politics but largely vanished elsewhere in Western society. To have a career of her own was difficult for all but the most determined women; while the economy was propped up by the cheap labour of maids, laundresses, cooks, and nannies, most professions of more social standing (such as teaching) still enjoyed a marriage bar requiring employers to fire women once they were married. There was also a negative perception of women 'stealing' jobs from men who came home from fighting in the Great War.

Verney Wheeler was already more than an Edwardian woman advancing and propping up her husband. She entered her marriage with a serious, if informally ended, education of her own, and by the time

---

[1] Technically, Caerleon was still in Monmouthshire (England) in 1926–7, but as it is now part of Wales and was in every way a Welsh project, it is included here under that country's aegis. This also reflects the view of the Welsh books on nationalism and identity cited throughout this chapter.

the Wheelers left Wales, she was an equal partner in their practical endeavours. Wales may be justly considered her 'graduate work', since it led to the FSA that she and others saw as her professional qualification.[2] She was not alone in this; a glance through the title pages of books by the Wheelers' contemporaries shows few doctorates, an academic innovation still suspect at that point. Instead, authors list BAs, MAs, the occasional D.Phil. or D.Litt., and FSAs, in that order. Kathleen Kenyon never received or accepted a Ph.D. and openly said she considered them 'an American affection'. The appropriate thing socially was to receive an honorary D.Litt. at the end of an illustrious career, as a sort of academic retirement present—Margaret Murray being one of many examples.

Cardiff's National Museum, officially founded in 1907, encompassed art, archaeological and geological specimens, fossils, and miscellaneous antiquities in its remit (much as it does today). An elaborate stone building in Cathays Park was planned for the museum as early as 1905 and a foundation stone actually laid in 1912, but thanks to the war and the ensuing general economic depression it was still nothing more than a façade in 1920. Despite this, the objects destined to form the core collection of the unfinished new museum had already been transferred into its ownership, incorporating the old Cardiff municipal Museum of Natural History, Arts and Antiquities into the Museum of Wales as the 'Cardiff Collection'.

The use of archaeology in Wales (and elsewhere in the British Isles) to help create a unified national identity was in full flower by 1907. The University of Wales, based in Cardiff but still amorphous, had been founded in 1893. There was a conscious desire, as Wales industrialized, to create a national identity that was modern and still recognizably, historically Welsh.

The modern Museum owes much to Wheeler and his successor, Charles Fox. The two Englishmen established a permanent scholastic tradition there emphasizing:

> a major break with the romantic antiquarian approach to Welsh antiquity that had dominated the previous century; it was an account of the archaeology of a national territory, but its rigorous, scientific concern for the evidence made no concessions to national mythology or nationalist pretensions.[3]

---

[2] Dever (2004: 527).   [3] Champion (1996: 132).

Wheeler recognized and revelled in this political-historical remit, defending his hastily written 1925 book *Prehistoric and Roman Wales* as serving 'its frankly political purpose, as a primary medium of integration'.[4] Welsh intellectuals and labourers were all beginning to recognize the need and presence of a larger Welsh identity, based in a shared language and ethnic culture as well as geography. There were other social factors at work in the 1920s: a major plague of unemployment across the social board, especially in South Wales, the growing restiveness of women who missed their wartime indepen- dence and working responsibility, and a loss of young Welsh people to emigration abroad.[5] Shared history, taught to intellectuals through a university and displayed to the general public via an attractive, modern museum, was a way for the Welsh to formulate and acknowl- edge a unique identity as a people. There was also a tied desire to create a native intelligentsia that could celebrate the *gwerin*, an untranslatable Welsh term that roughly refers to national ancestors as seen in a semi-mythical romantic light; the *gwerin* are similar in cultural placement to the popular image Americans have of the pioneers on the Oregon Trail.

> the heroic Welsh people rising from their subjugation to claim nation- hood [. . .] classless and free of the conflicts associated with industria- lization . . . a world-view which emphasized the common language, culture and religiosity of the Welsh people [. . .] a common people, in harmony and at prayer until the 1930s.[6]

Plaid Cymru, the nationalist political party, was founded in 1925 and continues to be active today in Welsh politics and culture. From the beginning it has openly justified its existence and established its iden- tity with reference to a glorious shared heritage, often to the extent of creating further divisions within an increasingly multiethnic region.[7] This arose from opposition to the English government of London, but also from a desire to unify a group of very small valley-states that had historically ever been at one another's throats. For Wales to act nationally abroad in Britain, it needed to *think* nationally at home.

---

[4] Wheeler (1955: 69).
[5] See Davies (1989), Fevre and Thompson (1999), and Adamson (1999) for a variety of solid perspectives on the development of Welsh identity and nationalism in the twentieth century.
[6] Adamson (1999: 58–9).
[7] Davies (1989: 31); see also C. Williams (1999).

In response to this growing, local, political competition, as David Adamson points out, the Liberal government of London made an effort to be moderately supportive, with practical, if stingy, financial funding of the University and National Museum.[8]

Why does this excursus into the politics of Celtic nationalism matter in the context of Tessa Wheeler's life? It is important to recognize that the Wheelers were part of this cultural-nationalist movement, because it is very closely related to what they tried to achieve on their next curatorial project at the London Museum: a universally useful historical identity for their shared home town. In Cardiff, the Wheelers saw an institution consciously trying to present a varied people with a shared identity to be proud of. The lesson was not wasted.

Until the Cathays Park structure was finished, the collections were held haphazardly at the Cardiff Free Library. The prior Keeper of Archaeology, John Ward, had held the post for many years, until a long illness effectively retired him and left a backlog of donations and acquisitions uncatalogued. This is the first clear picture of the Wheelers working together—a vignette often varied from that point on.

> He [Wheeler] flung himself into activity: his room in the old Museum quarters at Cardiff Library, to take a detail, had camp-beds where he and Tessa, whom he had married in 1914, slept when it was too late to go home.[9]

The Wheelers would not find permanent housing in Cardiff until 1921, when they rented a flat on Cathedral Road. The camp beds in the offices probably reflected that necessity as well as their joint devotion to the task at hand; and the persistent image of them working together in domestic companionship late into the night was to become the norm.

A minor question in these years is what became of Michael Wheeler while his parents sorted fossils. He was only six when the family moved to Cardiff, not yet at boarding school. Was he also sleeping in the office; or were other arrangements made?[10] It seems doubtful they could have afforded a nurse; a Welsh student of Wheeler's remembered Verney Wheeler and Michael accompanying

---

[8] Adamson (1999: 61–2).
[9] G.C.Boon (1977b: 172).
[10] Carol Wheeler Pettman to the author, 5 February 2007.

his university excursions. Michael seems to have stayed with his parents whenever possible; photographs from 1921 show him in the museum workshop and on-site at Segontium (Fig. 3). His daughter, Carol Wheeler Pettman, feels that the family probably did camp out in the library occasionally but not on a regular basis. In her view, it is more likely that Wheeler stayed there often, and his wife and son joined him at times. She thinks her father would have seen it all as a great adventure.

It is not clear whether Verney Wheeler initially had a Welsh office of her own, as she was to have later in London. There is no record of one. With space at a premium in the Library, it is doubtful. She never appeared in any official staff photographs, and was not mentioned in the Annual Report for 1926, which recorded Wheeler's departure with regret.[11] But she certainly had an accepted quasi-official place (as became apparent in 1926 when the Wheelers left Wales), and at some point she began to receive her considerable amount of 'official' archaeological mail at the museum, where there would be space for her to have a room of her own, and where the amount of work she was doing would require one out of sheer practicality. Her letters from the museum are extensive and written on official notepaper, dealing especially with the Caerleon excavations and its associated funding questions.[12] Later, a new Keeper of Archaeology, V. E. Nash-Williams, turned to her more often than Wheeler for help with the site.[13]

Wheeler's career at the University College of South Wales is of less concern here than the Museum. Verney Wheeler was not closely involved with his university students at this time. The amount of work her husband had before him was impressive, as he tried to make the very new subject of archaeology an acceptable academic discipline. Simultaneously, he was attempting to identify those students who could be successfully trained to be the new generation of excavators. He badly wanted to implement his ideas about method and practice. But not even Wheeler could do all he set himself, and the museum and excavation work that overflowed his plate began to fall primarily

---

[11] National Museum of Wales Annual Report, 1926.

[12] The archive of letters at the National Museum of Wales testifies to this, and is quoted extensively below in the section dealing with Caerleon.

[13] See e.g. TVW to V. E. Nash-Williams, 15 and 20 March 1930. Caerleon site archive, NMWA.

Figure 3. Young Michael Wheeler in Cardiff, holding an unidentified object. The reverse reads, in Michael's adult handwriting: 'In the workshop. Note the Bronze Age war [illegible] I am mending! Sept: 1921.' The background shows the disorganized state of the Museum of Wales at the time.

to Verney Wheeler more and more as time went on. She began to develop links with her husband's younger colleagues, focusing on those serious enough to get past her bombastic spouse and into the field. He had strict ambitions for his pupils, and even at this early time was as ready to discourage the unsuited as encourage the suitable.

One of the pupils to benefit—perhaps more than any other Welshman—from the joint oversight of the Wheelers was V. E. Nash-Williams. He was only three years younger than Verney Wheeler, and came to university after war service abroad. He shared with Wheeler a military past and a need to earn his living—although one of Wheeler's first students in archaeology in 1920, he expected to become a schoolteacher simply because that was the traditional job a university degree qualified him for. Instead Wheeler swept his teacher's schoolbooks into a convenient wastebasket, and him into the National Museum.[14] An interesting monograph could be written on Nash-Williams' life, an early example of the rise of the professional rather than dilettante or volunteer curator. His correspondence with Verney Wheeler had a more personal aspect as well—she admonished him for over-working, advised him how to dress and act when appearing at the Society of Antiquaries, and usually began her letters to him with a maternal 'Dear Old Lad'.

There is one story of Verney Wheeler at the college, remembered years later by Violet Audin, a former student of Wheeler's who did *not* go on to make archaeology her career. Besides vividly illuminating Wheeler's first teaching lecture series and developing style, it also gives us a brief, rare glimpse of young Michael Wheeler.

> We [students] were about eight in number, and certainly we were important as we helped to launch Dr. Wheeler [. . .] into the world of Archaeology. It was the year 1920 when, after being advised by the Professor of History to take a two years' course in Archaeology, I first met Dr. Wheeler [. . .] He was certainly handsome, but looked somewhat older than his years, so that I didn't then realize that he was [only] about ten years older than his students. The lectures were extremely boring. We had to provide ourselves with the three Guides to the Stone, Bronze, and Iron Ages. Dr. Wheeler, with the help of projected slides, lectured on these. He was always late for his lectures [. . .] We went for a few field excursions in the neighbourhood of Cardiff [. . .] His first wife Tessa and their young son used to accompany him on these excursions. She also came to our lectures when they were held at the Old Museum in Cardiff [. . .]When in 1923 I wrote to him re my desiring to take up Archaeology as a career he strongly advised me against it, saying it was not a suitable career for a young woman. He said teaching was more suitable. It was![15]

Mortimer Wheeler was a man of his time, but he was ahead of it (generally speaking) in his recognition and encouragement of talent regardless of gender. Perhaps in this case he was letting his correspondent down easily. By 1923 he was making frequent, grateful use of his own wife's talents in archaeology, and throughout his life he was usually happy to advance young women professionally. Part of

---

[14] Wheeler (1957: 6–7).

[15] Violet Audin to Jacquetta Hawkes, 6 April 1982 (J. B. Priestley Library, University of Bradford). The passage quoted comes from a short essay Audin sent to Hawkes, in the letter already referenced. It is headed: 'This was written after the death of Sir Mortimer Wheeler.'

that evolved thinking stemmed from his tendency towards romantic and sexual affairs, but it had a stern basis in serving his chosen discipline.

SEGONTIUM: 1921–1922[16]

[T]hese affairs of administration constituted an increasing and not particularly congenial diversion [from archaeology ...] my *venue* had been moved from Essex to Wales but my purpose remained unchanged: namely, to integrate a given portion of Roman Britain by selective excavation, and at the same time to evolve an adequate technique with Cranbourne Chase [the Pitt-Rivers estate ...] as my pattern.[17]

While Wheeler had been involved with and even directed brief digs from his undergraduate days on, these had been scrappy and under conditions he could not control.[18] Since then, two factors had changed. He had survived the First World War, and at the same time survived all but two of his contemporary pre-war archaeological colleagues. Wheeler's reaction was common to men in his situation; he felt, and declared openly, that he had to succeed not only for himself, but also for the dead.[19] Of the five participants in Wheeler's university excavation at Wroxeter, only he remained.

The other new influence was more pragmatic: he had become conversant with the works of General Lane Fox Pitt-Rivers, the pioneering Victorian archaeologist. Pitt-Rivers' excavation maxims of careful order, strict planning, and extensive, timely publication had been mainly forgotten, even by his own students, but Wheeler took them as his own.

Nobody paid the slightest attention to the old man [Pitt-Rivers]. One of his assistants had even proceeded to dig up a lake-village much as

---

[16] The modern name for Segontium or Caernarvon is Caernarfon. The Wheelers' names for sites will be given throughout this work, e.g. 'the Brecon Gaer' rather than 'Brecon Gaer'. In all cases, the difference is very minor.

[17] Wheeler (1955: 71).

[18] Ibid. 34, 64–6.

[19] Ibid. 66. J. R. R. Tolkien, who served on the Somme and lost two of his three closest friends in the War, felt the same subsequent drive to succeed in his field as Wheeler did, and phrased it in almost the same way as Wheeler did in *Still Digging*. See his letter to G. B. Smith on 12 August 1916 (Tolkien 1995: 8–11).

Schliemann had dug up Troy or St. John Hope Silchester: like potatoes.
Not only had the clock not gone on, but it had been set back.[20]

He continued to reference the General as a predecessor for the rest of
his career.[21]

The first chance to apply these new ideas came with an invitation in
1921 to continue the excavation of the Roman fort of Segontium, near
Caernarvon in Gwynedd. A. G. K. Hayter (FSA) had begun exploration of the site in 1920, with its work being paid for by the 'Segontium
Excavation Fund' of the Segontium Excavation Committee. The
Cambrian Archaeological Association was a primary donor, and
yearly reports were published quickly through its parent journal
Archaeologia Cambrensis. It was an excellent, contained situation,
and the Wheelers made the most of it in excavations undertaken
during their summer vacations in 1921 and 1922. Segontium was the
first of many such working holidays, usually undertaken in the
summers when student labour was easier to obtain and the weather
more reliable. Years later, Michael Wheeler could remember only two
non-archaeological vacations as a child: a trip to a resort near Calais,
and a Mediterranean cruise. He believed his father hated the French
trip, and indeed it is easy, if malicious, to imagine Rik Wheeler pacing
impatiently up and down a seaside promenade.[22]

In 1924 Wheeler published a synthesis of all the work in *Segontium
and the Roman Occupation of Wales*, with the aid of the London-
based Society of Cymmrodorion. Segontium has been re-examined
and re-excavated since the Wheelers left it, resulting in a minor but
essential readjustment of the dating of the periods of occupation, and
some doubt of Wheeler's theory that the fort was unoccupied or
abandoned during the third century. This has come mainly through

[20] Wheeler (1955: 66–7) is referring to St George Gray, later a minor rival in Dorset.
[21] He even considered writing a biography of Pitt-Rivers with Jacquetta Hawkes
towards the end of his life, but the project never materialized (Hawkes 1982: 371).
[22] This breakneck pace eventually began to contribute to Verney Wheeler's chronic
health problems (Hawkes 1982: 85). A letter of Verney Wheeler's to Nash-Williams,
written on 15 March 1930, may be related to one of these trips. She advises that no
excavation be undertaken at Caerleon in the coming season, saying there is no money
in hand and no destructive development planned that might encourage donors. She
also asks Nash-Williams to look after the printing of that year's appeal for funds,
saying that Wheeler is 'overworked' and she hopes to get him away for a little vacation
in April. Like most wives of the period (and many wives today), she was not above
fulfilling her own needs through ostensible attention to her husband's. (TVW to V. E.
Nash-Williams, 15 March 1930. Caerleon site archive, NMWA.)

researchers working with the finds archive, who have also advanced questions regarding the dating of Samian ware and other pottery. On the whole, the report is still of value to modern readers; new criticisms are levelled mainly at dating, rather than excavation technique or organization. The raw materials of study—pottery, coins, sections, and so forth—were excavated in such a way that they may be re-examined today without difficulty, echoing Pitt-Rivers' definition of an archaeological dig's first priority.[23] This achievement became a hallmark of the joint Wheeler digs.

The astute reader will have noticed little mention of Tessa Verney Wheeler in the last few pages. At this point, she was still invisible in most respects; but that was about to change dramatically.

The archive for all of the Wheelers' Welsh work is held by the National Museum in Cardiff. Verney Wheeler is conspicuous by her absence in the Segontium files. This stands in sharp contrast to all the other sites she and her husband were involved in, Welsh and other-wise. By the next major excavation in 1924, her work is easily trace-able through the site archive and daybooks. Wheeler acknowledged her routinely in his book on Segontium, and not at all in the interim reports.

> Finally, this page [of acknowledgements] would not be complete with-out a reference to the continuous assistance of my wife, of whom I will say no more than that she carried out the administrative duties of the excavation and has shared in all stages of the work.[24]

These stock references at the end of acknowledgements were com-mon at the time; Nash-Williams' reference to his wife in the report of the 1927–9 Prysg Field work is very similar.

> Finally, I ought not omit mention of my wife, who, as well as drawing the Samian potters' stamps, has assisted in all stages of the report.[25]

These simple sentences are difficult to interpret without further evidence; they may describe a wife who worked as hard as her husband or the paid diggers, organized and washed the small finds, drew the illustrations, paid the bills, and in short 'shared in all stages

---

[23] See Simpson (1962) for pottery; Casey (1975) for a discussion by the next excavator on the site; and Boon (1976; 1977a) for a re-examination of the finds and a thoughtful general discussion of the 1920s excavations.

[24] Wheeler (1923: 13).

[25] Nash-Williams (1932: 48, n. 1).

of the work'.[26] They may also describe a wife who always made the tea, brought out meals on time, helped in small professional tasks, and generally 'domesticated' the camp; a charming, non-archaeological participant in dig life. The models may be accurately considered as Hilda Petrie versus Agatha Christie Mallowan; the latter is the most delightful exponent of this non-archaeological type, but even she was drawn into cleaning finds with her face cream and nail sticks, as she wrote in her 1946 memoir *Come, Tell Me How You Live*.[27]

By looking carefully beyond the Segontium site archives, which type Verney Wheeler tended towards in this developmental phase of her career can be determined. The most interesting of the references that amplify and expand on Wheeler's short statement comes from George Boon, who re-examined the excavation of Segontium a half-century after the Wheelers left Wales. In a 1977 discussion of the numismatic evidence, published by coincidence in the same issue of *Archaeologia Cambrensis* as his obituary of Wheeler (which focuses on the Welsh years, and includes Verney Wheeler as an important player), Boon described his experiences trying to sort and identify inter-war numismatic finds during a renovation of the Segontium Museum.

> Only the 1920 coins have envelopes with letter-by-letter descriptions, done by A. G. K. Hayter, who was then in charge of the diggings. In later years, the coins were identified by Dr. and Mrs. Wheeler as they came to hand, but doubtful specimens were afterwards submitted to Harold Mattingly of the British Museum.[28]

Note the association of Verney Wheeler with small finds, an area she would become particularly expert in at Verulamium. It is clear that

---

[26] The traditional and enduring association of women and small finds is beginning to draw some attention; see Root (2004: 12–15) for an overview of recent work on the subject.

[27] At the time of writing (March 2011), the British Museum had just purchased a collection of small Assyrian ivories excavated by Mallowan between 1949 and 1963. Some were cleaned by Christie and are described in detail in Christie (1977). The association with a perennially popular author undoubtedly led the previous owners, the British Institute for the Study of Iraq, to seek an even higher price than that normally associated with such rare and precious objects. The group, comprising one third of the total collection, is the second most expensive acquisition by the British Museum in the last ten years. The BISI made a generous gift to the Museum of another third, and the last third will be returned to Iraq. (http://www.britishmuseum.org/the_museum/news_and_press_releases/press_releases/2011/nimrud_ivories.aspx, accessed 14 March 2011.)

[28] Boon (1977a: 40).

she was appealed to as someone with specialist knowledge of the site and its objects, as well as the general subject.[29] The logical conclusion is that she was active on the excavation. There is also Jacquetta Hawkes' description of Segontium.

Altogether the Wheelers must have been satisfied with the results of their first joint venture in 'archaeology from the earth'. They were feeling their way in growing confidence, he particularly in the uses of stratification, she in the handling of and recording of artefacts. Presumably, too, responsibility for the commissariat and for looking after the needs of the few students employed on the dig already fell upon Tessa.[30]

Hawkes did not know the Wheelers in 1922, but she was a colleague and friend of theirs from the 1930s on. More importantly, her first husband, Christopher Hawkes, was involved with them professionally in Wales from an early date, beginning with his work on the Brecon Gaer as an Oxford undergraduate.[31]

Least important of all, but worth mentioning due to its source, is Wheeler's consistent use of the word 'we' when describing his Welsh work. It was a literary habit of his throughout his autobiography and archaeological writing. However, there are later instances in his autobiography (particularly in connection with Caerleon and Verulamium) where he is clearly referring to himself and Verney Wheeler.

Segontium was the pivotal moment of Verney Wheeler's life and career, and it cannot be left without a little further speculation. At some point during these two years in Caernarvon, she must have decided at a conscious or subconscious level to commit herself more fully to the work at hand than society would generally expect of a loyal wife. The talents nurtured by her teachers and courses at UCL had been long dormant during the World War, Wheeler's absence, and their son Michael's infancy. In this new setting, they came into play again.

It is unlikely that Tessa Verney Wheeler sat down one evening in the summer of 1922 and formally decided to devote her life to archaeology. It *is* a fact that she had already decided to devote her life to a man who, like his hero Flinders Petrie, had no room in his life

---

[29] Ibid. 172.
[30] Hawkes (1982: 85–6).
[31] See e.g. Wheeler (1955: 76): 'In July 1926 we moved to London and got to work [on founding the Institute of Archaeology].'

for anything outside his calling. Apart from her own intellectual interests, if she wanted her relationship with Wheeler to remain a central feature in his life, she had to join him in what mattered most to him. On a more conscious level, her socialization as an Edwardian woman must also have played a role. What really matters in the end is that she had the brains and knowledge not only to aid her husband, but also to partner him.[32]

THE BRECON GAER: 1924–1925

Moving on to the Wheelers' second joint dig, the Brecon Gaer, we find Verney Wheeler becoming more and more evident in the documentary site archives, though she is still officially only a mention in the final report. By their next dig at Caerleon, she and Wheeler have equal billing on the final reports, and she has begun solo publication.

The Brecon Gaer is also the site of a Roman fort, Segontium's counterpart in the south of Wales. Wheeler was eager to understand the southern part of the Roman road system in Wales, and the forts that garrisoned it. It was also politically expedient from the National Museum's standpoint as a unifying national institution. Wales was still 'an aggregate of parish pumps rather than a nation', as Wheeler observed pungently, and it was desirable to give both north and south equal attention.[33] Like a number of his contemporaries, at this time Wheeler looked for a Roman period in Wales (or Scotland, or any other liminal space) as a way of establishing it as an appropriately serious subject for major study.

The presence of the 'fishful Usk' nearby was also an advantage, and one Wheeler still remembered with pleasure years later.

---

[32] The opinion of Beatrice de Cardi, Wheeler's former secretary and an eminent archaeologist in her own right, differs somewhat from mine on this subject. Her view is that Verney Wheeler would have gone into whatever career Wheeler chose to take up with equal gusto and similar results, her example being architecture (interview with Beatrice de Cardi, 14 November 2006). I disagree on this point: Verney Wheeler's academic background in history led to her peculiar suitability for archaeology, and was the foundation of her ability to do independent professional work without Wheeler. However, de Cardi agrees fully with me on Verney Wheeler's archaeological abilities, especially her gift for teaching.

[33] Wheeler (1955: 73).

They excavated over the summers of 1924 and 1925. Wheeler remembered in 1955 that 'on the whole it was, I suppose, the happiest and least anxious of all my enterprises'.[34]

The sources for the Brecon Gaer are more varied and extensive than those available for Segontium. The National Museum of Wales holds a large archive related to the site, including the site diaries, correspondence, and bank information. Jacquetta Hawkes' first husband, C. F .C. (Christopher) Hawkes, and his friend and fellow New College undergraduate J. N. L. (Nowell) Myres also worked on the excavation, providing her with vivid memories for her biography of Wheeler.[35] Hawkes remembered his hope, or even expectation, of a wife like Tessa Wheeler, who could share his interest in archaeology. Myres remembered the site in even more glowing colours; for him, it was the first step in a long life in archaeology, and a liberating moment mentally. He is one of the first archaeologists who can be described as Verney Wheeler's student. She eventually arranged for his first site direction at Caerleon, and was one of the few people to whom he sent a copy of his first publication.

Young Nowell and Mrs Wheeler also developed a warm personal friendship that lasted long beyond the dig. Years later, he told Jacquetta Hawkes of his 'profound admiration' for her as a woman and a worker.[36]

> Tessa herself seemed to welcome it [their friendship], for she needed at that moment in her life an understanding friendship with someone, however innocent, on whose devotion and discretion she could place absolute trust [...] The work on the Brecon Gaer was on quite a modest scale and was not conducted in blaze of publicity. Rik himself treated the excavation as an agreeable background to a fishing holiday. He would begin the day by directing Christopher and myself, and the handful of unemployed Welsh navvies who comprised the labour force, what we were to find, and would then disappear, suitably equipped, in the direction of the river. In the evening he would return, not always overburdened with trophies of the chase, listen to what we told him of the day's work on the dig, and explain to us what he thought it meant. Meanwhile Tessa coped with all the organizational and administrative

---

[34] Wheeler

[35] In the event, even though his first wife, Jacquetta Hopkins, was also a young archaeologist, the marriage failed on personal grounds. His second marriage was to the early medieval and Dark Ages archaeologist Sonia Chadwick (Webster 1991: 164).

[36] Hawkes (1982: 91).

chores that a dig entails, including the provision of enormous picnic meals. Apart from their son Michael [. . .] and occasional visitors, there was no one else there at all.[37]

The site records, and Jacquetta Hawkes' research, suggest that Myres was slightly romanticizing the situation—several other students also assisted the Wheelers, and Wheeler did not fish all day, every day.[38] But the pattern of Wheeler proposing and Verney Wheeler disposing was becoming more and more pronounced, and workers on later digs would also notice and comment on it. Another pattern was also becoming apparent. Wheeler and Verney Wheeler's marriage was beginning to come under some strain, partially from his insistence that his archaeological work must always come first for them both. Verney Wheeler gave willingly, both from love of Wheeler and from her own intellectual interests, but she was already overworking herself physically and mentally. More delicate is the question of what Hawkes calls Wheeler's 'minor infidelities'. While there was little scope for such activities in an empty valley by the Usk, Verney Wheeler had most likely already had to deal with her husband's chronic unfaithfulness elsewhere in Wales. In time, this stress would also contribute to her ill health.

At this point in her life, Nowell Myres' intelligent, youthful admiration must have been very comforting. Three of the letters he sent to Verney Wheeler in 1927 after returning to Oxford are preserved at the National Museum of Wales. They are an interesting mixture of archaeological gossip, acute observations of college life and his work as a very new lecturer, technical questions, and intriguing personal details, especially those thanking her for various pieces of unelaborated 'wise advice'. He ends his letters with appeals to her not to forget to visit her 'two children' in Oxford, probably a reference to himself and Christopher Hawkes. At the time, their other student from the Brecon Gaer, Christopher Hawkes, had just published an article on Alchester, which he sent to Verney Wheeler for criticism.[39]

To return to the Brecon Gaer—the archives in the National Museum provide complete evidence for Verney Wheeler's involvement in the site. Newspaper reporters and antiquarian societies visiting the

[37] As quoted in ibid. 90–91.
[38] Ibid. 91.
[39] J. N. L. Myres to T. Verney Wheeler, 22 April, 8 May, 8 October 1927. Caerleon site archive, NMWA.

site attest to her presence and activity there, but more physical evidence also remains.[40] The work began with the usual letters back and forth between Wheeler (in his most official capacity), the local landlord, and other interested parties. Eventually, a contract was signed, the arrangements for funding were finalized, the appeals sent out, and an Excavation Committee formed. The money for the actual work was deposited at Barclays under 'Excavation Fund', in the name of Mrs Tessa Verney Wheeler. The neat, professional accounts, drawn up in black and red ink, were made up and signed by Mrs Tessa Verney Wheeler.[41] The only extant site notebook, a scrappy book of plans begun in its second year, is almost certainly in the handwriting of—Mrs Tessa Verney Wheeler.[42] Comparison of these running plans to those in the published report would thus seem to attest to the sureness of her on-site diagramming; for example, in the bath buildings, only one change appears, to the right of the apse.

The point where Verney Wheeler took over the accounts and the bank dealings for the Brecon Gaer marks the moment she was no longer acting merely an extension of Wheeler. By taking on the finances for the dig, she became responsible, legally and intellectually, for her actions there. The extensive auditing of the accounts by various financial supporters bears witness to that.[43] Fortunately, Tessa was excellent at sums—and even better at financial regulations.

Her physical involvement must also have increased. She is remembered today by those who knew her as a noted technical excavator and field conservator, a great finds archaeologist, and an excellent teacher of those skills.[44] As she was teaching and excavating independently by her next dig at Caerleon, Segontium and the Brecon Gaer must be where she learned basic technical methods. Still, Wheeler's acknowledgement of her in his site report, *The Roman Fort Near Brecon*, barely hints at her changing and expanding role.

---

[40] See e.g. the *South Wales News* of 15 August 1925, recording a visit by the Cambrian Archaeological Society.

[41] Brecon Gaer site archive, NMWA.

[42] Verney Wheeler also lectured on the Brecon Gaer in her presidential address to the Archaeological section of the Cardiff Naturalists' Society. She was their first female president. *South Wales News*, 20 March 1926.

[43] Brecon Gaer site archive, NMWA.

[44] Interview with Beatrice de Cardi, 14 November 2006; interview with Margaret Drower, 19 January 2007.

To my wife I am indebted for continuous co-operation both during the digging and in the classification and reparation of the 'finds'.[45]

The site report is in other respects exemplary for the period. Wheeler dealt logically with the materials at hand in six sections, whose subjects include a bibliography (written by V. E. Nash-Williams), the structural remains of the forts, the structural remains outside the fort (including the road it protected), a historical summary, detailed descriptions and drawings or photographs of the finds, and outstanding problems left unanswered. The material included is what a reader would expect from a modern report (barring scientific analyses and other innovations not available to the Wheelers). It holds up fairly well today, and remains the most complete excavation of the site. Later researchers and excavators compliment the 'perfect order' and careful recording of the Brecon pottery storage at the National Museum of Wales, but go on (as with Segontium) to use it to slightly re-date the Wheelers' chronology. This maintains a continuing pattern of slight re-dating at Wheeler sites.[46]

Before leaving this site, two of the 'occasional visitors' deserve more specific mention. Sir Flinders Petrie and his wife, Hilda, also preferred archaeology to more traditional holidays.

He had chosen 'stone circles' and cairns for his holiday task [. . .] on the first day I [Wheeler] asked him what instruments he proposed to take with him. A look of ineffable cunning came into his eyes as he produced a single slender bamboo pea-stick and—a visiting card. The pea-stick [. . .] gave him the line [. . .] the visiting-card [. . .] a right angle.[47]

In *Archaeology From The Earth*, Wheeler remembered the incident again under his description of necessary surveying equipment.

I saw some of his [Petrie's] results, and marvelled that they were not more inaccurate than they actually were. But then he was a genius.[48]

After dinner every evening, he would 'with the help of a logarithm-table [. . .] reduce them to a schematic diagram'.

---

[45] Wheeler (1926: 3). Wheeler's constant quoting of the word 'finds' in association with objects from the site is a reminder that the language of archaeological reports was new, and not rapidly made standard. Even Wheeler, whose reports can be considered cutting-edge for their period, found time for the odd poetic or rhetorical flourish.

[46] Simpson (1962: 19).

[47] Wheeler (1955: 74).

[48] Wheeler (1954: 144).

Verney Wheeler's memory of the Petrie visit was by chance recorded by Kenneth Collingwood Selly, who knew her at Maiden Castle in Dorset several years later. It is revealing in a number of ways, not least of the relationship between her and Wheeler, and of the differing expectations the visitors and visit placed on them. These seem to have been rather more stressful in Verney Wheeler's case. She was both their prestigious guests' social hostess and junior colleague. Occasionally she was also their keeper, as when both Petries were 'treed' by an angry bull whilst out surveying their stone circles.

> One day when many of us were eating in the mess hut, the Petrie's adventure with the bull came up and one of the girls said 'Tessa, you were very brave to mount guard with only a ranging-rod!' and Tessa replied 'I was much more frightened of what Rik would say if anything got damaged, than I was of the bull!' Which seems to suggest that the Petries' survey amounted to rather more than a 'visiting card and a piece of string.'[49]

Petrie was impressed by his young friend's wife, and said so in a letter to Wheeler. The approbation of the great excavator is phrased in an interesting way, considering his own wife Hilda's career.

> I [*unclear word*: regret *or* imagine] that family propriety has effaced any record [in the Brecon Gaer site report] of the unfailing driving power of Mrs Wheeler, which seemed the back-bone of the carry-on.[50]

THE MOVE BACK TO LONDON

Back in Cardiff, Wheeler's career advanced swiftly. When the Director of the Museum, Dr William Evans Hoyle, retired on grounds of ill health in 1924, Wheeler gained the position—a major step up for a man who was still only 33. His appointment was seen as a logical step for both the Museum and himself. It was now tacitly assumed that he would make his career in Wales. Wheeler lent credence to this idea with his devotion to his work, whether administrative, educational, or

[49] Hawkes (1982: 91); Kenneth Collingwood Selly to Jacquetta Hawkes, 7 December 1983 (J. B. Priestley Library, University of Bradford).
[50] W. Flinders Petrie to Wheeler, 30 October 1930 [?]. General Correspondence and Papers 1930, MOLA.

archaeological. The series of professional classes and summer schools he set up for provincial curators at the National Museum, which combined all three of these headings, were a particularly ground-breaking and popular innovation that called back once again to the Welsh nationalism and unity the Cardiff institution hoped to foster.

The great goal was to finish the Museum's new quarters and completely relocate its collections.[51] Wheeler applied to the Treasury in London for a building grant, but it was not enough. As Wheeler himself remembered it, only 'chance and Sir William Reardon Smith, Bart.—but especially Sir William Reardon Smith, Bart.—enabled [me] to meet it.'[52] Wheeler had been friends and allies for some time with Reardon Smith, the wealthy, self-made owner of a shipping fleet, and when he became Director one of his first moves was to remove the museum treasurer in 'open battle' and install Reardon Smith in his place. The ship-owner 'marked his appointment by coming to my office and writing a cheque for £22,000'—or rather, for £21,367 4s. 9d, the exact amount of the museum's bank overdraft.[53] At the time it was an anonymous gift; it was almost a whole year before someone spilled the beans to the press and Reardon Smith got his due credit. An appeal was also made to the public on a national (Welsh), rather than local, level, and they responded enthusiastically in a reflection of their new cultural unity.[54] The museum building was begun again, and opened by King George V in 1927; it remains in use today.

Naturally Rik and Tessa benefited personally from the promotion, most of all from the higher salary the position of Director commanded. They left the Cathedral Road flat and moved to Y-Bwlch ('The Pass') on St Michael's-road, a house with a garden that they had built for themselves in the suburb of Llandaff. Tessa and Michael were delighted with the change.[55] After ten years of rented rooms outside various army barracks, cots in museum offices, and small city flats, it

---

[51] Parts of the Cathays Park building were in occupation as early as 24 October 1921, when a newspaper review records that the art, botany, and zoology departments were all in their new homes, while geology is on the site but in temporary occupation (*Western Mail*, 24 October 1921). But one Stephen Coleridge writes to the same newspaper on 19 April 1923, to complain about the obstructive trees planted around the 'half-finished public museum'.

[52] Wheeler (1955: 70).

[53] Ibid. 70. *Western Mail*, 10 December 1925 and 23 October 1926.

[54] National Museum of Wales Annual Report, 1957.

[55] Jacquetta Hawkes (whose interviews with Michael Wheeler provide much of this first-hand detail) is probably projecting her own personality on to Tessa a little.

is hard not to imagine Tessa's happiness in a family home that was entirely their own.[56] As it happened, they would live in it for less than two years.

Wheeler had always missed London, and only two years after he accepted the Directorship of the National Museum of Wales, he quit the post in favour of the Keepership of the London Museum.[57] Cardiff had provided considerable excitement at first, with the struggle to establish and fund Welsh archaeology followed quickly by his promotion and fight to open the Cathays Park museum. He was honest about his ambitions and motivations: he still wanted above all to establish a modern, nationally influential Institute of Archaeology, and he believed that could only happen in London.[58] Cardiff was closing in on him, no longer providing enough stimuli or 'open battles'. He manoeuvred successfully to have his Cambridge friend Cyril Fox appointed in his stead. The Directorship was and is generally considered a terminal position; Fox stayed in Cardiff for the rest of his career.[59]

There is a parallel here to Wheeler's quick move to Wales in 1920, after the Royal Commission refused to give him a raise. Further back, there is a rapid departure from a moderately well-paid position as publications secretary to the Provost of UCL, in favour of the new, underpaid Franks Studentship in archaeology. Each time, he abandoned a safe career with a relatively dull future to strike off in a new direction in hopes of a challenge.

It was becoming abundantly clear that, unless I made a determined move, I should become a permanent cog in the machine [of UCL].[60]

All the friendship and co-operation which I had left behind me in Cardiff, and indeed in Wales generally, were inadequate compensation (in the eyes of a young man) for the limiting environment of the Cambrian highlands.[61]

---

[56] Hawkes (1982: 95).

[57] Wheeler to Cyril Fox, 19 September 1924. See also C. Fox (2000).

[58] Wheeler (1955: 76).

[59] When illness forced his retirement, both he and his archaeologist wife, Aileen, were much missed.

[60] Wheeler (1955: 34, 68).

[61] Ibid. 83. At the same time, and for the same reasons, Wheeler records turning down the Abercromby Chair of Prehistoric Archaeology in Edinburgh (where he had spent his early childhood).

What role did Verney Wheeler play in this major career decision? London was her home too; she had been raised and educated there. However, when the Wheelers returned to the capital Verney Wheeler was the person who kept up more long-term links with Wales, especially with Nash-Williams and Caerleon. Perhaps she would have been happy for Wheeler to remain a noted provincial archaeologist and curator, rather than accept a much lower salary on the chance of accomplishing great things. Her self-effacement throughout her life points to a different kind of ambition than his—to simply do a job well, not to receive praise or attention for it. She also lacked Wheeler's ghastly wartime experiences, and his consequent visceral need to create a new archaeology not only for his living students but for his dead colleagues.[62] For that to happen, he needed her practical ability as much as she needed his pushing to publicize her work.

The museum staff marked their departure personally by presenting written testimonials to both Wheelers, along with matching silver cigarette cases. Verney Wheeler was a heavy smoker throughout her life, even in neck-deep ditches in the rain. Wheeler was no better; at 80, he was still dispatching younger colleagues to find him Balkan Sobranies in unlikely seaside towns.[63]

The Welsh archaeological community, rather more practically, organized a testimonial fund that was well subscribed to. Its handover was described in the *Western Mail* newspaper. The Chairman of the fund, Dr D. R. Paterson of Cardiff,

> handed over to Mrs Wheeler a cheque for a substantial sum as a token of their friends' appreciation of their services to the Principality. Mrs Wheeler, in response, said the ambition of her life was to be helpful to her husband in his archaeological researches and the kind words which had been spoken helped her to think that she had not altogether failed in that ambition. (Hear, hear).[64]

In the *South Wales News*, Dr Paterson's speech was reported more fully.

> In Mrs Wheeler Dr Wheeler had a wonderful chief of staff, one thoroughly interested and capable, and he (Dr Paterson) had great pleasure

---

[62] Ibid. 66.
[63] *Western Mail*, 29 June 1926; Grahame Soffe, pers. comm.
[64] *Western Mail*, 22 June 1926.

in handing her the cheque subscribed by archaeologists. (Applause.) Mrs Wheeler, in replying, said she had always endeavoured to be a part of the shadow behind her husband. The people in Wales had made it easy for her to fulfil that ambition.[65]

In the posed photographs of the event, Wheeler is shown receiving the cheque. Verney Wheeler stands beside him, looking both wry and uncomfortable.

The Wheelers' decision to leave also prompted a flurry of biographical news articles, many of which paid unusual attention to Verney Wheeler and made much of her partnership with her husband. The most interesting of these appeared in the *South Wales News* on 20 March 1926. The paper's 'Lady Correspondent' seems to have interviewed the reticent Verney Wheeler most successfully. A wealth of details emerge: Verney Wheeler's birth in Johannesburg, her work during the war as an assistant surveyor of income tax, and her election as the first woman President of the Archaeological Section of the Cardiff Naturalists' Society. She was active in the various social and intellectual societies that were such a feature of the period, when unemployment left more and more people with free time for study, and when improved primary education made the man and woman in the street more enquiring about the world about them.[66]

> Dr Wheeler's removal to London will be a double loss to Wales, and particularly to archaeological circles in the Principality, because of the valuable work which Mrs Wheeler has done in co-operation with her husband [...] To Dr Wheeler's schemes [...] she has brought her keen enthusiasm and specialised knowledge [...] For three seasons they excavated at Carnarvon and other fields where they have worked include Margam Mountain [...] the hut circle at Blaenrhondda, Ely Racecourse, and Castell Morgraig [...] On these and other subjects she has lectured extensively throughout the Principality. She takes a keen interest in women's part in public life and is a member of the council of the Cardiff Women Citizen's Association.[67]

The mention of other excavations in this article, apart from the three discussed here, is a reminder of the huge amount of relatively trivial work for which archival records do not survive, and hint at Wheeler's

---

[65] *South Wales News*, 22 June 1926.
[66] Thomas (1988: 24).
[67] *South Wales News*, 20 March 1926.

enduring habit of accepting responsibility for excavations in which he played a purely supervisory, and in some cases long-distance, role.

ISCA AND CAERLEON: 1926–1927

Cardiff could not be instantly abandoned. Wheeler was still eager to continue his Welsh archaeological campaigns, at least until they could be handed over like the Museum to trustworthy successors like Cyril Fox.[68] With representative forts in the north and south of the country explored, Wheeler had his eye on completing the picture with the legionary fortress of Isca that partially underlay the village of Caerleon.[69] The site was particularly attractive thanks to its small Roman amphitheatre, still covered completely in velvety green turf in 1926 and set into the ground like a dish. Locals called it 'King Arthur's Round Table', a nickname Wheeler instantly and ruthlessly exploited for funding. It was decided that the amphitheatre would be the first point of archaeological contact with Isca—a familiar type of site, easily contained, and above all 'likely to attract the considerable funds required for a long–term program of work'.[70] A trial excavation in 1909 by the Liverpool Committee for Excavation and Research in Wales and the Marches had shown it to be in excellent condition.[71]

Matters were brought to a head at the end of 1925, when land in the centre of the town was sold for development. The Caerleon Excavation Committee was formed in response, under the leadership of Lord Treowen and the Bishop of Monmouth.[72] Verney Wheeler served as its secretary and chief fundraiser until 1931, long after she had left Wales.

Caerleon was Verney Wheeler's site, perhaps more than any other. Her contribution is still rarely acknowledged, with the majority of the credit going to Wheeler. But by any measurement it was she who

---

[68] Fox and his wife, Aileen, became lifelong friends of the Wheelers. They were another husband-and-wife team, and Aileen also excavated independently at Caerleon (A. Fox 1941).

[69] Wheeler (1955: 73).

[70] Ibid. 75.

[71] R. C. Bosanquet and F. King [excavators], with appendix by George C. Boon (1963).

[72] Wheeler and T. Verney Wheeler (1928: 111).

accomplished the actual excavation of the amphitheatre that interested the public in Caerleon, and thus paved the way for the archaeological work that has continued there intermittently ever since. The
amphitheatre remains the most completely excavated in Britain.[73]

Verney Wheeler's responsibility for the amphitheatre is not a
matter of conjecture, as it is with Segontium and even the Brecon
Gaer. It is straightforward. She was on-site for eight months, far
longer than the other two site directors, and 'alone' most of that
time; Wheeler was in London, pursuing his new ideas, coming up
for rare nights and weekends.[74] Nash-Williams, who took over Caerleon after she finally moved permanently east, kept in constant
correspondence with her regarding the site. He was in need of her
expert opinions. She was also the 'honorary secretary' (which in a
contemporary context simply meant unpaid) of the Caerleon Excavation Fund, a post she held until 11 July 1931.[75] Even after she left
Wales behind her, she continued to help with more than good advice
by personally facilitating non-Welsh donations; a 20 March 1929
entry in the minutes of the Society of Antiquaries of London lists a
gift of £10 to Mrs Wheeler for 'Caerleon'. Caerleon was also important to her on a less altruistic level, as it was the justification for her
election as a Fellow of the Society of Antiquaries.[76] For the rest of her
life, Verney Wheeler would sign articles, books, registers, and formal
letters as Mrs Tessa Verney Wheeler, FSA. It was the only inscription
on her grave.

Caerleon, to Verney Wheeler, represented more than an excellently
excavated and almost unique site of European importance. It was
birth as a separate intellectual identity, distinct from her husband,
working with him but not for him. It is the high point of her Welsh
career, and marks the moment she emerged definitively from her
husband's shadow. The overwhelming personal and professional

[73] Boon (1972: 89).
[74] See e.g. the quotation from one of Verney Wheeler's Caerleon notebooks below.
[75] Official announcement of the Caerleon Excavation Committee, 11 July 1931.
She also attempted to resign the Secretaryship in January 1927, but was prevented by a
committee vote. Cyril Fox to A. H. Lee, 31 January 1927. Caerleon site archive,
NMWA.
[76] 'Qualification [for the Society of Antiquaries]: Has taken part in numerous
Roman + other excavations in Wales, and has herself superintended the excavation
of the amphitheatre at Caerleon'. 'Blue paper' or candidate nomination for TVW,
7 November 1927, SALA.

justification with which the site provided her must be constantly kept in mind as her work there is examined.

The basic history of the site was straightforward and well established. Caerleon, like Segontium and the Brecon Gaer, was a well-known former Roman settlement, and like those of the Brecon Gaer and of Cardiff itself, its Welsh name reflected that early history.[77] The settlement of Isca dated from about AD 75, when the *Legio II Augusta* was stationed in the area as part of Roman movements against the Silures. From the beginning, Isca was a successful permanent settlement, its timber and earth buildings quickly replaced by stone. It had a good port on the Usk River with access to the sea, stone bath buildings, an extramural settlement of camp followers and soldier's families, and generally reflected the height of Roman military achievement in the area. By AD 90, the first version of the amphitheatre already existed, and Isca was established as a centre of regional Roman occupation.[78]

The village that grew out of the Legio II fortress prospered moderately in the medieval and modern periods. Its association with antiquity was continuous, both with the Roman past and with King Arthur. This was thanks to medieval identifications of the grassed-over amphitheatre with the Round Table, and Tennyson's local composition of the *Idylls of the King*. Fortunately for the excavators, the village had not grown to the extent of completely covering the Roman fortress, as at York and Chester. Much was made of this in appeals for funding.

There had been a good deal of recording and antiquarian work on the site since the seventeenth century. A successful Victorian businessman named John Edward Lee had founded a Caerleon Antiquarian Association, as well as a Caerleon Museum of Antiquities to house interesting fragments properly. The museum opened in 1850, its objects well catalogued and illustrated by Lee in two volumes, and the Antiquarian Association ran the museum from its founding until its 1930 incorporation with the National Museum in Cardiff.[79] There was no shortage of educated local eyes on the Wheelers' work.

It was clear from the beginning that Isca would be expensive to excavate. Wheeler was quick to bring its romance to the attention of

---

[77] Nash-Williams (1927: 378–9).
[78] Boon (1972; 1987); Knight (2003).
[79] Lee (1862; 1868).

the press, promising the *Daily Mail* exclusive updates on their Arthurian progress in return for substantial financial support.[80] Contrary to general belief, the Caerleon news reports were not all written by Wheeler. J. N. L. Myres, much less interested than his former teacher in promoting archaeology through the press, was annoyed to find that part of his work included writing daily reports for the *Mail*. However, judging from the homogenous quality of the newspaper articles that appeared over time, almost all the reports were reworked by a *Mail* staff writer. There is usually no by-line, though very occasionally one is 'From Our Correspondent'. Wheeler did contribute several longer, credited articles synthesizing the evidence in what was becoming his trademark public style: racy, emphatic, and certain.

Over the course of the excavation the *Mail* spent more than £3,000 in total, and in the end the newspaper simply purchased the site and presented it to the nation via Cadw's predecessor, the Office of Works. Cadw (the Welsh historic environment service) continues to maintain the site today. An American group, the Loyal Knights of the Round Table of America, was also successfully approached under similarly disingenuous grounds. No one with any real knowledge of the site, in America or Britain, seems to have seriously believed the amphitheatre was Arthurian, but everyone enjoyed the romance of the idea.

Many smaller and more local donations were also received, and a small admission charge made to view the excavation 'in action', an innovation frowned upon by the Wheelers' colleagues that proved very profitable over time (though it did incur the extra expense of paying a permanent caretaker).[81] It is uncertain who thought of this last innovation. Given Verney Wheeler's control of donations and accounts for the site, and Wheeler's genius for publicity, either or both could have come up with the concept.

Wheeler was accused at Caerleon, as elsewhere, of being too mercenary, too personally publicity-hungry, and generally of what modern critics would call 'dumbing down'. He defended himself throughout his career with the argument that the public paid for archaeology, one way or the other, and that they deserved to know what they got for their money.[82] This debate also produced a

---

[80] Hawkes (1982: 100); Caerleon newspaper archive, NMWA.

[81] Wheeler and Verney Wheeler (1928: 111–12).

[82] Wheeler (1955: 104). Hawkes (1982: 97–8) has an even-handed discussion of both sides of the issue.

justifiable criticism frequently made of Wheeler: that in his desire to make a good, saleable story of his material, he was often guilty of hasty and oversimplified interpretations.

This was the Wheelers' most important and far-reaching Welsh excavation. Segontium and the Brecon Gaer were interesting, small-scale places to hone various methodologies. Caerleon was a major legionary fortress, impressive by any standard. It was by far their most ambitious work to date in terms of prestige, size, and length of ancient occupation. The timing of the excavation meant it also had to provide an unequivocally positive note on which to leave Wales.

The immediate problem was who would begin the work. Wheeler himself was fully tied up in London with his new commitments. Verney Wheeler was, at least for the first few months of the move, similarly engaged, though she set up the plans and preparations for the first summer season, and was present on site as much as possible (as in her letter of 16 May 1926, below). The most obvious and best-qualified candidate, V. E. Nash-Williams, gave them six weeks at the outset of the campaign. But he was founding his own archaeological career, and could not yet spare the time he later devoted to Caerleon. The Wheelers' method of training the young in their own methods later led George C. Boon and other colleagues to consider a season with them 'almost a qualification' by the 1930s, but in 1926 there was not yet a large backlog of professional former students to rely on.[83]

There were some, though. Verney Wheeler solved the difficulty by establishing a continuing Wheeler policy of entrusting responsibility to former or current students, both to relieve herself and her husband and as part of their training. She suggested J. N. L. Myres to Wheeler, and personally asked the young man to 'come to her rescue', as Jacquetta Hawkes' interview with him on the subject puts it.[84] Myres is clear that Verney Wheeler was his main reason for coming to Wales again. He was 23, busy with his first academic fellowship (at Christ Church Oxford), and deeply, romantically attached to Verney Wheeler. She combined an appeal to his chivalry with a motherly reminder that it would be excellent practice for future archaeological work. He came for the summer, staying until he had to return to Oxford in October. His site diary survives, beginning on 29 July with a beautifully lettered title page and

[83] Boon (1977a: 172).   [84] Hawkes (1982: 100).

growing gradually more frantic, scribbled, and unreadable as time passes. His careful, pasted-in drawings of the stratigraphic layers he encountered, though, reflect his Brecon Gaer training.[85] He records three visits by Wheeler, of which this is a typical example.

> July 31–August 1 – (1) Dr. Wheeler examined the 5 drums of the engaged column [...] (2) Dr. W. also examined the 'steps' leading down to the arena in Entrance A [...][86]

Wheeler is also mentioned regarding pottery identification on 14 August and 17 September.

Myres did his work creditably, and got a crash course in site management in return. He seems relieved to hand over responsibility and the notebook to Verney Wheeler on 22 October 1926. Wheeler, though, does not mention him at all in his autobiography in connection with the site.[87] It is unclear why. He may have felt Myres' time was too short to take up space in an already rushed account of his early career in Wales, or have remembered the young man's contribution as less central than Myres himself did. The acid argument concerning Verulamium the two had in print immediately after Verney Wheeler's death may also have played a role, though by the time he wrote *Still Digging* Wheeler had forgiven him. In any case Nash-Williams is (quite properly) much more associated with the site.

Due to bad weather, active excavating soon had to be postponed to the spring of 1927, but consolidation of what was already exposed continued without pause.[88] At that point Verney Wheeler took complete personal control, to the extent that one of her former workers remembers her as present from the beginning (Fig. 4).[89] Wheeler was a vital part of the dig, but a remote one, paying flying visits from London. Verney Wheeler was the one who carried out the real work, and she should be held primarily responsible for its high quality.

Factory and pit closures meant unemployment in Caerleon was a serious problem in 1926, as it was elsewhere in South Wales. There

---

[85] J. N. L. Myres, Caerleon site notebook 1. Caerleon site archive, NMWA.
[86] Ibid.
[87] Hawkes devotes two pages to Myres' work in Caerleon, mainly because of his strong memories of the site.
[88] T. Verney Wheeler to V. E. Nash-Williams, 17 November 1926. Caerleon site archive, NMWA.
[89] Interview with Cecil Davies, 1 December 2006.

Figure 4. The Caerleon team in 1927. Verney Wheeler stands in the centre, holding a book. V.E. Nash-Williams and Cecil Davies sit in the front row, second and third from the right.

was no shortage of the cheap untrained labour also used at the Brecon Gaer; archaeology compared very favourably to the ditch-digging and other physical work the government could sometimes find for unemployed men desperate for any job.[90] It continued to be a fairly major employer in the depressed little town on the Usk for some time; a large part of Nash-Williams' correspondence after taking over the site deals with applications from potential workmen, most of them ex-servicemen with good war records. He could only take a small number at a time, and was forced to make not just secondary but tertiary lists of potential stand-ins. A major practical obstacle to 'being fair' about distributing these jobs evenly over the years was the necessity of hiring back workers he had already trained, in order to save time and money. Nash-Williams, himself an ex-serviceman, felt the difficulties facing these men keenly. It was incredibly difficult to watch the men who had come back damaged from the terrible battles of the Great War diminish and die away in their own fields and yards.[91]

A gravity-powered light railway was designed and laid down by the general site manager and clerk of works, J. V. Bowen, who had

[90] Thomas (1988: 24). Interview with Cecil Davies, 1 December 2006.
[91] See V.E. Nash-Williams' letters from 1927 on, Caerleon site archive, NMWA.

worked for the Wheelers since the Brecon Gaer summers. A young farm boy named Cecil Davies was also hired with his father's horses to pull carts of debris.[92] Technically the excavation was conducted along the basic lines of a modern area excavation, with the entire surface removed in regular layers. The small size of the site made this method possible, and the aesthetic (and commercial) potential of being able to walk into the amphitheatre made it desirable. Generally there was about two inches of turf to be removed, followed by a charcoal layer.

Davies, 14 and 15 during the dig, clearly remembered the work up to the end of his life. His memories of Verney Wheeler were unreservedly warm and admiring. Davies' recollections of Wheeler were less positive. 'He' would come once a month to look over the dig 'dressed up like a dog's dinner'. Davies' father told his son that Dr Wheeler thought he was better than the workmen, and although this is somewhat at odds with Wheeler's personality as seen elsewhere, an impression strong enough to last eighty years deserves mention. It was probably not entirely the fault of Wheeler's manner or his suits; the workmen as a group were jealously devoted to Verney Wheeler— as Davies said, 'I fell for her'. He particularly remembered a bus trip to Newport that she paid for herself, so that the men could see themselves in a newsreel made of the excavations.[93]

Davies was quickly promoted from driver to the surveyor's and Verney Wheeler's Boy Friday, and saw something of everything that went on at the dig as he accompanied her around it. According to his account, every morning Mrs Wheeler, or in her absence Bowen, would assign the day's places and work. Men would work separately at clearing their given patch, and when they found something interesting, put it aside until Mrs Wheeler came to explain it. If it was a very good piece, she took it away into the site office (a hut located on the same spot as the modern toilets) and cleaned it. The men worked from eight to five, with a half-hour for lunch, and got a shilling and twopence per day, plus another shilling if they found a coin. Cecil Davies found an inscription one day, and got a shilling and sixpence.[94] The pay, even before these incentives, was comparable to the wages previously paid by the local industrial corporation.

[92] Brecon Gaer site archive, NMWA.
[93] Interview with Cecil Davies, 1 December 2006.
[94] Ibid.

Verney Wheeler's site notebooks are radically different from those of Myres. She is obviously more accustomed to archaeology, and treats her work at Caerleon systematically. Myres' book is arranged like a traditional journal or diary, but Verney Wheeler's are technical and businesslike, building on the very similar book she kept at the Brecon Gaer. The Caerleon book is not organized by day but by site feature—for example, 'Bath bdg H', followed by a list of information concerning the feature, plans and sections of it, and useful general information about the excavation. It is a synthesis of work as it is being done, and the overwhelming impression it gives is of confidence. Verney Wheeler knows what to look for as she walks around the site. Occasionally complete paragraphs in longhand break the notation to clarify a single feature, and she seems to be drafting her report as she walks. Her sketches are not as elaborate or finished as Myres', but her plans are much more scientific and technical, closer in appearance to those in a modern site report. She does not draw her plans separately and paste them in as Myres does, but sketches reduced diagrams and dimensions directly onto the page in a firm hand.[95] It is, in short, the work of someone familiar with Romano-British archaeology and able to interpret it on the spot.

As she had done ever since her university days, Verney Wheeler occasionally turned a book upside down, or turned to the blank pages at the centre, and listed personal notes or to-do lists. She retained this habit through her professional life, sometimes ticking things off (presumably as they were accomplished). These mundane, endearing lists often illustrate the variety of her responsibilities and concerns on a site. The reverse of Caerleon notebook two is fairly typical, with addresses of donors, stonemasons and other useful local contacts, a schedule for October 1926 ('24th: J.N.L.M. T.V.W. [R.E.M.W. all day to tea] + Miss Wms.'[96]), a memorandum on postage costs, an invented Latin inscription copied out in Verney Wheeler's handwriting and honouring the work on the amphitheatre of 'ego, J.N.L. Myres', notes on some Roman coins found in a Caerleon house's garden, and items from an 1880 book on local historical traditions that she wishes to follow up on later.

Most unusually, there is also a carefully copied Welsh prayer beginning, 'Grant, oh God, thy refuge, and in thy refuge, strength'.

---

[95] Verney Wheeler, Caerleon site notebook 2. Caerleon site archive, NMWA.
[96] Ibid.

It is worth some attention as it is one of the very few instances of anything remotely like religious feeling appearing in either of the Wheelers' writings. He in particular rather prided himself on being the only atheist in the foxhole. The prayer, also known as the Druid's Prayer or Gorsedd Prayer, was the work of Edward Williams, the eighteenth-century Welsh antiquarian, stonemason, and poet. Under the bardic name Iolo Morganwg, he supported a fusion of Christian and Arthurian traditions that proposed the essential survival of the Welsh bardic tradition from the mythical Celtic period (not dissimilar to what is frequently seen in Caerleon's tourist traps today), and was the inventor of the modern Gorsedd of the Bards. He also authored a series of long-lasting forgeries alleged to date from the pre-Roman period, in a similar spirit to the slightly earlier Ossian poems of Scotland. Like Wheeler, he perceived the Romans as imperialists; but unlike the Englishman, he saw that as negative. He was, in fact, representative of the romantic and inaccurate antiquarian tradition in Wales that almost met its match in the scientific, archaeological approach of the Wheelers and their successors. The poem Tessa copied is by far his best-known work today, attributed by him to the early bard Talhairan and first published after his death in 1848. It has been sung in the modern period as a hymn, and that may have been Tessa's point of contact with it. She included several clergymen among her friends and admirers, though none could tempt her to obviously religious behaviour.[97]

In the same way the workers kept pieces to show her, Verney Wheeler occasionally kept a shortlist of objects and questions for her husband on his brief visits, usually alongside other memoranda. Wheeler was not the only person she asked; Nash-Williams also appears. A representative list from just after her takeover of the site (with her original punctuation and spacing) reads as follows. The last three notes are particularly interesting in light of Caerleon's funding.

To show Rik:
(1) Room B Docecus Donancus
(2) Culvert A pottery –
(3) look at section over culvert A.

---

[97] See Morgan (1975: 51) for a general discussion of Williams. Champion (1996: 128–32) discusses the conflicts between archaeology and the romantic past.

Ring up N.W. [Nash-Williams] to get photographs – send in mercury to
   DM [Dennis Morgan?]. √
Warning re. amphitheatre details appearing in press. √
N.W. – ask about shale bowl handle.
N.W. – get essential information.
Draft an appeal.
Consider post-cards.
Write to Archbishop.√[98]

Verney Wheeler did not rely too much on outside advice, even at the
beginning. Her later reputation as a technical expert on small finds
had its beginnings here, prefiguring the split-second identifications
and after-hours cleaning lessons remembered by Margaret Drower
and Beatrice de Cardi.[99] For the most part, she made her own
judgements and interpretations in the neatly turned prose of her
site notebooks. Wheeler was rarely present, and it was impossible
for her to regularly turn to or depend on him. Given the confident
tone of the site archive, this seems to have benefited her development
as an archaeologist; being forced to rely more on her own abilities
strengthened them. Despite the ongoing belief that Wheeler excavated Caerleon, Verney Wheeler was the one who did the real work:
eight months of it in total, in contrast to Myres' four months or Nash-
Williams' six weeks.

The proof of all this is in the full excavation report, presented to the
Society of Antiquaries by the Wheelers on 26 January 1928 and
published later in the year, some time after Verney Wheeler's solo
summary report. It is co-authored by both Wheelers. In terms of
organization it represents another small step forward towards modern archaeological reports, with a history of the site, discussion of it
archaeologically, and series of separate finds reports on coins, pottery,
and so forth authored by experts in each field. Compared to a recent
report on Caerleon, Edith Evans' 2000 *Caerleon Canabae*, it is
scrappy but full of solid information.

The report exhibits throughout the firmness of language and
slightly journalistic tone normally associated with Rik Wheeler's
writing.

---

[98] TVW, Caerleon site notebook 2. Caerleon site archive, NMWA.
[99] Interview with Margaret Drower, 19 January 2007; interview with Beatrice de
Cardi, 14 November 2006.

It is at Cardiff, therefore, on the one hand, and at Richborough on the other, that we must look for the history of Caerleon in the fourth century, and it is possibly in the amphitheatre which lies buried outside the walls of Richborough—the only other British amphitheatre known to consist partly of masonry—that the lost century of 'King Arthur's Round Table' may yet be found.[100]

This should be compared to the ending of the shorter site summary Verney Wheeler wrote for *Archaeologia Cambrensis* in June 1928. The obvious similarities between the solo and the joint publication point to greater stylistic as well as material input from the author of the first version. That sole author was Verney Wheeler, the woman who wrote such charming and fluent letters, in which she showed herself quite as capable and articulate as her husband with a pen.

It is at Cardiff, therefore, on the one hand, and at Richborough on the other, that we must look for the history of Caerleon in the fourth century, and it is possibly in the amphitheatre which lies buried outside the walls of Richborough that the lost century of 'King Arthur's Round Table' may yet be found.[101]

Verney Wheeler sometimes insisted that Wheeler made the grand leaps of synthesis and interpretation, and was responsible for the literary qualities of their report, but her Caerleon summary and her letters concerning the site correct this.[102] The final article is, in its most important aspects, her work. She shows an unexpected firmness in her brief report, overcoming her personal shyness and a little opening awkwardness. As in the site diaries, she knows what she is talking about, and is confident enough to acquit herself well on her first published outing.

Nash-Williams took over Caerleon in 1927, and the amphitheatre finds were handed over to the Caerleon Museum. Nash-Williams continued to rely on Verney Wheeler for both archaeological and mundane information. Her occasional, specific questions in the site diary pale beside the number of letters he sent her asking for, and receiving, detailed help and advice. He also wrote to Wheeler, but

---

[100] Wheeler and Verney Wheeler (1928: 155).
[101] Verney Wheeler (1928: 32).
[102] Sources as diverse as Jacquetta Hawkes and Beatrice de Cardi often took her assertion at face value, in the teeth of all the evidence. Carol Wheeler Pettman, the Wheelers' granddaughter, contributes a similar family tradition. Hawkes (1982: 136); interview with Carol Wheeler Pettman, 10 January 2007.

only occasionally and mainly to ask for political advice dealing with museum staff. The weight of his reliance archaeologically was on Verney Wheeler. She continued to raise money for the site and help him decide what to do next, even as she moved on to other sites. Verney Wheeler's letters, preserved together with Nash-Williams' replies, are always indefatigably cheerful and helpful. Her entire Caerleon correspondence illustrates her gently asserted authority and her tact. These brief examples all come from that source, and date from before she is 'officially' on-site. From the beginning she was in all respects in charge.[103]

> [Verney Wheeler to Nash-Williams on 16 May 1926, regarding a very overblown report in the *Western Mail* of a volunteer finding a valuable necklace:]
> [...] the finds, which do not include a necklace (one bead of normal type) are in my possession duly labelled. The occasional 'helpers' here are often trying. I expect you know.
>
> [Verney Wheeler to Dr Cyril Fox on 22 April 1926, on an article for *Archaeologia Cambrensis* he had sent her with the note: 'Please read and alter where needful!':]
> The Arch. Camb. Article is great. My caution suggests only slight alteration of words re the *Daily Mail* supply of funds for the excavation of the amphitheatre. Perhaps you would approve an added paragraph by improving the one tentatively attached [lost]?
>
> [The same to the same on 26 March 1926, on whether Nash-Williams and his staff should be insured:]
> Yes. This should have been done at the start. The number of workmen is immaterial. The policy is taken out on an estimated expenditure in regard to wages.

A three-cornered conversation between Wheeler, Verney Wheeler, and the 'Old Lad' on 30 November 1929 is intriguing evidence of Verney Wheeler's continuing Welsh authority at the ground level. Its subject is a coin cache from Caerleon that must be appraised to see whether it falls under the complicated and draconian treasure trove laws of the day. Wheeler outlines the procedure for Nash-Williams, prefacing a long dissertation on the subject by saying that his wife is just off to speak with the appropriate Treasury official. A letter written by her later on the same day explains how much the finder and the Crown must be given for the hoard. Both Wheeler and

[103] Caerleon site archive, NMWA.

Verney Wheeler emphasize the necessity of rewarding the finder immediately and generously. Verney Wheeler adds, practically, 'if we have to give any more to the finder [after the coins are formally assessed], we shall in future be suspect in the matter.' She also has information about potential intriguing around the hoard by Nash-Williams' workmen, which Bowen has brought to her in London rather than him in Cardiff. She has tried to redirect him to Nash-Williams, but Bowen sees her as a more powerful authority.

In another letter of 19 June 1929, Verney Wheeler recommends Christopher Hawkes to Nash-Williams (as she had recommended Myres to Wheeler) as a safe person to involve in the excavations at Caerleon, saying he will not 'poach'. She goes on to suggest that offprints of the amphitheatre report be kept there for immediate sale to visitors. Other considerations were taking Verney Wheeler away from Wales, though. Later in 1929, when Nash-Williams asked Verney Wheeler to deliver a lecture she agreed, but complained that it meant finding substitutes for four lectures she was due to give in London (3 October 1929).

In a larger sense, Verney Wheeler's years in Wales are an accelerated symbol for the development and normalization of woman archaeologists in the inter-war years. Her time as a silent, helpful wife at Segontium quickly gave way to the more official role of the account keeper and recorder at Brecon Gaer. Following hard on the forts' heels, her independent direction of the Caerleon dig and publication of the site report, culminating with her formal recognition by the Society of Antiquaries, made her an archaeologist in her own right. Her husband, colleagues, and students, the people best qualified to judge, all agreed on that point. It was time to return to England and express herself on a larger scale.

6

London (1928–1936)

With the move to London, the Wheelers' lives sped up as their commitments multiplied and changed in nature. Verney Wheeler was as personally involved in the London archaeological community as she had been in Cardiff, but at an appreciably higher level. In Wales, she had been the President of the Archaeological Section of the Cardiff Naturalist's Society. In London, she eventually sat on the Research Council of the Society of Antiquaries, a group capable of national influence. The years from 1926 to 1933 were hectic, simultaneously containing the rejuvenation of the Museum of London, the founding (at first only on paper) of the new Institute of Archaeology, and the excavations at Lydney Park in Gloucestershire and St Albans in Hertfordshire. This last large-scale excavation, one of the most central to both Wheelers' careers, could easily overwhelm this period in their lives. But Verney Wheeler's less photogenic activities in London are just as, if not more, important, and deserve full attention before moving on to Lydney and St Albans.

Verney Wheeler's life was full of interconnecting circles; no one aspect of it can ever be fully separated from the others. Her connections at the Society of Antiquaries provided the opportunity and some of the funding for Lydney and St Albans, and her work at the Museum of London brought some of her only paid lecturing. The Society was a familiar fairy godmother for the Wheelers; the alert reader will recall that the Antiquaries also funded the Franks Studentship that enabled Rik and Tessa's engagement.

In the interests of clarity, these various circles will be teased apart here, and each examined in some isolation. While this is not strictly logical chronologically, it is the most sensible approach from the perspective of archaeological history. The fact that this chapter must be prefaced by this type of discussion is a testament in itself to the complexity, richness, and—more than anything—excitement of the Wheelers' professional life. Their personal life was correspondingly complicated. It should be said now that the complications were primarily (but not exclusively) due to Rik's failings as a husband. His serial infidelities were growing in frequency and number. While the situation affected Tessa cruelly in this period, it must not be allowed to wholly prejudice our judgement of their working partnership. Nor can his actions be completely ignored.[1] It was a factor in their life together, but by no means the only one; and while it is impossible not to sympathize completely with Tessa—to 'side' with her, as so many of their friends and colleagues did—it must be remembered that, despite the heartbreak and professional difficulties his behaviour caused her, she never left him or (as far as can be known) considered divorce. Indeed, of the many worries his affairs caused her, the most personally frightening was that one of his girlfriends would convince him to leave her and Michael.[2] Contemporaries of the Wheelers like Beatrice de Cardi cannot imagine them legally separating; it would have been socially and professionally disastrous for both husband and wife at that time and place, especially since all their acquaintances would have known why. It was much more in line with Tessa's personality to doggedly endure pain rather than leave Rik, whom she loved sincerely as a wife and respected most as an archaeologist.

It is dangerous work to attempt an understanding of any marriage from the outside, and the effort is rarely crowned with success. Any attempt here will be limited strictly to the times when their home life shows a provable impact on their work.

PROFESSIONAL RECOGNITION: THE SOCIETY OF ANTIQUARIES

The work at Caerleon propelled Verney Wheeler to election as a Fellow of the Society of Antiquaries in March 1928; straightforward

---

[1] Jacquetta Hawkes outlines this side of Wheeler without undue prurience in her 1982 biography. Hawkes (1982: 9–13).
[2] Carol Wheeler Pettman agrees with this assessment. Interviews with Beatrice de Cardi, 14 November 2006, and Carol Wheeler Pettman, 10 January 2007. Hawkes (1982: 135–6).

words for a complex process. The Society of Antiquaries of London was (and is) a venerable institution of the British intellectual scene. It was officially founded by Royal Charter in 1751, but its creation really should be dated to July 1707, when it held its first meetings. In the summer of that year, a group of friends (including William Stukeley) began meeting at the Mitre Tavern in Fleet Street to discuss their joint interests in antiquarian pursuits. Such coffeehouse societies were a feature of the age, and the modern Society still retains a vague, pleasant flavour of the *Spectator*. Eventually, the Antiquaries found a permanent home at Burlington House on Piccadilly, where they continue to maintain committee minutes going back to their earliest meetings.[3]

When Verney Wheeler was proposed for membership in 1928, the Society was going through a series of quietly momentous internal changes. Two of the most important concerned her directly: the place of women in the Antiquaries, and the place of the Antiquaries in the developing discipline of British archaeology.

The former problem had been largely resolved by 1928 after a certain amount of inner writhing. Papers written by women had been read to the Society fairly regularly by their husbands and brothers, though the ladies themselves had been carefully excluded from the proceedings, sometimes by those same husbands and brothers. Other men wished to change the status quo.

The professed *ability* of at least some women could not be seriously doubted. John Evans (the father of Arthur and Joan) famously raised the issue of female guests' attendance at meetings in 1901. As he grew older, his last wife, Maria Lathbury Evans, had begun attending Society meetings with him. She would probably not have been seen as more than decoration if she had not been an Oxford-educated classicist with strong opinions of her own. It was impossible to consider Maria Evans as merely an invisible appendage to her husband, and her presence began to feel threatening. On 14 March 1901, her husband brought up the subject—it is still not quite clear whether he was pro or con her attendance!—and those present voted 44 to 7 to exclude her.

In 1906, John Evans made another gynocentric proposal, this time that women authors be permitted to read papers accepted for submission to the Society, or at least attend the meetings at which they

---

[3] Evans (1956: 51–2).

were read. This was also refused, with shades of the difficulties Beatrix Potter's uncle found in reading his niece's paper on mycology to a scientific audience.[4] But change could not be held back forever. With the passing of the Sex Disqualification Removal Act in 1919, the Antiquaries decided to voluntarily admit qualified women before unqualified ones were forced upon them. It was more than an intellectual debate: Burlington House was let to the Antiquaries rent-free by the government, and the Society was worried that any apparent refusal or slowness to comply with the Act could jeopardize that situation.[5] A list of six suitable women was proposed at the governing Council meeting of 25 February 1920, and the first four on the list nominated *honoris causa*. Eventually four out of the six accepted nomination and were duly elected, including the famous traveller and adventurer Gertrude Bell.

On the whole, the Antiquaries were ready to admit their wives and daughters to full membership. Once the decision was made, there was no need to hurry; Gertrude Bell was proposed at a meeting on 17 March 1920, but not officially elected until almost a year later on 13th February 1921, and Nina Frances Layard (another well-known nominee, a member of the remarkable Layard family that included Austen Henry Layard of Nimrud) was the last of the test group to be inducted, on 3 March 1921.[6] To understand this length of time, the reader should bear in mind that during this period the Society of Antiquaries held elections for membership every few months. Each election held up a dozen or so names for consideration, of which most were usually accepted without demur; such a long time for consideration was unusual.

After that, the Antiquaries rested on their feminist laurels. While willing to accept women, they were not to be rushed. They blackballed the first ordinarily proposed woman in November 1920.[7] However, it ought to be noted that they printed new ballots with the wording 'h___' rather than 'him', so the hypothetical possibility of female members was at least maintained. On 4 February 1926, they finally elected their first woman member, Mrs Reginald Lane Poole, by the ordinary difficult process of balloting and vote. On 1 March 1928,

[4] Ibid. 388.
[5] Ibid. 388–9.
[6] Council Minutes, 1920–21, SALA.
[7] Evans (1956: 389).

Verney Wheeler became the second to go through the procedure successfully.

Burlington House preserves Verney Wheeler's 'blue paper', the ballot proposing her for election and recording the numbers of votes for and against her. It makes interesting reading. She was proposed by the eminent A. W. Clapham, an old friend and supporter of Wheeler's from the Royal Commission on Historical Monuments, and nine other prominent members of the Antiquaries also supported her election. Wheeler, who had become a Fellow in 1922 and gone to the Research Council soon after, could not sign the paper, but other familiar names leap out.[8] C. R. Peers, the Director, was the second to add his name, followed by R. G. Collingwood, John Myres (father of Verney Wheeler's protégé Nowell), E. Vincent Evans, J. P. Bushe Fox, T. Davie Pryce, O. G. S. Crawford, Cyril Fox, and E. E. Darling. It is still a prestigious list. There is, unsurprisingly, nothing written under 'Addition, Profession, or Occupation', but where the form calls for 'Qualification' Clapham has written:

> Has taken part in numerous Roman and other excavations in Wales and has herself superintended the excavation of the amphitheatre at Caerleon.[9]

Verney Wheeler was elected with a small but decisive majority, and 'FSA' stands after her name in her publications in the same way that it does after her husband's.[10]

There were more tangible benefits than prestige. The Society of Antiquaries, while not rich, was extremely well connected. It provided the Wheelers with several vital services, putting them in contact with potential new excavations and funding sources, and providing an outlet for the subsequent publications. Their next excavation at Lydney Park in Gloucestershire was the first example of this process.

The minor hiccough in Verney Wheeler's election was not due exclusively to her sex. The Wheelers were in the forefront of the second of the Society's difficulties: the conflict between an older generation of antiquarians and a rising generation of archaeologists.

---

[8] Hawkes (1982: 125).
[9] Ballots for 1 March 1928, SALA.
[10] Ibid.

Jacquetta Hawkes, along with her first husband, Christopher (elected in 1932), was definitely of the second group.[11]

> The Antiquaries was becoming more sharply divided between the old antiquarian Fellows, with interests well represented by *Archaeologia* [the house publication], many of them gentlemanly amateurs and devoted to mediaeval studies, including heraldry, and the rising party of the archaeologists, who had mud on their boots, potsherds in their pockets and 'science' on their lips. These 'dirt archaeologists' might also in fact be scholars and gentlemen, but they roused the hostility of the more die-hard antiquarians.[12]

Needless to say, the Wheelers, their friends, and their pupils were 'dirt archaeologists'.[13] The dichotomy is most swiftly understood through the opposing personalities of Rik Wheeler, pre-eminent 'Digger', and M. R. James, long-time 'Herald'. Both were Fellows during the same period. James, a Cambridge expert on and cataloguer of medieval manuscripts, lover of heraldry, and lifelong bachelor inhabitant of bachelor academic institutions, is best known academically today for his editions of medieval apocrypha. He was also, of course, the author of an impeccable series of terrifying and witty ghost stories, many of which take thinly disguised Fellows and recognizable versions of university libraries as their protagonists and settings. James's archaeologists or amateur artefact-hunters, such as the lead characters in 'Oh, Whistle, and I'll Come to You, My Lad' (1904) and 'A Warning to the Curious' (1925), inevitably find that their disturbance of ancient objects and locations results in malevolent pursuit from beyond the grave. Digging into the physical past, in an M. R. James story, is always bad and occasionally fatal. Perhaps the urbane James was engaging in some mild wish fulfilment—though in fairness, the dreadful item in his stories is occasionally a manuscript.

During Verney Wheeler's lifetime, peace was more or less kept between the 'Heralds' and 'Diggers'. She had occasionally attended the regular Thursday lectures at Burlington House prior to her election, usually signed in as Wheeler's or Clapham's guest. As a

[11] Christopher Hawkes was elected in 1932 (Webster 1991: 173).
[12] Hawkes (1982: 125).
[13] In 1949, a difficult presidential election brought matters to a head once more, as Wheeler fought the 'Herald' Sir James Mann for the position. He lost, but became Director instead, and thus balance was maintained. Evans (1956: 437–8); Hawkes (1982: 265–6) has a more personal account of the affair.

Fellow, her attendance rose sharply.[14] She attended almost every Society lecture from 18 September 1928 through 1929, and presented her first paper on 14 November 1929: a report on the Lydney excavations, alongside Wheeler and their partner William Hawley. The two men had perforce presented the first report on Lydney without her on 26 January 1928.

Interestingly, Wheeler's regular attendance drops sharply once Verney Wheeler starts going as a Fellow, able to represent their interests fully before their peers. However, both Wheelers were very closely involved in the Society's funding and organization of the excavations at Lydney and St Albans, even before beginning physical work at the sites. Verney Wheeler served time on the Society's Council, and was appointed to the Research Committee on 4 April 1935.[15] Her importance to the Antiquaries is best attested to by the unusually long obituary notice it gave her via Charles Peers after her sudden death in 1936.[16] She had died less than two weeks before; as had been foreshadowed in Wales, it was only when she was gone that those around her really recognized, or were allowed to recognize, her extraordinary gifts. In the new President Sir Frederic Kenyon's anniversary address for 1936, a tribute to Verney Wheeler also played a large part. It focused mainly on her work in the field and founding the Institute of Archaeology, paying homage to her 'radiant and gallant personality'. Kenyon also announced the creation of a scholarship in Verney Wheeler's name, which the society continues to administer today.[17]

> the fund [is] raised to commemorate the work and personality of our friend and Fellow Tessa Verney Wheeler, to whom the successful foundation of the Institute [of Archaeology] was in so large a measure due. The income of the fund will be devoted to assisting those who desire to be trained for the serious study of archaeology [. . .] It will be a fitting memorial of one to whom students in the past owed so much.[18]

The Society was not the only place Verney Wheeler sat on a prestigious committee. In 1927 she joined the committee of the British School of Archaeology in Egypt, a position that brought her

---

[14] Clapham and Rik always signed Tessa in as Mrs Wheeler; she always signed herself in as T.V. or Tessa Verney Wheeler. A small, significant point.
[15] Special Committees minutes, 4 April 1935, SALA.
[16] *Antiquaries Journal* 16 (1936), 327–8.
[17] http://www.sal.org.uk/grants/tessaandmortimer
[18] *Antiquaries Journal* 16 (1936), 256–7.

into further contact with the Petries, Margaret Murray, and many other old acquaintances.[19] Flinders Petrie had established the group in 1906, as a way of freeing himself from the immediate control of the Egypt Exploration Fund with which he had worked since the early days of his career. His recent summer at the Brecon Gaer was no doubt connected to this invitation, otherwise a little distant from Verney Wheeler's own research interests.

It was an interesting but increasingly difficult position. The School's main objective was to support the Petries' work in Egypt and Palestine, and as their lives centred more and more in the Middle East, it became harder and harder for the committee back in London to keep up with the elderly couple's accounts (and vice versa). By 1935, Verney Wheeler was the Chairman of the School's Executive Committee. It was an awkward post, where she often had to justify autocratic financial decisions the Petries had made to the Committee that should have made them.

> [She] found herself embarrassed at having to answer to the Joint Archaeological Committee for decisions and actions taken by the Petries without her knowledge, and they on their side complained that 'London' was acting too high-handedly'.[20]

The Executive Committee was formally dissolved in November 1935, and replaced by a smaller body located in the Petrie's new home base, Jerusalem. Verney Wheeler was no longer involved after that point. It was a sensible move, and no ill-feeling seems to have arisen between the Wheelers and Petries from it. On the contrary, around the same time, Verney Wheeler collaborated (or perhaps conspired) with Margaret Murray to send their mutual student M. V. Seton-Williams out to the current Petrie excavation in Sinai, and Wheeler and Petrie began to work together towards the physical establishment of a London Institute of Archaeology.

THE LONDON MUSEUM: LANCASTER HOUSE

Having got far ahead in time in considering part of the impact of Verney Wheeler's death, the story now returns to the Wheelers' paid

---

[19] Drower (1985: 295).
[20] Ibid. 409.

work in London: specifically Wheeler's new job as Keeper of the London Museum. It was a post he would keep (at least nominally) for eighteen years, until going to war in 1940 and then to India in 1944.

The London Museum, today amalgamated with its old rival the Guildhall Museum as the Museum of London, was originally the brainchild of two men: Viscount Harcourt and Lord Esher. Both came from long-established aristocratic backgrounds, and Lord Esher's friendships with several members of the royal family ensured that the new museum received the helpful patronage of King George V, Queen Mary, and Queen Alexandra. Both men also enjoyed influential government connections, leading to equally useful support from that quarter. Their goal was to found an institution devoted solely to the history of London, while recognizing London's importance to the country as a whole: a national/municipal museum. For a model, they took the Museé Carnavalet in Paris, opened in 1881 along similar lines.[21] It was the kind of populist project the Wheelers always found appealing.

After the usual vicissitudes were overcome, the museum was opened in temporary accommodation at Kensington Palace in 1912, thanks mainly to Queen Mary's personal interest. It was a stopgap, but allowed the first Keeper and Secretary, Sir Guy Laking, to begin making purchases and accepting donations for display. In late 1913, the collection was moved to a slightly more permanent residence at Lancaster House, formerly Stafford House, a beautiful Georgian building presented to the nation for that purpose by Sir William Lever. The Museum was established in the building on a twenty-eight-year lease—its supporters hoping that by the time the lease expired, the institution would be so entrenched the government would be unable to move them out. As events played out, the lease expired in 1940 while the Museum was closed for the duration of the Second World War. The staff found themselves homeless in 1945; as the interloping Foreign Office, which had used the building during

---

[21] Sheppard (1991: ch. 3). Francis Sheppard's book on the history of the Museum of London cannot be too highly recommended, as both an excellent discussion of a fascinating subject, and a larger examination of the ways in which twentieth-century public museums came into practical, funded existence and were integrated with the communities they represented.

the war, claimed right of possession through established use in exactly the way the Museum had meant to.[22]

It was to Lancaster House that Wheeler went in 1926. The Museum was at that point in some disarray; Wheeler compared it obliquely years later to the Augean stables. In his autobiography, he addresses his time there directly very briefly, preferring to move straight on to the founding almost ten years later of his beloved Institute of Archaeology.[23] Although the Museum is dismissed as 'the basis of our operations [to found the Institute of Archaeology]',[24] the pair were closely linked at the latter's beginning, thanks to the presence of the Wheelers. The teaching at the Museum was the real beginning of the Institute.

Wheeler had not been Lord Esher's choice. He preferred the assistant keeper, his son, Colonel Maurice Brett. However the appointment to the Museum came directly from the Treasury, via the recommendation of a committee of trustees. Wheeler's supporters at the Society of Antiquaries threw their weight and their names behind him in a series of enthusiastic letters, and were ultimately successful.[25] In the long run, father and son took the new broom's advent in fairly good spirit, and Brett worked well with the Wheelers during their reign. Lord Esher did stop liberally funding new acquisitions, but replacement benefactors were eventually found.[26]

The museum's holdings continued to be varied, ranging from the early accession of a dugout canoe found at Mortlake to the carved medieval doorframe of St Ethelburga's Church, Bishopsgate. Costume was always a major focus of collection, at a time when that was more unusual, as were London's decorative arts, architecture, and theatrical history. In short, the diversity of the metropolis was and is mirrored in its museum, and it continues to act as a conscious cultural identifier for a diverse and ever-changing urban population. The Museum of London remains a clear connection point for developing nationalist and cultural concepts, as well as illuminating the curatorial movements responsible for the modern

---

[22] Ibid. 75–9.
[23] Wheeler (1955: 84–7).
[24] Ibid. 84.
[25] Sheppard (1991: 102–3).
[26] Ibid. 104–5.

preference for audience- (rather than object-) oriented 'educational entertainment' displays.

The slight sideshow flavour was enhanced by Sir Guy Laking, the first Keeper, who was fond of theatrical touches that occasionally appeared at the expense of the historical object's dignity or even period. It was Laking who dressed the Mortlake canoe with a life-size model of a heavily bearded prehistoric Briton, and showcased a lurid 'working' model of the Great Fire of London, providing objects of fascinated terror for a generation of city children. Wheeler took some pleasure in removing the Early Briton, but relented when it came to the diorama. It survived to burn on command almost to the present day.[27]

CARDINAL MANSIONS

It is easy to imagine Verney Wheeler's relief at buying her last return ticket to Wales. Commuting between Caerleon and London cannot have been easy. In 1928, she returned to a recognized place as a published archaeologist and Fellow of the Society of Antiquaries, to a husband at the forefront of his profession, and to her childhood home. On the other hand, there was an immediate downside. By the time he left Cardiff, Wheeler was being paid £200 for his University lecturing and £400 for his curatorial work. While Wheeler was offered exactly the same salary by the London Museum, £600, the cost of living in London took a much greater proportion of their income.[28] The difference was great enough that the Wheelers originally planned to save on rent by their old trick of living at cavernous Lancaster House itself. However, one of the conditions of the twenty-eight-year lease was that the building would be available for purposes of government hospitality, and the consequent pressure for space foiled their hopes. Instead, they found a cheap basement flat at 2 Cardinal

[27] In recent years, the Great Fire diorama was finally replaced with an interactive touch-screen display on the same subject. It is, in the opinion of this writer, far inferior to the original papier mâché model, whose increasing fragility has made it impossible to regularly display. Sheppard (1991: 52); Hawkes (1982: 109); Wheeler (1955: 85).

[28] His salary at the London Museum rose to £900 in 1930. R. E. M. Wheeler to Cyril Fox, 19 September 1924; Hawkes (1982: 107).

Figure 5. 2 Cardinal Mansions, Carlisle Place. The front windows of Number 2 can be seen through the iron railings in the lower right-hand corner.

Mansions, Carlisle Place (Fig. 5)—one, as Hawkes points out perceptively, very similar to those Wheeler had lived in as a child in Bradford.[29]

Universally considered gloomy, Cardinal Mansions and successive London flats figure largely in later writers' criticism of Rik and Tessa's relationship. Jacquetta Hawkes' indignation on Tessa's behalf over the abandonment of their Welsh house was perhaps personal, but Francis Sheppard, in his history of the Museum of London, lists the 'depressing basement flat off Victoria Street', alongside Rik's unsociable working hours and affairs as examples of the difficulties he submitted his wife to by returning to London.[30]

By modern housing standards, the quiet corner flat is spacious and even airy. It has two large studies or sitting rooms, two bedrooms, a drawing room, eat-in kitchen, and a tiny afterthought of a bathroom reflecting pre-war priorities. On a recent grey April day, it was

---

[29] Ibid.
[30] Sheppard (1991: 110).

unexpectedly sunny; due to a position on a corner and next to a light well, it is well lit from three sides. Tessa herself remembered it fondly, as Hawkes in fairness recorded.

> much later [in her life...] she told a young confidante that they had been very happy together when poor, living in a basement flat and 'giving friends bread and cheese—when there was any cheese.'[31]

Hawkes, Sheppard, and others assumed that part of Tessa and Rik's habit of spending long days and nights at the museum derived from a reluctance to return to such an unaesthetic home. This is certainly possible, but once again we must resist the temptation to project onto Verney Wheeler. To imagine her as a brave little woman sacrificing her overwhelming feminine desire for a traditional hearth and home to her husband's professional ambitions is just as dangerous as assigning her a right-on first-wave feminist disregard for domestic life. Neither can be said in fairness to predominate. Nowhere else in her personality is this enigmatic woman more difficult to read.

The situation should be examined with a reminder of their attempts to gain housing in the museum itself before moving to London, and their similar working habits at the National Museum of Wales. This is a continuation of a previously set pattern, which leads to a suspicion that it might simply be the way the Wheelers preferred to work. The museum needed all the time they could give it, and the family atmosphere engendered by the 'mother–father' dichotomy of their leadership led to success in both the gallery and the field. Neither made their private home the first priority of London life, though they opened it generously to family and friends. Rik's father, Robert, used it as a base in central London, typing an affectionate letter to Tessa one afternoon in 1930 when she was at St Albans and he was in Cardinal Mansions. He signed it, sweetly, 'Your Dad'.[32] A less welcome visitor was a hard-luck case picked up by Tessa, H. E. Cheeseman, who actually moved in with them in 1930 while she tried to help

---

[31] Hawkes (1982: 106–7). I have been unable to determine who this 'young confidante' was. Hawkes's archives in Bradford do not identify her or include the full text of the interview. It could have been Hawkes herself, who knew Verney Wheeler at the end of her life, though they were not especially intimate and thus this seems improbable. Veronica Seton-Williams, whom Verney Wheeler was very fond of and worked closely with, is also a possibility. Hawkes also says that Michael Wheeler remembered the flat as 'of a fair size but gloomy'.

[32] Robert Wheeler to TVW, 5 August 1930, VMA.

him repair a life whose (unknown) disasters had caused his wife to leave him and his seven children to be placed in a Catholic children's home. Tessa seems, for some unknown reason, particular worried by the religion of the children's home, the only time such a prejudice appears in her writings. She paid off Cheeseman's furniture debt of £104 (no small undertaking for the cash-strapped Wheelers), found a 'private benefactor' to cover the basic bills of his old Belfast home through the end of 1930, and enlisted the help of V. E. Nash-Williams, with whom she often conspired in unobtrusive charity. Even Rik was pressed into finding the hapless and helpless Cheeseman a place. Eventually Tessa found him a post as secretary on a new Spiritualist magazine, and he vanished into history, complaining he would have preferred a job 'with the oil companies'.[33]

THE LONDON MUSEUM: NEW DIRECTIONS

The Wheelers professionalized the London Museum. The Early Man was removed from the Mortlake dugout, the haphazard system of accessions numbering was abandoned in favour of the running system still in place, regular activities for schoolchildren and lectures for their teachers were scheduled, and the general public was attracted to the museum by a series of special exhibits—a common enough trick today, here pioneered.[34] Wheeler wrote populist catalogues for sale at the museum, both for special exhibitions and for the permanent collections, these last with straightforward titles like *London and the Saxons* (1935). They offered a chance for the kind of synthesis of history and archaeology he enjoyed, with the ready get-out clause of a popular audience whenever stricter academics (especially J. N. L. Myres) remonstrated with him on his treatment of the subject at hand. An example is a letter from Wheeler to E. Jeffries Davies on 16 July 1935.

> I do not imagine that my views will meet with any more acceptance than anyone else's views on this subject—but then no one ever will agree with

---

[33] TVW to V.E. Nash-Williams, 3 June 1930, NMWA; H. E. Cheeseman to TVW, 29 July 1930, VMA.

[34] Sheppard (1991: 104–9).

anybody else about the Dark Ages. That, as I take it, is their most attractive feature.[35]

In January 1930, the fledgling Royal Commission established to inquire into national museums and galleries presented a report on the London Museum to Parliament, saying that it 'should set a national standard for other Museums of its kind [...] a model local museum'.[36] The model London Museum is now gone, but the Wheelers' effect on it can be seen in the Museum of London. This amalgamation faithfully preserves the innovations and the motivations that they drove ahead, especially in the realm of children's education. All sorts of attempts were made to draw in schoolchildren: an essay competition, with one prize for a boy and another for a girl, was established in 1928 and became particularly popular. Newspapers covering the awards were mildly surprised to learn from museum staff that the girls' essays tended to be slightly better.[37]

Verney Wheeler's presence at the London Museum is not difficult to determine, but the evidence for the exact nature of her place there is mainly secondary, somewhat anecdotal, and open to a degree of interpretation. Two radically opposing views are those of Beatrice de Cardi (Wheeler's secretary from 1936 on) and W. F. Grimes (his successor as Keeper). Beatrice de Cardi is somewhat dismissive of Verney Wheeler's role at the museum, but their overlapping time there together was very brief, and de Cardi worked exclusively with Wheeler.[38] W. F. Grimes, on the other hand, attributed the resurrection of the museum entirely to Verney Wheeler, in an unpublished interview with Jacquetta Hawkes. This view should also be tempered: Wheeler had irritated Grimes in a variety of ways for many years. The latter's first position had been at the National Museum of Wales as assistant keeper of archaeology in 1926, and thus he had been following the other man (though not by choice) for some time. Their tempers were not compatible. Perhaps Wheeler was a little too dashing, and Grimes a little too Pooterish—but in the best and most

[35] R. E. M. Wheeler to E. Jeffries Davies, 16 July 1935. General correspondence and papers 1935, MOLA.
[36] As quoted in Sheppard (1991: 103–4). They also said that it would be impossible for the London Museum to truly achieve its potential unless the staff was enlarged.
[37] Hawkes (1982: 117); *Morning Post*, 4 December 1928; *Times Educational Supplement*, 8 December 1928.
[38] Interview with Beatrice de Cardi, 14 November 2006.

complimentary sense of that much-abused word, one reflecting a kindly man who did his duty in admirable quiet and with modest personal ambitions.[39] Most important was Verney Wheeler's general lecturing work. Regular gallery and school lectures by Colonel Brett had always been a part of the museum's educational remit. He never enjoyed the work, and his schools talks had shrunk to a half-hour in length.

when the Treasury mandarins realized that Colonel Brett's lectures to the school parties were only of half an hour's duration, they actually reduced his salary in July 1925.[40]

His father, then Chairman of the Board, reassigned the work to Verney Wheeler on 25 June 1928, and from 1931 she was paid £190 annually for it.[41] She would continue to take on a great deal of this type of unsung, ephemeral public speaking, outside the museum as well as within it, and on a wide range of subjects.[42] Many of these lectures were general in nature, given to the same types of local societies she had often spoken to in Cardiff, but their importance was considerable and the seed they sowed took root. The great archaeologist Sheppard Frere vividly remembers hearing Verney Wheeler lecture on Verulamium at his Sussex school as a child; he would go on to excavate the site himself in later years.

Talks of this type were another way to draw people into the museum, and to interest them in the past. The object was not to create a museum for the elite, but for everyone. The number and frequency of these lectures may be assessed by Verney Wheeler's letter of 3 October 1929 to Nash-Williams, in which she agrees to

[39] More modern readers should become acquainted with the Gissing brothers' masterpiece of reluctant admiration, *The Diary of a Nobody* (1892). To sneeringly dismiss it as a middle- or upper-class misunderstanding of the 'clerking class' is to quite miss the book's point; it may have begun as a mockumentary of small ambitions, but it ends as a panegyric to the very simple, very timeless value of loving home, family, and friends, even when they are driving one mad. It is, in fact, the Edwardian ancestor of the popular US version of the television show *The Office*, which departed from the UK original in showing characters happy in their believable mediocrity (although not always aware of it). JHA; Gill (2004), accessed via the online edition at http://www.oxforddnb.com/view/article/67870.

[40] Sheppard (1991: 101).

[41] Committee minutes book, entry for 25 June 1928, MOLA; Sheppard (1991: 108–10).

[42] Sheppard Frere, pers. comm., 18 December 2006.

give a lecture for him in Newport, but grouses that it means finding four substitute speakers for as many talks in London.

> Cursed be lectures. You nodding sympathetically. Rik can't possibly, the force of his argument nearly blew me through the door. And if I come it means, on either date, finding substitutes for 4 lectures here. If you personally are very hard up for a programme, I would help out on Dec 4th but as a last resort and at your own peril.[43]

While back in Wales for a moment, it should be noted that while there is no record at the National Museum of Wales of Verney Wheeler being paid or an official member of staff, the amount of official and professional mail she received at the museum is proof that she must have been present almost every working day, and strong supporting evidence that she must have had or shared an office on-site. The London Museum has no comparable cache of correspondence, though in the manner of good archives everywhere, it preserves a random copy of a bill for refinishing the bathroom of 2 Cardinal Mansions, SW1, made out to Mrs Wheeler at that address.[44]

According to her contemporaries and the London Museum's secondary archival materials, her position there was constant and even quasi-official. Together, she and Wheeler dominated the building. When Hawkes interviewed staff from the Wheelers' time there, they all remembered Verney Wheeler vividly as a constant presence, with two small offices of her own.[45] Touchingly, the porters called her 'the Angel'.[46] Wheeler's paternalism was matched by Verney Wheeler's maternalism, and staff responded with a familial loyalty and drive, despite the regular absences of 'father and mother' during the digging season, and of 'father' all round the year as he pushed the cause of archaeology on a national level. This type of management would be considered impossible today, but in the 1920s and 1930s it was not only acceptable but also immensely successful. Hawkes gives a glimpse of the 'family meals' staff shared, reminding modern executives that the best team-building exercises are always spontaneous

---

[43] T. V. Wheeler to V. E. Nash-Williams, 3 October 1929. Caerleon site archive, NMWA.

[44] General Correspondence and Papers 1930, MOLA.

[45] Hawkes (1982: 118). Hawkes conducted extensive interviews with former museum staff. Her notes are preserved in her eponymous archive at the J. B. Priestley Library in Bradford, but sadly they are often near-illegible.

[46] Ibid. 119.

expressions of a real desire to spend time together. Her painting of the scene in domestic tones is evocative.

> An important feature of the domestic regime of the museum was a communal lunch, at which all the salaried staff, the researchers who were found working space in the museum, and friendly visitors ate their packed meals together. The Wheelers' sandwiches were daily fetched [. . .] from Capella's, an Italian restaurant just across the way. These gatherings kept everyone in touch with one another's doings and ideas. Later in the day tea would be brewed in the governmental kitchen.[47]

While Verney Wheeler is not immediately obvious in the museum's archives, they do provide some glimpses of her that are generally interesting more for their implications than their actual content. They come mainly from Wheeler's official correspondence as Keeper. Here are three examples, the earliest from 1928–9, when Professor Percy Flemming, who became one of the cataloguers the museum was desperately in need of, first approached Verney Wheeler for a job. He wrote as much to Wheeler on 2 January 1929.

> When I suggested, in writing to Mrs. Wheeler, that I might possibly be of some assistance to the Museum, I naturally though of myself as a voluntary worker—And when Mrs. Wheeler wrote in reply, *asking me to join her in making the catalogue* [my italics], I gladly accepted.[48]

He ended up doing the work for 10s. 6d. an hour; the job was so large that he was urged by the Wheelers to take an honorarium.

When Harry Plowman accidentally broke a glass Tudor jar that supposedly belonged to Lady Jane Grey's mother Frances, he turned to the London Museum for help restoring it. He was a member of the Society of Antiquaries and a good friend to the museum. It was in their interests, as well as their good manners, to give him the best help, and that meant Verney Wheeler (then at St Albans digging). Martin Holmes, then Wheeler's secretary, wrote to Plowman regarding the request on 20 June 1933.[49] At this time conservation was still very much a catch-as-catch-can department, and many repairs were made by either Verney Wheeler or by the 'handyman porter' David Sagar in the museum's basement.

---

[47] Ibid. 118.
[48] General Correspondence and Papers 1929, MOLA.
[49] He stayed at the museum until retiring in 1965 as senior assistant keeper, and became an expert on theatrical history. Sheppard (1991: 111).

The broken glass jar will be seen to by Mrs. Wheeler herself as soon as she returns at the end of this week.[50]

That Verney Wheeler took on the role of repairwoman is unsurprising. Conservation was still in its infancy; in April 1936, the same month as Verney Wheeler's death, Wheeler hired a 14-year-old school leaver called Arthur Trotman as 'boy learner'. One of his duties was to assist Sagar in what would today be called general objects conservation. Trotman eventually retired in 1986 with the title 'chief conservation officer of the amalgamated Museum of London'. Through study, ability, and constant application, he had become a master of the many, widely differing branches of conservation and restoration that the museum needed. His career is a fine monument to the way conservation used to be learned—on the job.[51] Until recently, no academic institution was able to match the intense learning experience of the museum lab, in a nice parallel to the practical fieldwork necessary to archaeology. It is only in the last twenty years that specialist fields of conservation have become commonly regularized in degree courses; when the author's mother, Cristina Balloffet Carr, began her career as a textile conservator at the Metropolitan Museum of Art in 1978, she was a good seamstress with an undergraduate background in art history but no more specific training. The chief conservator of the time, Nobuko Kajitani, preferred raw ability in new hires, and trained her workers according to her own specific needs rather than coursework requirements. Both systems have advantages and flaws; a combination of the two is, as in archaeology, always to be preferred.

Wheeler's letter to George Eumorforpoulos (another FSA) on 7 February 1934 gives a hint of the extent of Verney Wheeler's lost correspondence. A similar archaeological sample can be found in the upcoming discussion of Lydney Park.

Percival David, just before he went away, mentioned in a letter to my wife that he would like us to consider the possibility of arranging for occasional meetings of the Oriental Ceramic Society [. . .] at Lancaster House.[52]

[50] General Correspondence and Papers 1933, MOLA.
[51] Sheppard (1991: 111).
[52] Correspondence and Papers 1934, MOLA. They were granted permission cheerfully, and convinced the government office that also had to be applied to that it qualified under the Government Hospitality proviso of the lease.

Why do no letters from Verney Wheeler survive in London? There are a large number of them in Cardiff relating to her archaeological work, dating well into the 1930s, though the extent of her presence or involvement at the museum there is unclear. Contrarily, it is known she had offices and semi-official duties at the London Museum, and there is not one letter remaining there signed by her or in her hand. Perhaps all documents relating to her archaeological work were moved elsewhere, but plenty of letters from *Wheeler* relating to excavations are preserved. It is possible that after Verney Wheeler's death her letters were returned to her husband or son; but surely such sentiment would not extend to carbon copies of business letters. The least poor explanation that can be offered is that staff and students at the London Museum approached her in person rather than by mail. Occasionally people like Percy Flemming refer to decisions made with her in conversation (as above).

Hearsay, as relayed by Jacquetta Hawkes, also refers to her acting as her husband's editor. Wheeler's pretty wit was ever at odds with his pragmatic political instincts.

> [Verney Wheeler was an] effective censor when she heard some particularly angry or scathing letter being dictated to an individual whom they could not afford to antagonize.[53]

There is one letter in the London Museum that may reflect this—a draft written by Wheeler to Lord Esher on 10 October 1929 or 1930, regarding financial estimates he has sent to the Treasury and proposed changes in the Museum he wishes Esher to support. These include increased educational outreach. Someone has annotated it in pen—writing 'Yes', 'Very satisfactory', and other, more detailed comments of correction and approval. It is likely that this editor was Verney Wheeler; he or she uses her usual choice of pen and flair, though there is not enough of a handwriting sample for it to be conclusive. Of the alternate candidates, only the Assistant Keeper (and Lord Esher's son), Colonel Brett would have been senior enough to criticize the Keeper in this free way, and it is unlikely that Wheeler would have asked for (or put up with) his advice. The annotation is crisp, authoritative, sensible, and encouraging, all qualities associated with Verney Wheeler's written style. There is a particular interest on the writer's

---

[53] Hawkes (1982: 116).

part in a suggestion of Wheeler's to make the Museum free every day but one, to attract the hoi polloi but also keep them out at scheduled times. The unknown writes 'I agree. All days free except Tuesday.'[54] Whoever this person is (and it is almost certainly Verney Wheeler), he or she is integrated fully in the Museum, and taking a firm role in its running.

Still, the general archival absence of Verney Wheeler remains inexplicable. Surely she must have signed at least one museum note during the years 1927–36? She often used London Museum stationery and envelopes in other contexts, for example when sending materials or finds back to Lydney Park. The coins returned to Lydney after the relevant publication was completed went there courtesy of His Majesty's Service and at His Majesty's expense, via London Museum stationery. That was one reason the Wheelers so often used Museum notepaper: it travelled free.

Verney Wheeler received some official recognition in 1931, when she began to receive the previously mentioned £190 a year. The money was derived from the rent the museum received from the London Society.[55] This salary was in return for the public and school lectures she had given from 1928 and continued to present, and the only time she was officially paid for her regular work.[56] She also took over Dr Flemming's part-time assistantship and lectureship in March 1931. It is unclear whether she was paid for this, but it is likely since Dr Flemming had been. In the minutes of the meeting, at which she was not present, it was noted that:

> Mrs Wheeler has, by invitation of the board, given most of the Museum lectures for the past three years.[57]

Wheeler was a man on a mission. He saw the Museum as forerunner and eventual satellite of his larger 'blueprint' for a great Institute of Archaeology, with university accreditation and scientifically trained students. In his vision, the Society of Antiquaries and UCL would be enlisted in support, as would the Royal Commission on Historic Monuments, and the Wheelers themselves would make sure that younger archaeologists gained field experience. All of the things he loved best

---

[54] Draft of letter from R. E. M. Wheeler to Lord Esher, 10 October 1929 (?). General Correspondence and Papers 1930, MOLA.
[55] Sheppard (1991: 110).
[56] Ibid.; Board minutes book entry for 25th June 1928, MOLA.
[57] Board minutes book entry for 27 March 1931, MOLA.

about his boyhood and his London education would be combined, as a tribute by a 'lone survivor of the Missing Generation' to the potential colleagues and friends he had lost in the war.[58]

Before that was accomplished, the Museum had to be dealt with. Verney Wheeler's role here was (as usual) to do a great deal of actual work, though Wheeler was never idle. He proposed that 'the London Museum [. . .] be cleaned, expurgated, and catalogued [. . .] turned into a tolerably rational institution'. Verney Wheeler started the conservation work, hired Percy Flemming, and did a great deal of the cataloguing herself. Wheeler thought 'contacts at the Society of Antiquaries [. . .] had to be established or confirmed by lecturing and committee work'. Here both he and Verney Wheeler served on committees and gave and attended lectures. He wanted to guide the Royal Commission through Roman London, and he did.

How much input did Verney Wheeler have in the original creation of the above list, which Wheeler included many years later in his autobiography? It seems unlikely that he really returned to London with a 'pocket bulg[ing] with the blueprint of the Institute of Archaeology [. . .] the next obvious step in the development of our infant but growing science'.[59] But it is quite likely that he returned with a definite aim, and that he and Verney Wheeler together felt their way to its completion. We cannot know how much or how intensely Verney Wheeler felt about their London work, and whether for her it held the deep emotional charge Wheeler felt. Here, as elsewhere, we must look at the intensity of her labour to understand the intensity of the feelings that inspired it. While love for a husband might have provided the initial push, by this point her intelligence and her love of the work must have been as centrally motivating.

It is of limited use to speculate on Verney Wheeler's motives; without being able to question her personally, all *is* speculation. All that is certain is that her work was good, and that it would be difficult for any of us to strictly identify and rationalize all the motivations that ever sustained us, personally or professionally.

One more London task now awaited the Wheelers. University College, where Wheeler was still a Fellow and both were alumni, had to be strong-armed into creating a proper, practical university degree in archaeology. There were other Heralds in London to be

---

[58] Wheeler (1955: 84).
[59] Ibid. 83.

found and fought, and throughout his life Wheeler was always capable of creating opposition if he could not find it. Most importantly,
potential young archaeologists had to get their hands in the earth; and
here the Wheelers worked constantly together to bring their students
into practical contact with the past.[60]

THE LONDON MUSEUM AS A
PROTO-INSTITUTE OF ARCHAEOLOGY

At the British government reception for the [...] first international
congress of archaeologists in 1932, the evening was only enlivened by
[...] the lady dressed in cream and gold who was making her way
towards me [Howard Kilbride-Jones]. It was Tessa. 'I haven't seen you
before,' she said. I explained that I was reading archaeology at Edinburgh University, and she continued, 'In that case I think we should
have a talk'. She led the way to Wheeler's study, where we chatted for an
hour or so. Her viewpoint was entirely different from [V. Gordon]
Childe's and I listened to her attentively. The result of that talk was
that I became hooked on archaeology [...]Tessa was a very sincere
person, considerate, and those who were fortunate enough to know her
loved her. She was her husband's back-up, the rock upon which he built
up his reputation. Whilst her husband was out and about [...] she got
on with the job.[61]

One of the most important aspects of the joint Wheeler legacy is the
Institute of Archaeology at University College, which stands today
(albeit in a different location) as one of the couple's most permanent
memorials.[62] The physical Institute was officially opened in 1937,
almost exactly a year after Verney Wheeler's death, but its genesis lay
as far back as 1927, and the paper foundation was in 1934. It is one of
the accomplishments most firmly associated with her today, and was
(along with Maiden Castle) one of the projects upon which she was
engaged at the time of her death.[63] It was also (like the Verulamium
Museum and the Maiden Castle report) dedicated to her memory.

---

[60] Ibid.
[61] Kilbride-Jones (1990: 20).
[62] Originally the Institute was a separate organization within the general University of London group, but it was always very closely associated with UCL in structure,
staffing, and geography. It became a formal department of the College in 1986.
[63] See e.g. Crawford (1955: 183).

Studying archaeology in Britain in the 1920s was a chancy business. Few degrees carried an archaeological component, and students interested in gaining technical experience had to do what C. F. C. Hawkes and J. N. L. Myres did—find someone to provide them with an introduction to an excavator who needed assistance. Any ensuing practical activity would have to be carried out during vacations and on the student's own (unpaid) time. There was no question of receiving formal credit in the academic world for whatever was done outside it. Archaeology still looked suspiciously like hard work to traditional classicists—many of whom were also 'Heralds'. There were a few dedicated departments of study, as at Cambridge and Edinburgh; but there was no well-organized institution devoted to producing a regularly increased number of practically trained field archaeologists, who could take practical manual skills as well as intellectual abilities back out into the world.

Making a living out of archaeology was even more difficult, with few paid posts available and those that did exist focusing on museum curation rather than field excavation. Wheeler's exploitation of his museum vacations was typical of the way he and contemporaries like O. G. S. Crawford and Cyril Fox found a way to parley their official commitments into fieldwork. There were other ways into archaeology for interested parties who were not of the university class, but these were even more rare. William Wedlake, who will appear soon at Maiden Castle, was an isolated example of that process.

It was obvious that such a state could not continue. Archaeology was swiftly becoming a teachable, scientific skill, not just a way to obtain attractive museum displays or book illustrations. It required an environment in which it could be taught like any other academic subject.

It has been previously established that an Institute of Archaeology, centred in London, was a long-term preoccupation of Wheeler's, far outweighing the London Museum in his hindsight of 1955. O. G. S. Crawford records as much at the time as well, as in his diary for 10 October 1927, when he writes that he and Wheeler lunched together 'to discuss the School of British Archaeology'.

the whole of the work of creating what eventually became the Institute of Archaeology [. . .] was carried out by Tess and Mortimer Wheeler, who founded it [. . .] The chief problem, as always, was money; this was eventually solved by Tess, who found most of it from a voluntary

Figure 6. St John's Lodge today.

source; the University of London gave the scheme its blessing, but at first little more than that. After seven years of struggle the Institute was founded in 1934, and Wheeler became its Honorary Director.[64]

The struggle was largely Verney Wheeler's. She was the partner who engaged in the endless fundraising needed to support the Institute, and the one who eventually found it a physical home at the government-owned St John's Lodge in Regent's Park (Fig. 6).[65]

The building was in poor repair. It had been a hospital in the First World War and essentially abandoned since, but was lovely in its bones, potentially cheap, and most important, large. Flinders Petrie had come bounding on board the Institute scheme in 1932 with the immense and unwieldy gift of his extensive personal archaeological collection. He also brought the £10,000 donation he had been given to maintain it, but the money, while helpful, was not nearly enough.[66]

[64] Ibid.
[65] St John's Lodge is now a private home, though its beautiful grounds are open to the public.
[66] Hawkes (1982: 129–31).

Of greater value was the Petrie name and collection. This was mainly of Palestinian origin, one reason the Institute's focus shifted at the start to include Near Eastern (rather than exclusively British) archaeology. The assembly would fit very neatly into the Lodge's ballroom, and the Wheeler machine swung into action surrounded by packing cases full of Near Eastern pottery.

> My wife has stirred up Crown Lands, with the result that the lease of St. John's Lodge is, I am told, being 'speeded up', a very relative term![67]

Ultimately, Verney Wheeler's efforts with Crown Lands meant that the Institute was charged only a nominal rent for the Lodge, though it had to pay for renovations to the decaying building. She was aided by the First Commissioner of Works, William Ormsby-Gore, later the fourth Baron Harlech. He had a considerable amateur interest in archaeology and could understand her devotion to its study.[68]

The plaque that dedicated the Institute to Verney Wheeler's memory at its official opening in 1937 was entirely just, for both the building it was placed in and the money that enabled its foundation were a result of her work.[69] Wheeler took on the engagement of teaching staff personally, but Verney Wheeler did the greater part of all the other work, as he was the first to admit.[70]

The continuing story of the Institute of Archaeology after its physical opening is one of intense interest, but it is rather outside the remit of this work chronologically.[71] What is more interesting in terms of Verney Wheeler's life is the pivotal role she played in its founding, both in working towards the physical establishment of the Institute and in teaching with the body of students that began to form around both Wheelers at the London Museum. The Museum was essentially the proto-Institute, a centre for teaching and also for hands-on work. There Wheeler was the academic, 'winter' teacher. In the summer, students migrated to the great excavations at St Albans

---

[67] R. E. M. Wheeler to Sir George Hill, July 1935. As quoted in Hawkes (1982: 132).

[68] Ibid. 131.

[69] This plaque was transferred to the Institute's new purpose-built home at Gordon Square when it moved there in 1958, and remained on display for some time. I was unable to find it there in April 2008, but hope that the upcoming anniversary of 2012 (see note below) will encourage its reappearance.

[70] Wheeler (1955: 89–90).

[71] As the Institute approaches its 75th anniversary, that is changing; time and attention will be devoted to both Wheelers in the celebrations of 2012.

and Maiden Castle, and found Verney Wheeler waiting as the practical, 'summer' teacher.

As usual, this division suited their personal preferences and strengths well.[72] Verney Wheeler was not interested in parts of the 'work' that made her uncomfortable, particularly those that brought too much public attention. At the outset of her career, it was impossible to avoid some of this exposure, but as she grew into her professional personality she became more and more confident in getting her husband or assistants to take on tasks—such as presswork, discussed in a moment—that she had no interest in. An interesting point of comparison is the professional career of Dorothy Garrod, the first Disney Professor of Archaeology at Cambridge and a contemporary of the Wheelers. While a fine teacher in more informal settings, Garrod found departmental lecturing a great strain. Dealing with an all-male bureaucracy and engaging in the petty politicking of academia was also very difficult for the pleasant, shy woman, and her teaching declined as a result. Verney Wheeler had the advantage of her marriage: she was able to teach excavating, which she loved and where her strength lay, and when possible leave major political manoeuvring (an example of the type she did engage in is the personal appeal to the Commissioner of Works, above) to her husband (who enjoyed all kinds of fighting very much). The downside to this lies in Verney Wheeler's subsequent lack of recognition by later archaeologists, while Garrod is (quite rightly) celebrated as a visible pioneer.

Let us close this chapter by considering three of Verney Wheeler's students, all of whom worked under her in the field. Pride of place will be given to a young woman who travelled an impressive distance to train with the Wheelers in London.

> Although nominally attached to University College [in 1934–5] and given the keys to their Yates Classical Library, we really had no base; this was before the foundation of the Institute of Archaeology and there was nowhere for the archaeology students to be. Wheeler taught at the London Museum, then housed in Lancaster House, but there was no library and nowhere to sit and work except in the Board Room which

---

[72] Smith (2004: 213–41). I am indebted to P. J. Smith for permitting me to read her unpublished 2004 D.Phil thesis, 'A Splendid Idiosyncrasy: Prehistory at Cambridge, 1915–1950', which deals in part with Garrod's academic career and is of considerable interest in all respects.

was not always available. Books were the real problem. It was to overcome this that we were encouraged to join the Royal Archaeological
Institute, membership of which gave us reading, but not borrowing,
facilities within the Society of Antiquaries [. . .]Wheeler taught the
main outline of British prehistory and the Aims and Methods of
Archaeology as well. In our spare time, if we had any, we were supposed
to get up to the top of the London Museum and help Delia Parker and
Ione Geddye with mending the Maiden Castle material [. . .]Working
with the Wheelers one was at the centre of the British archaeological
world, and by attending meetings at the Society of Antiquaries I gradually met all the leading figures in British archaeology.[73]

This peripatetic young archaeologist is M. V. Seton-Williams, then
studying at University College London for a Prehistory Postgraduate
Diploma. This precursor of a dedicated archaeological graduate degree was a joint Wheeler brainchild; he had convinced the college to
establish it after it granted him an archaeological lectureship in 1928.
Rik Wheeler believed strongly that archaeology should only be taught
as a postgraduate subject, and that archaeologists were better served
by related but more wide-reaching first degrees (like history or
classics).[74]

A shy Australian girl who hated 'parties, pretty clothes and people
[. . . and] preferred old clothes, animals and solitude', Seton-Williams
had wanted to study Egyptology since her childhood. There was no
related degree in Australia at the time. Instead, she studied History
and Political Science at the University of Melbourne. Another Australian she knew, Nancy de Crespigny, had been working for the
Wheelers in England, and promised Seton-Williams a personal introduction to the couple. The result is a testimonial to the Wheelers'
growing reputation, for by the summer of 1934, Seton-Williams was
in London and enrolled for the next term at UCL.

As an archaeology student, she found her life revolved around
the Wheelers, the London Museum, and the Society of Antiquaries. Her memoirs of Maiden Castle, where she became a site
supervisor, are of special value; but at the moment she is of
more interest as an example of the type of student the Wheelers
were beginning to attract and influence. Seton-Williams is quite
clear that it was *the Wheelers*, not just R. E. M. Wheeler. Their

---

[73] Seton-Williams (1988: 23–5).
[74] Hawkes is right when she attributes this to an 'essential humanism' (1982: 128).

influence over her was so great that, although she had come to
Britain to study Egyptology, she switched to prehistory essentially
because the Wheelers told her too. The reader should be aware that
when Seton-Williams refers to the Wheelers, it may be taken that
she means both; she always makes a distinction in writing between
Mrs Wheeler, Wheeler or Sir Mortimer Wheeler, and *the* Wheelers.

> They told me that I could never hope to get a job in Egyptology as a
> woman and promised that they would see that I got something if
> I changed horses.[75]

It was one of the few instances where either Wheeler mis-stepped in
judging a student; Seton-Williams always stayed true to her first love,
and made her archaeological name eventually in Egypt and the Middle
East. The Wheelers might have initially told her she would never get a
job in Egyptology, but it was Verney Wheeler who used her position as
current Chairman of the British School of Archaeology in Egypt to get
Seton-Williams sent to the Petries in Sinai in 1935.[76]

Seton-Williams became particularly close to Verney Wheeler;
when she dedicated her autobiography to the three teachers who
had most influenced her, we find Verney Wheeler next to Margaret
Murray and Jessie Webb. It is not hard to see why: many young
people found comfort as well as an education in Verney Wheeler at
this time. Most of her actual teaching went on in summer and the
field, and her great contribution to establishing the Institute lay in her
endless practical work and fundraising, rather than in lecturing. But
she was a warm presence in students' winter lives nonetheless.

> Somehow I passed my examinations [in 1935, for the diploma]. During
> this time Mrs Wheeler was immensely kind to me. Many nights I had
> dinner with the Wheelers at the large Lyons in Piccadilly where
> I regularly ate a chicken omelette costing about 1s 3d. Mrs Wheeler
> wanted me to move into their flat in Park Lane but I wished to preserve
> my independence.[77]

The maternal feelings Verney Wheeler held for her students occasionally made their lives difficult as well as easier: when Seton-
Williams decided to visit Russia in 1935, she went there almost

---

[75] Seton-Williams (1988: 23).
[76] Ibid. 34. Margaret Murray also threw her weight behind the younger woman.
[77] Ibid. 30.

secretly 'without telling the Wheelers or my mother as I was sure they would not approve'.[78]

Other young people also found a helping hand in Verney Wheeler; her instinct for unobtrusive help found its flowering in them. It could be a tip for a cheap dinner location, a recommendation for fieldwork, or something more prestigious: Gerald Dunning, who was the first recipient of the London Museum's prestigious Esher Studentship for his research into medieval pottery, owed the valuable award partially to her support. When she found he was living on almost nothing in order to save up for his marriage, he became 'the special object of Tessa's benevolence'.[79]

Another woman who found her feet with the Wheelers was Kathleen Kenyon, probably the best-known Wheeler student today. She was born in 1906, and her father was Sir Frederic Kenyon, variously director of the British Museum, president of the British Academy, chairman of the British School of Archaeology in Jerusalem, and of course president of the Society of Antiquaries during part of Verney Wheeler's time at that institution. It is no surprise that his daughter manifested her abilities early, becoming the first female President of the Oxford University Archaeological Society while an undergraduate in medieval studies at Somerville College. In 1929, she took part in her first professional excavation, working under Gertrude Caton Thompson in Zimbabwe; and so when she went to work for the Wheelers in 1930 at Verulamium, she was 24 and already experienced enough to be trusted with a special excavation and publication of her own (the Roman theatre there).

Kenyon's main work took place mainly in the Middle East, where she became a great proponent of a modified version of the Wheeler stratigraphic grid system (sometime referred to as the Wheeler–Kenyon system). She and Rik Wheeler worked closely together throughout their professional lives—most especially via the Institute of Archaeology and the Palestine Exploration Fund. In later years, after Verney Wheeler's death, they grew apart, a rift increased by Kenyon's support for the Palestinian Arabs during the Six Day War. Her work in that area had left her with many official and unofficial ties that worried or offended her British friends. Wheeler, at his most Brigadier-ish, thought that she was too partisan and would be unable to work with Israeli archaeologists. He consequently tried

[78] Ibid. 28.
[79] Hawkes (1982: 114).

unsuccessfully to block her prestigious appointment as Chair of the Council for the British School of Archaeology in Jerusalem. Kenyon found out about the attempt and reacted angrily, though the two were reconciled to a degree eventually.[80]

In this period, Verney Wheeler's first students also began to show the fruits of their early promise. In 1930, J. N. L. Myres published his first book: a report on the excavation he, S. G. Stevens, and C. F. C. Hawkes had completed in 1928 at St Catherine's Hill in Hampshire, near their old school Winchester.[81] It was the first major piece of independent work for either; Myres carefully kept an envelope of letters and review clippings relating to this volume his entire life, throughout the publication of his many more important works. He sent one of his few complimentary copies to Verney Wheeler (*not* her husband), and she acknowledged it in an unusually emotional letter that reveals how touched she was by the gesture.

> My dearest Child,
>   St. Catharine's Hill. I treasure it more than I can say. It is very dear of you to send it to me when it could have been sent doubtless to better purpose elsewhere.
>   It is a *first-class* piece of work. And it breaks new ground both in its results and its comprehensive finish.
>   I am *very* proud for you all.
>   Tess.
>   P.S. I have written to Collingwood. Have you ever known me to italicize my feelings before?[82]

This letter is entirely typical of Verney Wheeler's unique approach to her students. There is maternal pride in its salutation and first paragraph, and professional appreciation in its second; personal kindness in its tone; and practical thoughtfulness in her postscript. R. G. Collingwood was a brilliant and unpredictable Oxford professor of philosophy and ancient history, and in 1936 he and Myres would collaborate on the first volume of the new Oxford History of England: *Roman Britain and the English Settlements*. Verney Wheeler's

---

[80] See Dever (2004) for a longer account of this interesting woman, or Miriam C. Davis's new biography, *Dame Kathleen Kenyon: Digging Up the Holy Land* (2008). It is certainly time Kenyon was considered on a larger scale.

[81] Webster (1991: ch. 7). For the publication, see *Proceedings of the Hampshire Field Club and Archaeological Society* 11, 1930.

[82] J. N. L. Myres papers, Bodleian Library.

postscript hints at her role as catalyst for one of the most monumental works of British historical scholarship in the twentieth century—or rather, two of the most monumental works, considering that Myres rewrote his portion completely in 1986 as *The English Settlements*.

Wheeler may dismiss the London Museum years in his autobiography, but in all outside assessments of him and his wife it must figure largely. It was certainly the precursor of the Institute of Archaeology that they dreamed of and worked so hard for during the 1920s and early 1930s: an experimental classroom for both the students learning archaeology and the archaeologists learning how to teach it. When the Institute finally came into full being, it had already proved its worth in several years of graduates like Seton-Williams.

7

Lydney Park, Gloucestershire (1928–1929)

During this period, the Wheelers continued to engage in major excavations during the summers. In retrospect, Wheeler saw this activity as their priority, although it is as usual difficult for the modern observer to disentangle the working trinity of museum, archaeology, and teaching. As early as 1927, the Wheelers were sizing up their first potential 'English' excavation, and the first of many summer letters appear in the London Museum archives from secretaries apologizing for the Keeper's absence digging; as in a typical letter (probably that of the Assistant Keeper) to M. Laing on 22 September 1933.

> I gather that Dr Wheeler's movements are at the moment extremely uncertain, he comes here only when the weather makes work at St Albans impossible.[1]

By the time Caerleon was handed over to V. E. Nash-Williams in 1928, Wheeler and Verney Wheeler were already exploiting their growing links to the Society of Antiquaries to gain the excavation rights of another intriguing Romano-British site: the temple of Nodens at Lydney Park, Gloucestershire. Of all their excavations, it was the most atypical in some ways, lacking the public interaction and student presence that had already come to characterize their work. In terms of excavation technique, though, it represents another leap forward. That, along with the unique features of the site itself, more than recommends it. It is thus particularly regrettable that Lydney Park, of all the joint Wheeler sites, is the only one without a surviving site archive.

---

[1] General Correspondence and Papers 1933, MOLA.

Figure 7. The Wheelers' reconstruction of the Romano-British temple complex at Lydney Park.

This late Romano-British temple complex and iron mine in the Forest of Dean competes with the Brecon Gaer for the title of most naturally beautiful Wheeler site (Fig. 7). It stands on a small hill at the end of a long rise above the Severn, on land belonging to the Bledisloe baronetcy. The family, under their original name of Bathurst, has owned the site since 1723.[2] Behind their house rises a sharp promontory, known locally for many years as Dwarf's Hill and crowned by the stubby remains of the Roman buildings and iron-workings called Dwarf's Chapel. The ruins were a popular spot for the graceful neoclassical coin grubbing that foreshadowed the more rigorous antiquarian movement and, eventually, archaeology.

One of these proto-archaeologists was the first Charles Bathurst, who excavated the site to an unusually high standard in 1805 and wrote two long discussions of the buildings he called the Villa and the Temple. Those essays are now lost, but his descendant William

[2] The present manor house is Victorian.

Bathurst posthumously published a brief summary of both reports and a catalogue of the best finds in 1879.[3] The only part of the original 1805 work to survive completely intact is, appropriately enough, a descriptive catalogue of selected coins compiled by Charles's daughter Charlotte. This admirable woman even included the circumference of coins, a prescient action that earned her the gratitude of later editors.

> This 'Tribute of Gratitude' [the coin catalogue] has proved upon examination to exhibit such accurate knowledge of Numismatics, coupled with such intelligence in the selection of the pieces deemed worthy of selection, that it is here printed without further alteration from the copy than that instead of the outlined dimensions of the coins, the customary abbreviations for metals and sizes have been substituted.[4]

Charles Bathurst's manuscript was not quite as fortunate under the hands of either William Bathurst or his successor as its editor, the Cambridge antiquarian C. W. King. Most of what a modern archaeologist would call synthesis was eliminated, in favour of a focus on the most attractive small finds, mosaics, and inscriptions. It is a beautifully illustrated volume and a very useful one, though not without its critics over time.[5] The book is especially indispensable since a number of the striking mosaics it records are now lost, most regrettably a large mosaic inscription identifying the donor of the pavement.[6]

By the 1920s, the Roman ruins were once more overgrown and neglected. Charles Bathurst's great-grandson, the first Lord Bledisloe, invited the Society of Antiquaries to return to the work, and as early as 19 May 1927 the Research Committee of the Society convened to

[3] Bathurst (1879).
[4] C. W. King in Bathurst (1879: vi).
[5] An unaddressed, undated note pasted into the back of the edition owned by the Sackler Library at Oxford reads in its entirety as follows. 'I have looked through the case of 'finds' at Lydney, and find that King's book is incorrect in many things. Note especially that Plate XXVI which is described as Samian in text, is bronzen. Some very important objects are not even referred to in text.' The note is signed 'J. Ward', and stamped 'Ashmolean Museum'. This copy was originally owned by Francis Haverfield, before being acquired by the Ashmolean and eventually absorbed by the Sackler. J. Ward must be John Ward, author of *The Roman Era in Britain* (1920) and other volumes on the subject, and coincidentally Rik Wheeler's predecessor as Keeper of Archaeology at the National Museum of Wales. I have been unable to see the original Bathurst manuscript, and so cannot say whether Ward's criticisms should be laid at the authors' or the editor's door.
[6] Wheeler and Verney Wheeler (1932a: 102–3).

discuss the site's funding. As usual, the full amount was patched together from a variety of resources, including the Society's Research Fund. The Fund, in a testament to the site's importance, contributed £100 out of its £253 balance. The Director, now Sir Charles Peers, said that he was sure Lord Bledisloe could be convinced to donate a similar sum. Then the matter stalled for a year, until 20 April 1928.

> [C]ircumstances [...] had caused the postponement of this year's excavation, but [he] stated that he [Charles Peers] had little doubt that Lord Bledisloe would now be prepared to allow the work to proceed. Resolved: That a decision [...] be deferred until another meeting of the Committee [...] and that in the meantime Dr Wheeler be asked to estimate the cost of an excavation and the time it might be expected to take.[7]

Another reason to postpone the work was the need to wait until Verney Wheeler was free of the Caerleon amphitheatre and able to come to Gloucestershire. Evidence from the Society of Antiquaries' archives emphasizes the delicacy of the negotiations involved, and the early point at which the Wheelers became identified with the site. The Society was not only investing an appreciable amount financially at Lydney Park, but also providing what was rapidly becoming one of its best excavating team.

Elsewhere in their careers, the Wheelers dealt mainly with municipal land owned by more corporate entities such as St Albans, and with people who were either of their own social standing or their workmen. Occasionally the two became conflated, as in the case of William Wedlake. He began as the Wheelers' Maiden Castle foreman, very definitely of the 'diggers', but over the course of the dig transitioned in his own mind and that of others to a 'scholar'. In Gloucestershire the Wheelers had to tread a little more carefully than usual; by the subtle distinctions of the day, or even the stranger divisions of today, Lord Bledisloe was their social superior. He had two things they did not—money and land—and two things they did— connections, and an interest (if in his case an amateur one) in antiquities.

A potentially interesting subject in his own right, this first Lord Bledisloe served as Governor-General of New Zealand from 1930 to 1935, bringing home a respectable collection of Maori artefacts and

[7] Society of Antiquaries Research Committees minutes, 19 May 1927 and 20 April 1928. SALA.

an interest in subtropical plants. His subsequent azalea and rhodo-
dendron plantings alone make a spring visit to Lydney worthwhile.
He is remembered today in New Zealand for his unusual champion-
ship of and respect for the Maori tribes and their leaders, and his gift
to the nation as a whole of the land on which the important Waitangi
Treaty was signed between the British and native peoples. Less high-
minded and quite as well loved was his presentation of the silver
Bledisloe Cup, a rugby trophy still annually contested by New Zeal-
and and Australia. He was exactly the combination of imperial
sportsman and amateur antiquarian with whom the Wheelers could
find a wide number of points in common. More importantly, he was a
cultured man in the best sense of the word, and once he agreed to let
the Wheelers dig, he stood back and let them do so without attempting to direct matters from the sidelines.[8] Wheeler in turn acknowledged this wholehearted support by proposing Bledisloe's successful
election to the Society of Antiquaries in 1929.

EXCAVATING NEXT DOOR TO THE MANOR

Lydney differed from all the other Wheeler digs in that it was a
private affair. The site archives, kept by Lord Bledisloe and now
vanished into the corners of an old-fashioned country house, are in
their absence a potent symbol of that.

The excavation was conducted in good weather conditions during
the summers of 1928 and 1929. As Jacquetta Hawkes notes, the
physical labour cannot have been too tiring, as no major earth-
moving or deep sectioning was necessary. Another FSA, Lieutenant-
Colonel William Hawley, 'was with us throughout', though very
unobtrusively, and took special responsibility for an earthworks
excavation.[9] His role on the dig is an interesting one, mirrored by
other, secondary figures at Verulamium and Maiden Castle: it was,
essentially, to be depended on by both Wheelers in the way Wheeler
himself had depended on Verney Wheeler in Wales. With her growing importance as a supervisor, auxiliary 'wives' of both genders

---

[8] Guide to Lydney Park, undated.
[9] William Hawley to R. E. M. Wheeler, 18 June 1929. General Correspondence and
Papers 1929, MOLA. Hawley is best known for his work in the first half of the 1920s at
Stonehenge, also published via the society.

began to be necessary assistants on digs. Soon they would be found in bright students like Kathleen Kenyon, but at Lydney the Wheelers still had to look among their peers.

A group of FSA scholars, rapidly becoming the Wheelers' usual suspects, also contributed expertise and occasionally portions of the report. They included Dermot Casey, T. Davies Pryce, and R. G. Collingwood. A young Oxford professor was recruited to write a recondite paper on the philology of the name 'Nodens' and its possible Celtic roots; it was one of J. R. R. Tolkien's first important publications, and unknowingly ensured that a mint copy of the Lydney report can today be worth over £500 at auction. J. W. E. Pearce and Harold Mattingly acted as Verney Wheeler's references when she made up the coin catalogue. Flinders Petrie even reappeared on page 43 of the report, making a suggestion about a disputed temple structure 'during one of his visits to the site' (presumably with Hilda in tow).[10]

Most of the physical heavy lifting during the excavation was done by the same type of historically nameless Welsh navvies Verney Wheeler had overseen at Caerleon. Given the proximity of the two sites, she may even have re-hired some of the same workmen. The Wheelers were almost within sight of Nash-Williams and his work in Monmouthshire, though the new Keeper of Archaeology does not seem to have visited Lydney. Nash-Williams and Verney Wheeler occasionally mention the Gloucestershire site in their correspondence for 1928–30, and once he regrets that he cannot come to her there.[11] Another Caerleon connection, J. R. Gabriel, visited around 31 October 1929 to update them on gossip about the Cardiff Board of Celtic Studies.[12]

Information regarding the actual process of work at Lydney (as opposed to its result) is in general much more unclear than at any other Wheeler dig. Lord Bledisloe was enthusiastic about the Wheelers' excavation, but not the Wheelers' practice of excavation publicity. Hawkes observes acutely that it was easy enough financially to avoid the newspapers for once, as the additional funding they supplied was here replaced by Lord Bledisloe.[13] As a result there was (for the

---

[10] Wheeler and Verney Wheeler (1932a: 43).
[11] Caerleon site archive for 1928, NMWA.
[12] T. Verney Wheeler to V. E. Nash-Williams, 31 October 1929. Caerleon site archive, NMWA.
[13] Hawkes (1982: 149).

Wheelers) minimal newspaper coverage, depriving the researcher of one of the great sources of contemporary information. The site archives have also vanished—a real pity, as it would be interesting to see how much of the final draft report was due to Wheeler, and how much to Verney Wheeler. Some of the most 'Wheeler-esque' passages in the Caerleon final report were actually due to Verney Wheeler. The Lydney report would be even more interesting to break down, representing as it does one of the first British archaeological reports organized systematically on modern lines.[14] It would also be rewarding to examine the site notebooks, and determine how much, or if, they have changed from those at Caerleon.

While this process would be satisfying, it is not necessary to engage in it in order to prove Verney Wheeler contributed to the site; that is sufficiently indicated by her name on the report's cover. There are also two intriguing letters preserved by the Museum of London. The first is from William Hawley, who sent his report on the earthworks to Rik Wheeler at the London Museum in June 1929.

> I was so sorry to hear in your wife's letter a short time ago that you were not well at that time.[15]

This at least establishes Verney Wheeler's regular contact with the 'secondary' excavator. A little later in the year, Glen Taylor writes to Wheeler on another subject and mentions Lydney together with Verney Wheeler. Here, Taylor implies Verney Wheeler's greater presence at the site, and her growing role within their intellectual community.

> I see in the Mail that Dr Wheeler says the 'Digging' season has started. Does that mean that Tessa is at Lydney and you are digging in bachelor quarters? In a letter I wrote to Tess a few days back I asked her if she could give me any information about some drain pipes found on the site of an old road marked in a plan of 1600 [. . . *repeats details of query to Wheeler*].[16]

During this period, copies of letters sent and received by the Wheelers while excavating were usually kept in the local site archives rather

[14] Ibid. 147.
[15] William Hawley to R. E. M. Wheeler, 18 June 1929. General Correspondence and Papers 1929, MOLA.
[16] Glen Taylor to R. E. M. Wheeler, 24 July 1929. General Correspondence and Papers 1929, MOLA.

than the London Museum. In the case of Lydney, an appreciable number of letters are found in London, all in Wheeler's name, relating to Verulamium and Maiden Castle. The absence or purging of any surviving Verney Wheeler letters in the Museum of London archives may be linked with the scarcity of letters concerning Lydney or the work there. The missing material, as well as the references quoted here, indicates that Verney Wheeler must have been receiving and sending correspondence concerning the site. The site archives at St Albans and Dorchester help gauge the depth of her involvement at Verulamium and Maiden Castle, but the vanished Lydney site archive prevents this easy corrective in Gloucestershire. The surviving letters she wrote to V. E. Nash-Williams mentioning the site have already been referenced, as have third-party references in the Museum of London archives.

Some odd site ephemera does survive at Lydney, including many of the empty envelopes originally used to store coins now on display. There is also a large photograph album of the excavation in progress, put together by Lord Bledisloe from negatives taken by Wheeler (Fig. 8).

Figure 8. Verney Wheeler sweeping a pavement at Lydney Park.

Many of the album's photos feature in the final report, including Plate XI.B, a shot of the swallow-hole that collapsed the Romano-British temple. Verney Wheeler stands in the pit, in profile next to the range rod. She is not mentioned in the caption and it is not entirely clear why her figure is necessary—after all, the range rod's purpose is scale. The photographer, if it was Lord Bledisloe, may have been attracted by the novelty of that now ubiquitous symbol of excavation, the range rod; but this seems a little far-fetched, especially in a book designed for a professional audience who would all know what it was.

The Lydney album has another, full-face version of the same shot, a more personal one, in which Verney Wheeler holds a trowel loosely in her right hand (Fig. 9). She meets the camera with a quizzical smile, and her general expression seems to support the identification of her husband as the photographer. Something in her face suggests a gentle, dryly humorous, and above all complete knowledge of what she is looking at, without giving away too much about what she thinks about it all. Even in this candid snapshot, Tessa's face is secretive. As always, there is a point beyond which she will not allow the viewer. Or (more prosaically) perhaps she was tired, and not in a mood to have her picture taken.

Figure 9. Verney Wheeler in the swallow-hole of the Lydney temple.

The excavation was completed by the end of 1929, and publicized by the *Times* in a tasteful Bledisloe-approved article. The official report did not appear until 1932, and was the first of several Wheeler excavations to appear via the Society of Antiquaries monograph series. In the introduction the authors defend the decision to re-excavate in terms that are also a defence of their new methods of archaeology. The very way in which those methods and aims could now be clearly verbalized illustrates the extent of the Wheelers' leap forward from their work in Wales, where they could express their new ideas in actions but not always in print. The insistence on an objects-based chronology linked to historical events, on dating specific levels, and especially on rigorous recording at every level, is here given its proper prominence. This report is feeling its way towards a textbook, and towards a method that could be taught as a system.

> In view of the relative thoroughness of the earlier excavations, the decision to re-excavate may seem a bold one. That [. . .] the new excavations have succeeded in elucidating the main history of the temple and its environs almost as completely as if the site had not previously been cleared, illustrate the difference between the technical methods of 1805 and those of 1928. In 1805 the diggers worked down to a floor and then stopped. To the modern excavator, the primary value of a floor is that it seals the evidence beneath it, and the careful recovery of this sealed evidence by the partial removal of the floor is an inevitable feature of his methods. That methods is therefore necessarily destructive to a degree never envisaged by the older archaeologists and the responsibility of the modern excavator to observe and record the evidence which, in recovering, he demolishes for all time, is proportionately great. No excavator a century hence will be able to approach the major part of the Lydney site with the optimism wherewith Lord Bledisloe and his colleagues approached it in 1928.[17]

Before Verulamium, before Maiden Castle, before *Archaeology from the Earth*, we find the basic technical premise of the Wheeler Method realized fully here both physically and verbally. If they had never excavated again, this report and this paragraph would allow us to tentatively reconstruct that method as completely as a palaeontologist reconstructs a dinosaur from its thighbone.[18]

---

[17] Wheeler and Verney Wheeler (1932a: 2-3).

[18] Hawkes also discusses the Lydney report as a prototype; see Hawkes (1982: 147).

The report traces the beginning of settlement at Lydney to the first century BC; the original Roman remit was found to be too narrow for the site's occupation history. According to the Wheelers' report, a small pre-Roman embanked fort was replaced by a second- or third-century Romano-British settlement around the temple of Nodens. Both were probably due to the presence of easily accessed iron on the hill, whose streams are still rust-red. Wheeler was particularly taken with an intact third-century Roman mine, which they found complete with the marks of mining picks on its walls. The remaining mosaic floors were Verney Wheeler's special province; her special responsibilities for this type of find would increase at Verulamium. Christopher Hawkes made particular mention of her work in his review of the final publication.[19]

> Mrs Wheeler's skill and patience have given us a brilliant classification and an exhaustive but always readable description, fully and strikingly illustrated.

The report's delicate colour frontispiece of the floor of room XXXV in the baths is Verney Wheeler's work; she made similar paintings of mosaics at their next dig as well (Fig. 10).

Besides Noden's temple and its associated activities and structures, the site's most exciting aspect was the serendipitous find by Wheeler of a hoard of 1,646 tiny *minimi* coins from a fifth-century period that might be charitably described as *very* late Roman. The entire collection filled half of a hurriedly requisitioned teacup, and the account of their finding in *Still Digging* exhibits the author's curious mix of scientific rigour and literary romanticism. He finds the coins quite by accident in idly driving a pick into a cement patch, and drops to his knees beside them in delighted surprise. So far, so Robert Louis Stevenson. But Wheeler's next action is to lay a half-crown down for scale, have the coins photographed in situ, get a measured section drawn relating them to the mosaic, and only then carefully lift the little discs.[20]

Hawkes has a slightly drier view of the adventure.

---

[19] Hawkes (1932: 489).

[20] Wheeler (1955: 97–8). Some newspapers headed the coins find 'King Arthur's Small Change'—shades of the Caerleon amphitheatre.

Figure 10. Verney Wheeler's delicate scale watercolour of the mosaic found in room XXXV of the bath buildings.

> It was characteristic that, Rik having found the hoard in this extra-ordinary way, Tessa, with Michael's help, laboured over the classification and wrote the account of the coins in the Report.[21]

Verney Wheeler was always fond of coins; a few years later, she told an interviewer from the *Western Mail* that she preferred bronze coins to gold finds, because of the firm dating they could allow.[22] Her Lydney coins catalogue was mainly her own work, aided by J. W. Pearce, who assessed the first, smaller hoard found, and D. A. Casey, who

---

[21] Hawkes (1982: 149).
[22] *Western Mail*, February 1935.

contributed a brief discussion of the method of the minimi hoard's manufacture. It is an excellent example of its type, and in her long discussion of the dating of the *minimi* hoard (the second coin collection found) Verney Wheeler exhibits a confidence best shown by her firm use of the pronoun 'I'. She discusses the hoard on both archaeological and stylistic grounds. It is another rare example of her crisp personal writing when left unfiltered.

> In other words, from a stylistic no less than from an archaeological standpoint, the character of the Lydney hoard is just such as we should expect to find in the sub-Roman environment which, on general historical grounds, may be supposed, if anywhere, to have subsisted in the fifth century in the lands bordering upon the Severn. Here, to the westward of the earlier Saxon invasions and to the eastward of the main area of Irish raid and settlement, Gildas tells of sub-Roman kingdoms in the fifth and sixth centuries. Here on general grounds, as Haverfield long ago pointed out, we should expect to find lingering traces of sub-Roman life [...] To that century, perhaps to the earlier part of it, I venture provisionally to ascribe the Lydney hoard.[23]

Before the publication, the Society of Antiquaries enjoyed a series of progress reports in the form of papers presented. At the second of these, on 14 November 1929, Verney Wheeler made the first of many appearances before the Fellows. Wheeler had already read a paper on the Caerleon Amphitheatre for her on 26 January 1928, and this was undoubtedly timed to coincide with her election later in the year.[24] It would not have been lost on the Society that she was already (so to speak) working for them.

RE-EXAMINING LYDNEY: A (VERNEY) WHEELER MISTAKE?

Lydney Park was another Wheeler success; the introduction to the report was correct in its boast that future archaeologists would find little more to do at the site. A re-examination of the available evidence by P. J. Casey and Birgitta Hoffmann was conducted between 1980

---

[23] Wheeler and Verney Wheeler (1932a: 129).

[24] *Antiquaries Journal* 8.2 (April 1928).

and 1981, and published by the Society of Antiquaries in 1999. It was similar in nature and results to the re-examination of Segontium.[25] As usual, the Wheelers' assemblage of material is of a quality so high it allows succeeding generations to reinterpret a site without further physical action; a definite advantage in this case, as only the most minimal trenching was possible in 1980. Casey and Hoffman's object was thus to consider:

> incompatibilities between the chronology established by Wheeler from coin evidence and the subsequent cumulative evidence for the pattern of coin use and supply in the broader horizon of Roman Britain in the fourth century.[26]

Casey and Hoffman do not acknowledge Tessa Verney Wheeler's work at Lydney at any point. References within the text to the 1932 report are credited to Wheeler alone, though the bibliography correctly attributes it to both authors. One (joint) Wheeler mistake does stand out in the Casey–Hoffman re-evaluation, and interestingly it came via the minimal trenching permitted to the later excavators. If they are correct, it represents a rare technical goof on the earlier team's part.

> the present excavation found that the 1805 excavation [of the Bath House] had been tidied up when the site was opened to visitors by capping the backfilling of individual rooms with freshly dug clay. This now gives every appearance of forming part of an untouched ancient surface. It is not unlikely that coins thought to have been found in sealed contexts, or adhering to mortared surfaces, were the product of earlier backfilling. It is notable that of all the coins found in the Wheeler excavation only one is acknowledged in the annotations on the storage envelopes to have been seen in context by the excavator himself, suggesting this was in itself a noteworthy event.[27]

Whether the excavator in question was a himself or herself is unknown. But in the interests of fairness, this potential mistake must be noted. Verney Wheeler took responsibility for numismatic evidence from this site, and if Casey and Hoffman are correct, blame must ultimately rest with her for not recognizing the older dig's backfill.

---

[25] Casey and Hoffman (1999).
[26] Ibid. 82.
[27] Ibid. 112.

This is more likely than her misidentifying coin contexts after they were removed from the earth. It is deeply unlikely that she would have seen only one coin in its original context at Lydney, given her hands-on approach in her other digs. Probably the coin described above as seen by the excavator was singled out for identification in this way for some more petty reason.

Casey and Hoffmann use their discussion of the numismatic evidence and the *minimi* hoard to argue for an earlier abandonment of the site, the late fourth century rather than well into the fifth century as the Wheelers proposed. Both cases are based on the dating of the *minimi* hoard from the baths. Casey and Hoffmann also tie their theory to larger numismatic and economic theories being propounded on Roman Britain. Their conclusions are convincing, but it is interesting to see that (as at Segontium) they are able to criticize the dating but not the synthesis or (with the exception of the passage quoted above) the technical excavation of the site.

What the Wheelers set their hands to as a couple prospered. That was because they were very good at their jobs, but also because both Wheeler and Verney Wheeler always made sure they could meet a challenge before they undertook it. Self-supporting intellectuals of their type work without a financial safety net (even more in the 1920s and 1930s than today) and cannot afford failure on an economic or professional level. For the Wheelers, potential failure was not only personally disastrous, but might also endanger the future of the interesting new archaeology that they were inventing almost as features emerged on sites to challenge them. To do less than their best, to not meet their own intellectual expectations, would be to fail on such an impressive number of levels that failure itself simply ceased to be an option.

8

Verulamium, Hertfordshire (1930–1933)

Suetonius, however, with wonderful resolution, marched amidst a hostile population to Londinium, which, though undistinguished by the name of a colony, was much frequented by a number of merchants and trading vessels. Uncertain whether he should choose it as a seat of war, as he looked round on his scanty force of soldiers, and remembered with what a serious warning the rashness of Petilius had been punished, he resolved to save the province at the cost of a single town. Nor did the tears and weeping of the people, as they implored his aid, deter him from giving the signal of departure and receiving into his army all who would go with him. Those who were chained to the spot by the weakness of their sex, or the infirmity of age, or the attractions of the place, were cut off by the enemy. Like ruin fell on the town of Verulamium, for the barbarians, who delighted in plunder and were indifferent to all else, passed by the fortresses with military garrisons, and attacked whatever offered most wealth to the spoiler, and was unsafe for defence. About seventy thousand citizens and allies, it appeared, fell in the places which I have mentioned. For it was not on making prisoners and selling them, or on any of the barter of war, that the enemy was bent, but on slaughter, on the gibbet, the fire and the cross, like men soon about to pay the penalty, and meanwhile snatching at instant vengeance.*

Considering the quality of the Lydney work and report, the way that both Rik Wheeler and Jacquetta Hawkes pass over it seems a little unfair. But it is understandable when considered beside the next

---

* Tacitus, *Annales* 14.3. Translated by William Jackson Brodribb and Alfred John Church,. This popular 1876 edition was in common school use through the pre-war period, and is probably the English translation Tessa and Rik were first exposed to. It was reprinted by Random House in 1942, and is freely available online via Tufts University's Perseus Project (http://www.perseus.tufts.edu) in an edition edited by Sara Bryant.

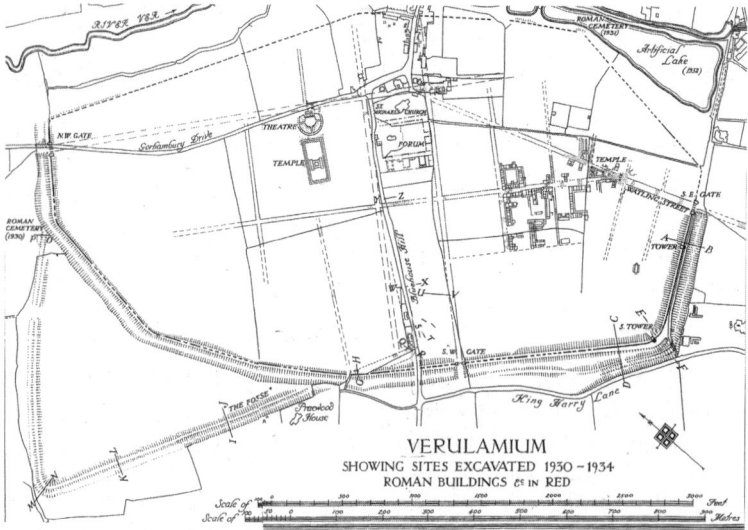

Figure 11. Plan of the Verulamium excavations, from the Wheelers' final publication of the work there.

Wheeler project: the excavation of Verulamium, one of the most important towns of Roman Britain, at the modern St Albans (Fig. 11). In terms of sheer physical size, Verulamium marked a departure for the Wheelers. In its ambitious remit, extensive publicity, and above all use as a teaching aid, it remains, with Maiden Castle, one of the most characteristic 'Wheeler sites'. For Wheeler, the excavation of Verulamium represented an overall realization of archaeological technique so ideal that he used it years later as one of his chief examples of 'tactics and strategy' in his textbook *Archaeology From The Earth*.[1]

In later years, Wheeler liked to see his pre-Second World War work in Britain as following a larger, prescribed pattern with a purpose beyond understanding the individual sites he worked at. He saw himself as deliberately selecting British excavations in a specific order that more effectively determined the history of Roman Britain and British civilization.

In a sense, our work at Lydney was an interruption in the ordered programme of fieldwork which I had mapped out. Already in 1926–27 a study of Roman London for the Royal Commission on Historical

---

[1] Wheeler (1954: 114–10).

Monuments had demonstrated simultaneously the interest and ignor-
ance of those Roman towns which mark the beginnings of civilization in
Britain [. . . these towns could provide] the recovery of social and
economic data on a formative scale. Of all places in Great Britain, the
obvious testing-ground for these larger issues was Verulamium.[2]

Whether or not Wheeler's ideas about how to study Roman Britain
archaeologically were quite as well worked out in 1930 as they were in
1952, Verulamium was the Wheelers' most important Roman site.
Their report alone has cast a shadow over the study of Romano-
British towns that has yet to entirely fade.[3] In the Council for British
Archaeology's 1993 volume *Roman Towns: The Wheeler Inheritance*,
Verney Wheeler is referenced extensively and the volume is dedicated
to her. Her central role in the museum's creation is remembered and
appreciated today, and the first thing a visitor to the museum still sees
is the plaque celebrating her contribution. It was also the last excavation that Verney Wheeler saw through finishing and publication (or
at least final proofs) before her death in 1936, and the last report on
whose title page her name appears.

The preceding chapter has shown how the technical basis of the
Wheeler Method was first definitively established at Lydney Park.
After that excavation, Verney Wheeler's working techniques continued to evolve, but were always based on that sturdy Gloucestershire
foundation. Wheeler's attitude towards his methods was often more
static (or more stubborn) than his wife's, and she developed more
flexibly than he did. The combination of his super-confident historical pronouncements and his super-masculine personality often made
it difficult for him to back down gracefully when wrong.

If Lydney Park represents a technical breakthrough, Verulamium
represents a social and educational tidemark. It was the first excavation at which the Wheelers fully engaged in that deliberate use of
students and the media that separated them from their contemporaries almost as much as their emphasis on strict stratigraphic recording. Lydney Park was a private excavation in the old-fashioned sense:
Lord Bledisloe insisted on only the most moderate and controlled
press coverage, and that via a conservative newspaper when the work
was done. The smaller size and obscure location of the site must also

---

[2] Wheeler 1955: 98–9.
[3] The volume is the result of a conference held in 1989 to mark the 50th anniversary of the Verulamium Museum (Greep 1993).

have predisposed the Wheelers towards mainly using paid labour as they had in Wales. At Verulamium, Wheeler and Verney Wheeler were freed from the constraints of a private owner, with the additional advantage of easy proximity by rail to their growing pool of pupils at the London Museum. The value of the new system of training was evident in 1934, when the Wheelers moved on to Maiden Castle and left their brilliant student Kathleen Kenyon behind them in Verulamium to excavate the pretty Roman theatre near the playing fields. The small excavation was concluded to everyone's satisfaction, and Kenyon's considerable professional benefit.[4]

As was becoming usual as their sites expanded in size and chronological remit, the Wheelers had a secondary co-director. This time, their old ally T. Davies Pryce stepped in from the Society of Antiquaries. A specialist in *terra sigillata*, he did not share their hands-on approach in actual excavation—but his expertise became invaluable once the time came to analyse the pottery finds. In their next excavation, the role of the co-director would expand yet more with Charles Drew.[5]

Maiden Castle is rightly the British site most closely associated with the Wheeler Method today. It was the first location at which the Wheelers expertly applied *all* of their new ideas *at once*. At Lydney, technical fundamentals were established. At Verulamium, these fundamentals were confidently applied as the Wheelers felt their way more uncertainly through the new problems and rewards presented by the combination of the press and their own protégés. By their next excavation in Dorset in 1934, they were able to set up camp and get straight to work with confidence in both the social and technical arms of their new methodology.

What set the Wheeler Method apart technically from other, more haphazard contemporary approaches to archaeology was its strict attention to gridded stratigraphy and detail, careful recording of objects, historically based analysis of an excavation, and financially conscientious insistence on an informed but openly selective

---

[4] See Kenyon (1934). The Wheelers' friend A. G. Lowther, who produced the reports plans, aided her. He also produced a guidebook aimed at a general audience entitled *The Roman Theatre at Verulamium: A Reconstruction*, a Kiplingesque series of drawings and vignettes from the various periods of the theatre's use (Lowther 1935).

[5] Although he is listed as a co-director, T. Davies Pryce was a pottery specialist rather than excavator and thus not a hands-on partner to the Wheelers in the way that Charles Drew was at Maiden Castle. Our interest in him is therefore minimal. Later criticisms of the pottery section of the final report can perhaps be laid at his door.

excavation of large sites. The Wheelers taught their students to look for a dramatic larger picture in the carefully documented details of their work. In a more universally applicable sense, the Wheeler Method was also about involving students and the public in the *process* of archaeology, not just its synthesized results. The fact that both Wheelers were so insistent on teaching is, counter-intuitively, sometimes more important than what they taught. They changed archaeology from a skill picked up on the basis of a hobby to one taught and tested in a formal setting. Along the way they also made it into a focus of public interest. And though they developed ideas and made decisions together, more often than not Verney Wheeler was the Wheeler actually turning theory into reality—conducting interviews with her reporters, lecturing her visitors, teaching her students, and meticulously recording her finds. The objects context sheets she drew freehand in her site notebooks became the model for a generation of students, and still appear familiar to modern archaeologists. This was Verney Wheeler's work, not Wheeler's; she was the 'details person' on sites, and such innovations belong first to her.

THE SITE'S HISTORY

Verulamium or St Albans is one of the longer-known settlements in England; Londinium, by contrast, is specifically stated by Tacitus *not* to be a ranking Roman settlement, despite its economic importance. Verulamium's first written reference is more prestigious—in book 14 of Tacitus' first-century *Annales*.[6] In his account of the Boudicean revolt of 61 AD, he describes the unfortified and unguarded *municipium* of Verulamium suffering the same wholesale slaughter and plunder at the hands of the Iceni as the commercial centre of Londinium. The dramatic literary passage perhaps excessively influenced the Wheelers' interpretation of their work at the site. The use of the word *municipium* to describe Verulamium is telling; it means a Romanized settlement with an imperial charter and connected set of rights for its inhabitants, the Belgic Catuvellauni tribe.[7]

---

[6] Tacitus, *Annales*, ch. 14.133.
[7] While the term 'Belgic' is not now preferred by historians and archaeologists, as it was used by the Wheelers throughout their report. I will adhere to it here for the sake of consistency. See Niblett and Thompson (2005: 24).

Archaeological finds over the years support this view of Verulamium. Scattered enclosed settlement in this fordable area around the
river Ver have been shown to predate the Romans, but by the early
first century AD a large enclosure on the river valley's floor lies on the
same site of the later Roman forum and basilica. A large number of
clay moulds found just outside this enclosure were at first thought to
have been the source of several interesting coin types minted by
Tasciovanus and Cunobelin, leaders of the Belgic Catuvellauni tribe,
and bear variations on the location name Vir or Verlamio. These
moulds are now thought to be intended for the production of stan-
dardized market weights, like the minting of coins a sign of high
status; associated argument makes the location a tribal site of either
royal or ritual significance.[8]

Around 10 BC the Roman-style Vir coins of the chieftain Tasciovanus begin to appear, and by 10 AD they give way to those of his
successor, Cunobelin. During the campaigns of the 40s Verulamium
may have been the site of a Roman fort; a fairly extensive quantity of
Roman military equipment has been found in and around the town,
pointing at least to a strong military presence. The idea of a formal
Roman fort there is now disputed; and Rosalyn Niblett's view is that
without the references to events there by Roman writers, archaeologists might not see the invasion at all in the physical record.[9]

By the period of the Claudian invasion, there was an *oppidum* or
enclosed settlement, another sign of the site's importance in the pre-
Roman landscape. Increasing Roman influence on the settlement is
apparent, even before the conquest, in coin design and luxury im-
ported goods. On the whole, Verulamium seems to have emerged
comparatively well from the Roman invasion.[10] Niblett goes to the
heart of the matter when she points out that even if Tacitus is
referring by *municipium* to a status granted by the time he is writing
rather than at the time he is writing about, early appearances of
Romanized buildings and luxury goods, as well as the attentions of
the Iceni, tell us that Verulamium was an early 'convert' to the new
lifestyle.[11] Its continued importance within the province is borne out
by extensive building, commercial activity, and the enclosure of the

---

[8] Niblett (2001: ch. 2).
[9] Ibid. 60.
[10] Ibid. ch. 3.
[11] Ibid. 66–7.

Roman town in the third century. The area walled in was larger than any other in Britain, barring Londinium and Corinium (Cirencester).[12] At this point the Roman town begins to decline, though again at what rate and to what degree is heavily disputed.[13] The town began to migrate uphill and north, towards the new shrine of the local martyr, Saint Alban. His abbey was eventually built there out of reused Roman brick. The ford was bridged, the town renamed more ecclesiastically, and its abandoned Roman section slowly declined back into green fields and scattered houses. But its classical past and prestige were never forgotten, and antiquarians like William Stukeley and John Leland continued to record remaining features and chance finds throughout the eighteenth century.

ENTER THE SOCIETY OF ANTIQUARIES (AND THE WHEELERS)

So matters rested until the 1930s, when growing expansion meant the Roman town was once more encroached upon. Almost half of the site of the old town was bought by the Corporation of St Albans in 1929, with the intention of laying it out as a park and playing fields for the rapidly increasing working-class population of the neighbourhood. The incumbent of the local parish of St Stephen's, the Reverend Harold Omer Cavalier, provides one of the best descriptions of the state of St Albans when the Wheelers were at work there.

> This is a new city, dropped from the clouds on my green fields, and I am the chief agitator for roads, lamp-posts, post-offices, schools, relief, and entertainments. I see a new meaning in *Tantae molis erat*. Your work has done wonders in opening the minds of the people here. My kindest remembrances to Mrs Wheeler.[14]

Cavalier swiftly became close to both Wheelers after the work began, and wrote one of the letters of condolence Rik treasured most after Tessa's death. He was a man of antiquarian leanings and erudite

[12] Niblett and Thompson (2005: 1).
[13] See Niblett (2001: ch. 5) for a full discussion of the many opinions on this topic.
[14] Harold Cavalier to R. E. M. Wheeler, 26 November 1932. Personal correspondence and papers, 1932, MOLA.

charm, who evolved a delightfully convoluted theory connecting the scallop shell apse mosaic and the Book of Revelation.[15]

As Rik Wheeler said much later, the Corporation 'had the enlightened thought' that it would be a good idea to have some 'tentative' archaeological work done before anything else. It was a very enlightened thought for that period, but as previously noted St Albans had a long knowledge of and interest in its Roman connections.[16] In the past, of course, this had mainly taken the form of admiring the quality of Roman brick and stone enough to comprehensively quarry the classical town for the medieval one.[17]

The local St Albans and Hertfordshire Archaeological Society was well connected in London via members it shared with Burlington House. Plots had been laid before the land was even available. Once it was, the Society of Antiquaries quickly sent its secretary, A. W. Clapham, to lunch with the Mayor. He was seconded in his mission by Dermot Casey and Rik Wheeler.

On their return, Clapham appeared before the Research Council to give an account of the visit.

> The Secretary reported that Dr. Wheeler and he had [. . .] examined the site. It was important that the remains of the town-wall should be cleared and preserved, and that such areas as the Corporation proposed to develop immediately for Park purposes should be excavated.[18]

While nothing appears prior to this in the Society of Antiquaries records connecting either Wheeler to St Albans, it is unlikely that it was either his first visit to the site or the first time he and Verney Wheeler had considered involving themselves with it. Wheeler maintained later that their work there was part of a larger, clearly envisioned campaign that he had had in mind long before they arrived in the town. Whether or not this is strictly true, they were swift to identify themselves with the excavation as early as possible, arguing some degree of premeditation on their part about the site. That early

---

[15] Harold Cavalier to R. E.M. Wheeler, 22 September 1930. Personal correspondence and papers, 1930, MOLA. Cavalier had the same quality of happy wit in correspondence as Rik and Tessa. It is a pity that space will not allow full reproduction of his letters here.

[16] Wheeler and Verney Wheeler 1936: 35–7.

[17] See e.g. the local monastic historian Matthew Paris, writing in the thirteenth century about the town's development.

[18] Society of Antiquaries Research Council minutes for 15 January, 1930, SALA.

identification was made possible, like Lydney, by their places within the Society of Antiquaries, and Burlington House continued to be the umbrella organization under which they excavated and from which they derived their status with the town authorities. The reverse was also true: the yearly Anniversary Address for 1931 mentions the work of both Wheelers at Verulamium as proof of the Society's success in its new support of archaeological excavations. As had become usual practice in the Lydney excavations, they presented yearly progress reports as part of the Society's usual Thursday series of lectures by Fellows.[19]

ARCHAEOLOGY FROM ST ALBANS?

As might be expected, Verulamium presented a new set of challenges to its excavators at the outset of work. The size of the future playing fields was a new test, and in addition the Wheelers were determined to understand not just the Roman town but also the ancient landscape in which it lay. Verulamium's connections with the Catuvellauni and identification with Tacitus' *oppidum* were long established. Both Wheelers had academic backgrounds in history and classics, which goes some way towards explaining their shared focus on tying the physical record into the written one. It was also a way to legitimize archaeology in the eyes of older members of the academic or intellectual establishment.

From the first pages of the report, they made it clear they were openly searching for a Tacitean *oppidum* and its potential relationship to the larger, more diffuse pre-Roman landscape.

> Throughout the task the excavators kept one objective in view—the recovery of the historical framework of Belgic and Roman Verulamium. This objective [...] led them across six miles of countryside, and only a careful selectiveness rendered a reasonably comprehensive achievement possible within the limits of four long seasons [...] Thus the present report is designed to be less a detailed illustration of the now familiar culture of a Romano-British city, than an attempted reconstruction of the social and economic evolution of a major civic unit during the four and a half critical centuries in which Britain passed from Belgic prehistory into Roman history and thence again into the darkness of Saxon 'protohistory'.[20]

---

[19] In 1931 and 1932 Wheeler read the papers; in 1933 and 1934 they presented them together. For details, see *Antiquaries Journal* 11–14.
[20] Wheeler and Verney Wheeler (1936: 4–5). Compare this to the quotation from *Still Digging* at this chapter's opening.

Apart from any larger historical aims, the Wheelers intended from the outset to use Verulamium as a training ground. It was close enough to London to draw the University of London students that were already clustering around the couple at the London Museum's proto-Institute of Archaeology. The large site was consequently quartered along the lines of the Roman town's *insulae,* and each *insula* given its own director from among the assisting students. *Insulae* were occasionally identified by their director's name, according to one press report, e.g. 'Miss Kenyon's house', but the site notebooks showing them to be officially organized properly via letter and number.

The students did not completely replace the navvies and workmen common to all contemporary archaeological sites; these appear again, with as little mention as before in the site records and reports. A contemporary news report describes them as out-of-work Welsh miners, suggesting that the Wheelers were still working within their familiar and trained pool.[21] There was mutual appreciation; at the close of works at Verulamium, Verney Wheeler gracefully accepted a dona-tion of two guineas and a letter of appreciation from the workmen.

In *Archaeology From The Earth*, Wheeler paid tribute to both groups in chapter 11, 'Staff'. He was in point of fact positively nostalgic on the subject of his old diggers.

> Today, in 1952, voluntary labour is Hobson's choice. The old-fashioned British labourer survives only in a few odd corners of the land [...] A note, therefore, which before the war might have run to some length may now be compressed into a few paragraphs, most of which are applicable to labour in general and are not confined merely to the (former) home product.[22]

Labour's face has changed over time. Jacquetta Hawkes notes that after the Second World War, students, volunteers, and the JCB replaced British navvies. The war's breakdown of the social system and the increased accessibility of higher education no doubt played a part in reducing the number of available ditch-diggers. Hawkes's and Wheeler's comments are, however, applicable mainly to Britain and the United States. In other countries (such as Italy and Spain), where a university education is not as automatically undertaken, the physi-cal labour that supports societies has often remained highly visible. It

---

[21] *Evening News*, 7 August 1931.
[22] Wheeler (1954: 148).

thus has yet to be romanticized or otherwise made permissible for the elite, and the old class barriers between diggers and supervisors sometimes remain.[23]

The pattern of work over the four years of the dig adhered closely to that of Wheeler the supervisor and Verney Wheeler the teacher. After the first year, the basic shape of the Roman town was established, and while the detailed exploration of the *insulae* continued under Verney Wheeler, Wheeler's role moved towards determining the placement of the town within a developing British landscape and narrative. Towards that end he broke completely free of the original playing field excavations and ranged across the ancient landscape on horseback or in his trademark grey Lancia, hunting for the original Belgic *oppidum*. It would be quite wrong to say he was never present, but Verney Wheeler always did the greater part of the physical organization and teaching on-site. This was apparent in their students' work as well as their own.

> Even from the outset, in the early 1930s, [Kathleen] Kenyon's close associates had observed that a good deal of meticulous recording and attention to section drawings—her trademark—was derived from [. . .] Tessa.[24]

This division is also reflected in the interim publications and reports. The first two interim reports were written and issued by Verney Wheeler alone via the *St Albans and Hertfordshire Architectural and Archaeological Society Transactions* of 1930 and 1931,[25] while the first two successful lecture-presentations of the Verulamium work at the Society of Antiquaries were made by Wheeler alone in 1931 and 1932.[26] The results are identical—the means of presentation, individual.

As at the London Museum, the Wheelers created a male–female leadership that their students and workers readily responded to. Wheeler was the active hunter, always on the move, a virile and occasionally

---

[23] Hawkes (1982: 156); Barry Cunliffe, pers. comm., November 2007.

[24] Dever (2004: 529). It is interesting that Kenyon references Wheeler but not Verney Wheeler in her 1961 textbook *Beginning in Archaeology*. The precision of the instructions contained in the book, and the emphasis on personal technique, are reminiscent of Verney Wheeler rather than her husband. Compare this to Wheeler's 1954 book *Archaeology from the Earth*.

[25] Verney Wheeler (1930; 1931). Wheeler did write a very brief introduction for the first piece.

[26] See the notes on his presentations in *Antiquaries Journal* 9 (1931) and 12 (1932).

dreaded presence even in his many absences. He shook things up,
upset people, corrected and praised them to an equally Jovian extent.
By contrast, Verney Wheeler almost always stayed 'at home' on the main
dig, teaching practical excavation techniques to students and organising
their housing and food. When Wheeler criticized flawed work, she
soothed the perpetrator and taught them how to do it right. They
cannot have been unconscious of the practical value of their dichotomy.
As at the London Museum, what we see here are two very clever people
deliberately working their (admittedly congenial) joint image as
mother and father to obtain the results they wanted out of others.[27]

The parental model was often carried to a positively Freudian
extreme by the Wheelers. Jacquetta Hawkes says that Rik had serious
love affairs with three of the eight young women who worked as
assistants at Verulamium over the years. When he moved on from
one of these girlfriends, it fell to Tessa to console them.[28] The dig *was*
a happy one by all accounts—but that does not mean it was not
sexually and psychologically fraught. Intelligent young women who
were drawn into the Wheelers' professional circle were taught how to
dig by Tessa, and presumably felt some of the affection for her which
was almost universal among her acquaintances. Did any of those
three young women feel guilt at any point, or did desire for Rik (or
his for them) trump maternal loyalty? These are very deep waters.

One consistent comment by those who knew the Wheelers is that
within the context of their digs, one was either for Rik or for Tessa.
Veronica Seton-Williams, of whom Tessa was so fond that she asked
the young expatriate to live with them in London, was definitely on
Tessa's 'side', perhaps partially because she was not personally inclined to respond to Rik emotionally. She never forgot Tessa, and her
relationship with Rik after 1936 was always coloured negatively by
memories of his treatment of his wife.

Verney Wheeler also played the conventionally feminine part of
gracious hostess to the many journalists who flocked anew to a more
public Wheeler excavation. She was the primary contact for the press
at St Albans, frequently interviewed by press services like the Associated Press that fed dozens of national newspapers. The result was
that one article featuring her might figure absolutely verbatim in
several different outlets. Occasionally, more personal pieces appear,

[27] Seton-Williams (1988: 30, 54–5).
[28] Hawkes (1982: 156).

Figure 12. Verney Wheeler in building III, room 4 of *insula* II at Verulamium, pointing at an infant buried in a small cist made from brick roofing tiles. She is demonstrating typical 1930s archaeological safety practices.

especially in the local *Hertfordshire Advertiser*. The Wheelers had a particularly close relationship with this paper during their years in St Albans, and the *Advertiser* reciprocated with effective marshalling of public support during the agitations for a Verulamium Museum.

The site was lightly wooded but otherwise not too physically difficult to uncover, barring some very deeply buried features in the old basilica site in the garden of St Michael's rectory. The excavation was organized to reflect the lines of the ancient *insulae*, with the better student assistants from London given a Roman house to excavate and explain. Verney Wheeler herself took charge of *insulae* I, II, and Site D (Watling Street) in 1930 alone, as an initial demonstration of good practice for students.[29] She is shown in building III, room 4 of *insula* II in one of her most charming and informal surviving portraits. Verney Wheeler hated to be photographed, but in this picture (Fig. 12) she stands smiling, cigarette in hand, and points excitedly at the infant cist burial she has just uncovered.

Verney Wheeler's 1930 site notebook shows some changes from the more private diaries of Wales. There are no more questions to herself, and the pages of the notebook are numbered and collated; for example, in the notebook dealing with *insulae* I and II, she adds a note to page 41 after its writing referring the reader forward to page 54.[30] One aspect that is reminiscent of Caerleon is its variety, which is a direct reflection of the variety of roles the writer took on. There is the now familiar mix of useful addresses, subscription lists, possible places for student accommodation, a copied extract from a 1848 essay on St Stephen's Churchyard (where she would be buried in six years), inserted sketches of Roman glass finds from 1813, and two homely recipes for 'shelac' (*sic*), probably for use on mosaic tiles.

This notebook is designed for easy use at a later date by others as well as herself, and as a teaching tool. Graph paper sections face some pages of text, a more technical version of her Welsh habit of facing illustrations with explanatory text (and vice versa). Most intriguingly, Verney Wheeler has sketched out the trench of two excavators identified only as Catlin and Dixon, apparently as she examined it. She is marking up their work.[31]

She must have found this teaching method fruitful, for it reappears, greatly expanded, in her next dig at Maiden Castle. It is yet another reminder that she, not Wheeler, took on the primary responsibility of practically teaching the students that were featuring more and more prominently at their excavations.

Margaret Drower, today one of the great ladies of Egyptology, also began her archaeological career with the Wheelers at Verulamium in the 1930s. Her friend Peggy Preston was a Wheeler student, and took her down to St Albans to share her tent and help clear pavements. Wheeler students were evangelical, and as Seton-Williams found it was not uncommon for them to co-opt or convert their friends. Drower

---

[29] Wheeler archive box A, notebooks 6 and 7, VMA; Wheeler archive box B, notebook 9, VMA.
[30] Wheeler archive box A, notebook 6, VMA.
[31] Wheeler archive box A, notebook 6, VMA.

spent two brief and hectic weeks being marked up by Verney Wheeler and photographed by the press. Her memories of the site revolve completely around Verney Wheeler—working with students, helping them develop technique, and in the case of the young Margaret Drower, astonishing them by her facility at identifying features and small finds before they were fully visible. Years later, Drower vividly remembers Verney Wheeler identifying late period wattle-and-daub at a glance.[32] It is interesting that Drower's memories of Wheeler are much more distant. Even now she is firm that at Verulamium, he was an overseer, not a teacher or an excavator.[33] Certainly Wheeler never identified himself with the specifics of the dig as Verney Wheeler did; there is no site notebook in his hand. He ranged (literally) over the big picture, while Verney Wheeler filled in the fine details.[34] Like everything in the Wheelers' life together, the Verulamium excavation is an instance of the instinctive and outstanding professional partnership the two shared. The relationship was always equal, and the roles were rarely identical. That was perhaps its greatest strength.

THE VERULAMIUM MUSEUM

The [Verulamium] Museum may be regarded as a memorial to that great scholar, archaeologist and beloved teacher, who planned it but never lived to see its completion.[35]

'The material we have recovered', she [Verney Wheeler] said, 'forms a complete unit in itself, and in my view should be kept on view as representative of the great site from which is comes. I look forward to a time when it will be possible to come to St. Albans to see not only the site of Verulamium but also the evidence of a civilization which has been recovered through the excavations.'[36]

---

[32] Interview with Margaret Drower, 19 January 2007.

[33] Compare this to Cecil Davies' similar memories of Caerleon in Ch. 3 above.

[34] See the discussion of *Archaeology from the Earth* for a consideration of how this dependence on Verney Wheeler as a site director influenced Rik's ideas about the roles of the various members of an excavation team, and how a dig should be generally conducted. His 1954 view of his own role as Director is perfectly in accord with his behaviour at Verulamium.

[35] Corder (1938: 123–4).

[36] *Daily Telegraph*, 25 September 1933.

The natural local outgrowth of the extensive work was a small, popular on-site museum, filled and organised as the dig proceeded. Both Wheelers were laudably generous in sharing themselves and their considerable combined experience in building a collection. In the short account of the Museum's opening by its first curator at the head of this chapter, the models of reconstructed buildings are credited to the University of London Institute of Archaeology—as usual, the Wheelers cross-refer-enced facilities and resources across various projects.

Their efforts focused first on the establishment of a permanent building, with its own curator. Wheeler and Verney Wheeler at-tended town meetings together to push for a purpose-built museum associated with a long-term plan for the site and finds. A few letters from Wheeler to various interested parties survive at the Verulamium Museum, and they make it clear that he was the secondary contact for the project. When he wrote to the Reverend Mitchell, vicar of St Michael's Church, in February 1935, it was because Verney Wheeler could not find the other man at the town clerk's meeting a few days before, and wanted to discuss some aspects of the stalling of the museum and consequent deterioration of the still-exposed mosaic pavements.[37] This is not surprising, considering the extent of his other museum obligations; Wheeler chronically overextended himself on as many fronts as possible.

The *Hertfordshire Advertiser* was also pressed into action by both, in a successful attempt to rally public support.

> My wife tells me that you [H. E. Carrington, the editor of the *Hertford-shire Advertiser*] would like to have a little ammunition for a demonstra-tion in favour of the new Verulamium Museum which the St. Albans Corporation is about the establish. I offer you the attached notes [a three-page memorandum], in the hope that they may be of some slight use to you—if I can help you further, please ring me up. I hope very much that the whole scheme may now have your powerful backing.[38]

As usual, Verney Wheeler was the driving force locally. Indeed, after her death, the museum was urged upon the town council as a memorial for the woman who had been so popular. It finally came into being in 1939, when Mary, the Princess Royal, and her husband

---

[37] R. E. M. Wheeler to the Reverend Mitchell, 12 February, 1935. Wheeler mis-cellanea, VMA.

[38] R. E. M. Wheeler to H. E. Carrington, 12 November 1935. Wheeler miscellanea, document 13, VMA.

the Earl of Harewood were dispatched to formally open the agreeable brick building on 8 May. It remains a useful part of the modern museum. A long ceremony and commemorative programme centred on the unveiling of a plaque honouring Verney Wheeler, by that point dead for almost exactly three years. Her ashes were buried a short walk away, in a grave built of Roman bricks at Harold Cavalier's church, St Stephen's. The memorial is still proudly retained by the entrance to the galleries, it is pleasant to note that when the plaque was unveiled once again on the museum's re-opening after expansion, its subject's granddaughters and great-granddaughter (also named Tessa) were present as the guests of honour.[39] The inscription remains an appropriate marker of the woman who remains in many ways the *genius loci* of the museum.

> In grateful and affectionate remembrance of Tessa Verney Wheeler, whose energy and enthusiasm contributed so largely to the success of the Verulamium excavations, this tablet is placed here by her friends in St. Albans. MCMXXXVIII.

'THE WHEELER INHERITANCE': VERULAMIUM IN THE LONG TERM

> The advances made by the Wheelers' work in understanding Roman Britain can hardly be over-emphasized. Prior to their arrival the account of the Roman town had hardly changed since [Joshua] Webster's [an eighteenth-century antiquarian's] time, yet seven years after the start of excavations in 1930, a detailed account of its history was published [...] for at least thirty years after the close of the Wheelers' campaign in 1934, the 'Wheeler model' coloured all interpretations of the town's past.[40]

While some of their conclusions regarding the town's development and decline are now disproved, the report remains one of the two

---

[39] Interview with Carol Wheeler Pettman, 10th January 2007.

[40] Niblett and Thompson (2005: 49). Rik returned to St Albans in 1949, to work briefly but profitably in the west corner of the Forum with Molly Cotton and several other old Wheeler hands. The excavation is of interest here as it was the first English excavation at which Wheeler introduced a new teaching innovation: regular, systematic lectures and technical instruction, as well as on-the-job excavation training. This natural evolution of previous Wheeler training digs had begun to unfold during his post-war work in India. Hawkes (1982: 267).

major sources of information on the site.[41] The other is Sheppard Frere's great series of excavations and their associated reports, which from 1956 on reworked the Wheelers' synthesis of the town's overall history.[42] The subject of greatest interest here is how the Wheelers excavated, so the debate surrounding their synthesis of Verulamium's history will be only lightly touched upon. The flaw in the crystal was that which dogged all Wheeler reports, whether joint or not: the desire to make archaeological evidence fit into their preconceptions about a site. Those preconceptions inevitably came from written historical sources, in this case the section of Tacitus discussed at this chapter's head. The Roman historian's vivid account of slaughter and mayhem coloured the Wheelers' interpretation of Verulamium from the start. It was a natural result of the historically based and historically biased academic background both Wheeler and Verney Wheeler came from.[43] Wheeler's early press publicity for the site also made much of its connection to Boadicea, harking back to his romantic Arthurian descriptions of Caerleon's amphitheatre.

Even at the time of the Wheelers' 1936 publication, uncertainties were voiced about their dramatic synthesis, with its focus on violent invasions and sieges. The first challenger was their former student J. N. L. Myres, who reviewed the report for *Antiquity* soon after its publication.[44] Myres criticized the selective excavation, and the guess-work the excavators employed to fill in gaps in the excavating and the archaeological record; he was suspicious of some of the dating and found the pottery illustrations inadequate, particularly galling considering their co-director was Davies Pryce. Myres wrote in his review that he felt he must point out these essential weaknesses, as the rest of the book was so impressive that its grave flaws might easily be overlooked. His criticisms were fair, and justified years later by Sheppard Frere's work on the site. Hawkes suggests that this unfavourable review was also subconsciously influenced by Myres' grief at Verney Wheeler's recent death, and his belief that Wheeler was partly responsible for her ill health. Perhaps Wheeler's intemperate response to criticism also had its foundation in her passing; this was their last major published work.[45]

---

41 Greep (1993: 1).
42 Frere (1972; 1983; 1984).
43 See the *Times* of 15 March 1930.
44 Myres (1938).
45 Hawkes (1982: 159–61).

The review also contained a great deal of praise for the book, subsequently overlooked in the fracas. Unfortunately, the article precipitated the type of storm in a teacup that magazines like *Antiquity* often produce. Wheeler wrote a nasty, and even mean, letter of response to the journal, and its editor (and founder), O. G. S. Crawford, published it without first showing a copy to Myres.[46] Comparing Myres obliquely to Bertie Wooster and sniping at his current employers, Christ Church, Oxford, was the least of the matter. Wheeler had an acid tongue, and he did not censor himself. The younger man took offence at both the letter and the editorial omission. He swore he would never again write for the journal while it was under Crawford's management, and he kept his word.[47]

Myres and Wheeler eventually repaired their relationship without too much trouble, and in *Still Digging* Wheeler humorously acknowledged the truth of his junior's criticisms. He attributed its failings to a growing personal disgust with the 'advertised *humanitas* of Roman civilization, which lay always so near to brutality and corruption'.[48]

A dig's life continues after the dirt goes back in. The synthesis of a site is always open to reinterpretation, and that reinterpretation is inevitable. Improved techniques improve technical understanding, and in addition what a culture needs from its history socially and politically changes.[49] It is best to accept this, do the best synthesis possible with the available evidence, and leave that evidence in a state that allows it to be re-examined and used again. This was and is not a new idea; Pitt-Rivers first articulated it in the Victorian period. Who can predict what future historians and archaeologists will value in their research? After all, when the first excavations at Lydney took place, there was no effort made to examine the earth features the Wheelers found so intriguing, and which they employed so usefully to reconstruct the site's buildings.

The depth to which it is still possible to examine the Wheelers' sites today is proof, if any were needed, of their accomplishment. Their specific, detailed work—the work we should mainly attribute to Verney Wheeler—remains applicable today.

---

[46] Ibid. 160.
[47] Ibid. 161.
[48] Wheeler (1955: 102).
[49] For a further consideration of these interesting concepts, see MacGillivray (2000), especially his Introduction.

9

Public Archaeology, Publicly Performed: Mosaics and Reporters

VERNEY WHEELER AND MOSAICS

Verulamium showcases the mosaics that were fast becoming Verney Wheeler's personal speciality, and to some extent her professional trademark (Fig. 13). Her facility in lifting tesserae is often returned to by those who knew her, and when Wheeler wanted to explain the preservation of mosaics many years later in a chapter of *Archaeology from the Earth* entitled 'Watch-Makers' Jobs', he simply included an article Verney Wheeler had written for the *Museums Journal* in 1933. Eighteen years after her death, her hand is still on his shoulder throughout the work.[1]

With their demand for precision and their detail, the overall excavation and preservation of these beautiful floors forms a useful metaphor for Verney Wheeler's approach to archaeology and indeed life. Her watercolour of the mosaic at Lydney establishes her early interest in the medium. It is fairly certain that she taught herself the skills she displayed at that site, perhaps basing her technique on her observation of Italian experts. Italian had been one of her subjects at UCL, and while no details survive of her travels abroad, casual references from various sources indicate at least two trips to the Mediterranean. Or she may have watched expatriate Italian artisans based in London do the work. Jacquetta Hawkes says that Verney Wheeler carefully watched the first set of mosaics being lifted at Verulamium in 1932, and was thereafter able to do the work herself.[2]

---

[1] Wheeler (1954: 111–13).
[2] Hawkes (1982: 157).

Figure 13. Verney Wheeler's watercolour of one of the most famous Verulamium mosaics.

Carol Wheeler Pettman, by contrast, relays a family tradition that Verney Wheeler learned the skill on a family holiday in Italy.[3] It is likely that both stories are true; it is unlikely that even a gifted conservator could learn the methodology during a single period of observation. Workers in Italy would probably be more willing to pass their knowledge on to an English student, whereas those based in London might see her as a potential competitor.

At Verulamium, as the population active on digs expanded, she had her choice of assistants for the first time—most especially, Dr Norman Davey, a young engineer and amateur archaeologist who eventually became an expert on the restoration of Roman wall paintings.

The presence of these assistants prompted Verney Wheeler to formally record her expertise in her 1933 article;[4] which, incidentally,

---

[3] Interview with Carol Wheeler Pettman, 10 January 2007.
[4] Verney Wheeler (1933).

gives her professional affiliation as 'The London Museum'. She writes
that she based her process at Verulamium on that of a London art
firm.

> The method here described was [. . .] experimental. It was based upon
> those used by Messrs. Arts Pavements, of Camden Town, who have
> most successfully removed three large pavements at Verulamium. In no
> case was I present at every stage of their work, and it is possible and
> indeed probable that my process is both under- and over-elaborate.[5]

Her twenty-five-step list is neither of those things, but extremely
detailed, specifying everything down to the preparation of various
glue types. It is a labour-intensive, precise process, requiring the
heavy-duty digging, draining, and drying of the pavement, followed
by a long series of more delicate tasks. Essentially, the excavator
lacquers the surface of the mosaic with thin glue, allows this to set,
applies a second layer of thick glue, and attaches a piece of canvas
directly to the mosaic's face. Verney Wheeler adds in a homely
footnote that 'actually a flour-sack cut down the seam was used'.
      This is allowed to set. The mosaic is then cut away from its bed, and
the whole floor peeled up like a transfer. It is removed to a wooden
frame that is backed in wet modern cement. The mosaic is flipped
again within its frame, at which point the glue attaching the canvas is
melted with hot water and removed. The archaeologist may then
choose to restore any breaks in the tesserae with modern replace-
ments, as long as these

> declare themselves as modern and so prevent deception. If restoration is
> not desired, the breaks should be brought to a smooth surface at the
> general level of the mortar bedding.

She warns that, depending on local conditions, the process may take
anywhere between three days and a week to complete, and describes it
as a 'recipe' based on her successful raising of a medium-sized, badly
fractured mosaic fragment at Verulamium in 1932. The sample floor
is probably either the small, well-preserved chequered floor from
building IV (room 10) or the *pelta* fragment from building IV
(room 8), both of which she dated to *c.* 300 AD.[6] The chequered

---

[5] Ibid. 107.
[6] Wheeler and Verney Wheeler (1936: plates XLVI.b, XLVIII.b).

floor seems more likely, as it is more complete and set in concrete.[7] We can therefore see that she took over the job early in the dig, probably immediately after the restoration of the three large pavements by Arts Pavements. The timing is a reminder that while Verney Wheeler's technique was refined and taught at Verulamium, her mosaic work at Lydney already displayed an expertise that her observation of the professional demonstration at Verulamium would have improved upon rather than replaced.

Maya Naunton, an objects conservator at the Metropolitan Museum of Art in New York City, kindly assessed Verney Wheeler's article from a modern perspective. Her opinion is that the method is primarily that employed today, barring the development of more subtle adhesives, and the modern policy of retaining architectural features such as mosaics in situ unless absolutely necessary.[8] Thomas Roby of the Getty Museum was also asked to contribute an opinion. In his account, a metal instrument replaces the fires as the tool for loosening the mosaic from its bed, but the adhesive-based removal method remains the same.

> I find [the article] very interesting, especially the use of fires to dry out the mosaic, certainly not a normal procedure today! Facings of mosaics are normally done with different layers of gauze and netting and adhesive, then mechanically removed underneath with a long metal instrument [. . .] to detach the bedding layers from the tesselatum.[9]

The second-century hypocaust mosaic of Building 8, *insula* IV, was excavated by Verney Wheeler in 1932.[10] She explored the terracotta plumbing system by crawling through its tunnels herself, before beginning the work of consolidation; she may have been the only person present small enough to fit *and* old enough to do so legally. The lovely geometric carpet was left in situ, and a purpose-built structure now protects it from the elements. There is a rare 'action shot' (Fig. 14) of Verney Wheeler sweeping the exposed mosaic still

---

[7] She mentions these under slightly different numbers in a memorandum on mosaic floors taken up between 1931 and 1933. Wheeler miscellanea, document 11, VMA.

[8] Maya Naunton, pers. comm., 14 May 2008.

[9] Thomas Roby, pers. comm., 13 June 2008.

[10] *Hertfordshire Advertiser*, 19 August, 1932.

Figure 14. Verney Wheeler sweeping the hypocaust mosaic after its exposure.

extant at the Verulamium Museum, which compares favourably to the delicate watercolour Norman Davey painted of it for the final report on the site and indeed the floor today (Fig. 15). The photograph of Verney Wheeler was probably taken by M. B. Cookson, a photographer who came in briefly from a London firm to do some piecework at Verulamium. His work was so impressive that the Wheelers requested him especially at Maiden Castle, and he embarked on a long and illustrious career as an archaeological photographer.[11]

While regular maintenance work has been carried out as appropriate, the quality of the floor's preservation is a continuing testament to Verney Wheeler's skill. Mosaics are notoriously difficult to consolidate and preserve in situ, and the quality of the initial conservation is vital to a floor's long-term survival.

The final paragraph of Verney Wheeler's article must be quoted in full.

[11] Hawkes (1982: 164–5).

Figure 15. The hypocaust mosaic today.

A word of warning, however, may be given about the appearance of the pavement before and after removal. *In situ*, the pavement is full of moisture and the colours of the tesserae, whether of stone or pottery, are brilliant. The drying process seems to reduce the colour to a dead level of greyness, and though, finally, the colours are found not to be affected by the heat, they are now over-dry and therefore much less vivid. A pavement removed has not the startling beauty of a pavement *in situ*. Experiments are being conducted, however, to discover the best method of bringing up the colours once more to their intended depth of tone.[12]

---

[12] Verney Wheeler (1933: 106).

When Verney Wheeler began lifting pavements in 1932, the *Evening Standard* was ready with a headline.

ONLY ONE PERSON IN ENGLAND CAN DO IT AND
THAT A WOMAN

Mrs Mortimer Wheeler, the famous woman archaeologist, is feeling very pleased indeed with herself just now, for she has done something that nobody else in England can do.

During the excavation of Verulamium . . . some magnificent mosaic pavements belonging to the spacious bathrooms of a Roman palace were found. They were richly coloured and in perfect preservation.

Mrs Wheeler, who has been superintending these excavations for her husband [. . .] wanted these pavements taken up and removed to the little museum on the site.

It was discovered that the only people who could do the job were a London firm of Italian mosaic specialists who for generations have lived and worked amongst mosaics [. . .] All the workmen are Italians and the craft of making and moving mosaics is in their blood, inherited from father to son [. . .] The work was difficult and costly. The expedition's purse is thin.

When the next floor was ready for removal, Mrs Wheeler decided to do it herself.

Experts were horrified. They even whispered 'Vandalism! It will be ruined.' [. . .]

And now she has taken up that floor successfully. It is just finished and not a bit is broken away. [Verney Wheeler explains the process she outlined in her *Museums Journal* article in more colloquial language.]

[. . .] It sounds so easy. But no one else has done it before except the Italians.[13]

There is much to consider in this article; the association of facility with nationality and the vague jingoism of an Englishwoman doing a job as well or better than an Italian; the celebration and surprise of her gender; and, from Verney Wheeler, the assumption that what she is doing is generally interesting, and ought to be explained to the working-class people reading the *Evening Standard* on their way home from work.

Wheeler was filmed during the same period for a Movietone news-reel, one of many, standing near the 'scallop shell' mosaic and comparing it favourably to the similarly bold use of primary colours by modern (1930s) artists. The newsreel is now on permanent display

---

[13] *Evening News*, 21st October 1932. The article's author is not personally identified.

at the Verulamium Museum; that institution is exemplary in its use of contemporary archival materials to explain the process, as well as the results, of archaeology. Together, this set of photographs, articles, and newsreel express their subjects' attitudes and reactions to archaeology as clearly as possible, and illustrate just one of the ways in which the Wheelers' widely differing personalities made them far more than the sum of their parts as an excavating team.

THE WHEELERS AND THE PRESS

Looking at the press coverage of the Verulamium mosaics provides a mental bridge to a subject central to understanding the Wheelers' innovations. While their technical work has always received the most attention in promulgations of the Wheeler Method, the couple developed two other concepts simultaneously that were just as groundbreaking. These two concepts are certainly as central to that Method, even featuring prominently in Wheeler's formal exposition *Archaeology from the Earth*. The first was their close work with and focus on students, already examined in detail. The second was their manipulation of the British press, considered now with examples taken from the extensive coverage of the Verulamium excavations.

It may seem odd to accord importance to the self-sought newspaper coverage of the Wheelers. Why need it be discussed at all? In a modern era of rampant self-promotion and a driving need to fill more and more programming hours, *not* documenting a process for the masses is the more unusual choice. And the Wheelers were not the first archaeologists to exploit the romance of archaeology for their own gain. Archaeology has always attracted larger-then-life characters; Auguste Marriette and Williams Flinders Petrie spring to mind among the generation prior to the Wheelers. It is no accident, either, that increased British press coverage of archaeology during the Victorian 'Petrie Period' coincided with a rise in literacy and education and the associated growth of cheap illustrated papers. Like today's television producers, newspaper editors in the fifty years prior to the Second World War were desperate for new material to fill pages—and it had to appeal to an increasingly diverse audience. Archaeology lends itself well to dramatic interpretations in both pictures and words, and coverage of new finds in Egypt, Italy, and even London received a gratifying response from a wide variety of readers. The use of press photographs and articles in this book has already helped to illustrate the Wheelers' life and work, and given them a contemporary context that is most important. This source is also an excellent record of the student society (in an anthropological sense) that grew up on each site around the pair. And there is an additional value in examining their presswork as a cohesive, developing policy that extends beyond the human interest it can lend to individual sites.

Of the Wheelers' contemporaries or near-contemporaries, perhaps Petrie was most alive to the funding potential of populism. He was an excellent speaker, and his popular lectures were sometimes used to make up the balance of funds for various digging schemes. Margaret Murray wrote tactfully that while Petrie was not 'cut out for the humdrum business of regular teaching', he was a spellbinding speaker who held his audience fascinated with accounts of his archaeological theories and work. His audiences occasionally responded to his lectures with standing ovations, a response as rare under the circumstances then as it is now.[14]

When it came to using the newspapers, the Wheelers were the spearhead of a growing movement, if one sniffed at by more reserved colleagues. Rik's rival in work and love, Alexander Keiller 'the Marmalade King', was a perpetually popular source for column inches. He would be in any period. Playboy heir to a Dundee-based fortune, the English-bred Keiller skied, had his private pilot licence before the RAF was founded, served in intelligence in the Great War, pioneered aerial photography, collected and raced cars, and was married four times. If that was not enough, he also openly had, as his biographer Lynda J. Murray puts it, 'more than a passing interest in witchcraft and criminology, and in exploring the range of sexual practices'.[15] Although the Museum of London archives preserves two January 1936 letters from Wheeler to Keiller that show a more humorous side to their relationship, generally speaking the two shared a liking for publicity, archaeology, and attractive women that ensured they competed viciously in all three areas.[16] People tended not to move from one man to another, whatever category their relationship with

---

[14] Murray (1963: 93).
[15] Murray (2004), http://www.oxforddnb.com/view/article/55071, accessed 16 March 2011.
[16] General Correspondence and Papers 1936, MOLA.

either fell into; William Wedlake was one exception, and he became an object of fierce contest.[17] As an archaeologist, Keiller resurrected the stone circles at Avebury, excavated across southern England, and made aerial photography into a useful tool for examining the tracks of history and prehistory across a broad landscape. Like Rik Wheeler, he enjoyed attention and courted that of the press, though for Keiller it was not a financial necessity.

That financial pressure, and a real moral sense, made the Wheelers carry media coverage to a much higher point than anyone else had to that point, working closely with newspapers and clearly recognizing the potential for public education and interest. While not the first media archaeologists, they were the first to fully, efficiently exploit the press. In the process, they both became public personalities. Tessa evolved into one with great reluctance, Rik with great enthusiasm, but both of their careers from Wales onwards were played out in part via the media. It is important to know how they used the press, and why they did—in other words, what they got out of the connection. That they got something also effectively explains *why* they maintained the connection—rarely have two people spent their lives less in superfluous, i.e. non-professional, acts. They literally did not have the time to waste on anything not of demonstrable use to their work.

To understand the relationship between the Wheelers and the press, it is necessary to go back to a very early point in Rik Wheeler's life—for the drive to publicize archaeology in this way is one of the few aspects of 'the Wheelers' that we can unambiguously attribute to him. While occasionally assisting his father as a teenager could hardly be called a newspaper apprenticeship, the fact is that Rik Wheeler literally came out of journalism. His early life was completely coloured by his father's profession; his first two years in London, immensely formative ones, centred fully on his father's *Yorkshire Observer* office. During that period, he discovered the city that became, with archaeology, one of the constant passions of his life, and the museums whose trusteeships and directorships he would later hold.[18] Hawkes notes that from the age of 11 to his graduation from UCL, there 'can have been very few years when he was not editing a magazine of some kind', usually an arts review. And he learned from

---

[17] Smith (2004: 151, n. 131).
[18] Hawkes (1982: 41).

his father to write for and to attract *ordinary readers*, a rare skill in his contemporary academic community. The crispness of Rik's later style originated in his father's habit of hovering over his son with a large pair of scissors as he wrote small insertions for the *Observer*.

> 'If you don't cut 100 words out of the middle, I'll just snip them off the end [Robert would say . . .] Write as though you were writing a cable-gram at a shilling a word.'[19]

This explains why Rik Wheeler turned so naturally to the press, as well as to universities and learned societies, to help support the Wheelers' earliest Welsh excavations. It also explains the ease with which he became one of the earliest academics to make a permanent career in media, setting a pattern for modern pundits like David Starkey and Julian Richards. There are two basic models for male media archaeologists today. There is the Virile: 'Watch as I rappel down this Iraqi cliff to determine the dialect of that inscription at its base!', and the Academic: 'Watch as I stroll through this lovely old town, pausing occasionally for an erudite joke about the private life of a historical figure!' Of course, an individual need not belong exclusively to one group. It can be argued that the patterns for both were at least partially set by Wheeler, whose post-war radio and TV work was extensive. Shows and documentaries featuring him still occasionally surface on cable history channels.

From the outset, then, the Wheelers were aware of the possibilities for funding and publicity that the press held out. Their excavation of the amphitheatre at Caerleon, funded as it was largely by the *Daily Mail*, gloriously confirmed the potential of this resource. While they would never again convince a newspaper to buy them an entire site, they would also never again offer a paper exclusive access to an excavation. After Caerleon, they used the press wire services to release large amounts of information or interviews to many papers at once. This is most noticeable at Verulamium: the London Museum's excellent press cutting service preserved endless, identical articles in various provincial and London newspapers on the site, distinguished only by their layout. Obtaining money directly from the press began to give way to the less conditional public money of publicity—and it did bring in money, as the accounts at Maiden Castle show. There

---

[19] Wheeler (1955: 29).

was a downside. The omnipresence of the press, and of the public via the press, did increase the pressure to make dramatic finds, and it is no wonder that the Wheelers occasionally discreetly 'saved' something until they felt a site needed attention. It never affected a feature's place in the final report, or in their own notebooks and records; but it allowed them to play the system a little. The Wheelers were clever about these small deceptions: there is only one extant instance of a reporter noticing them do it, in a brief notice included in the archives of the Museum of London.[20] One wonders if it would be possible today, when so many more forms of media outlets exist. A modern Verulamium student could email a picture from their camera phone to one of the many television channels and newspapers that encourage such free amateur submissions—though with camera phones, much more specific contracts for diggers have been developed to legally prevent workers from spilling the finds prematurely.

For Verney Wheeler, there was a private downside to site publicity. While she valued the press and what it brought, and worked closely with it to publicize sites, she hated the personal focus it placed upon her. Wheeler drove the media connection, but Verney Wheeler was often the one in the photographs. A woman doing something was and is News, especially when she is doing something traditionally associated with men—for example, physical labour, or studying the past. An appreciable number of articles about Wheeler digs appear under a headline like that of the *Daily Mail* for 23 August 1930: 'GIRL EXCAVATORS.'

These two examples from the Verulamium excavations are very typical. It is interesting to see the reporters' focus on Verney Wheeler's choice of dress, and the emphasis on her work with 'delicate' (i.e. feminine) small finds and women undergraduates. The voluntary nature of her work is also underlined as important; she is digging to help her husband, not because she has to financially. The two articles were probably released over a wire service; excerpts below are respectively from the *Daily Mail*, 9 August 1930, and the *Sheffield Independent*, 25 August 1930. All italics are added.

A woman with dark wavy hair and smiling brown eyes, dressed in a business-like brown jumper and skirt, brown stockings, and Wellington boots, is directing the important work of excavating the site of the

---

[20] The name of the journal is not clearly written, but it dated from 19 August 1932.

Roman city of Verulam [...] She is Mrs Wheeler, wife of Dr Mortimer Wheeler, Keeper and Secretary of the London Museum, who, with Dr T. Davies Pryce, a number of voluntary workers from various universities, and about 20 labourers [...] Mrs Wheeler, who is an expert in excavation work, is the chief administrative officer of the party. She organises the work, gives the men instructions in regard to digging, and is chiefly responsible for the sorting and marking of the large quantities of pottery and other relics which are being found [...] 'I like the work very much.' Mrs Wheeler told me. 'Reveille is at 6:30 a.m. We start work at 8 a.m. and do not finish until 6 or 7 o'clock. *I know of few better ways of spending a holiday.*'[21]

WOMAN EXCAVATOR: It is only fitting that woman should play her part in the discovery of Boadicea's city, but I believe that there is something unusual in having a woman to direct operations in excavation even in so suitable a site. This, however, is the work which has been undertaken this month by Mrs Mortimer Wheeler, whose husband is the keeper of the London Museum, and in charge of the important new digging near St Albans. Mrs Wheeler is an expert in excavation work, *so I hear she asked to be allowed to join the party and take charge of the more delicate side,* such, for instance, as the handling of the pottery and other fragile objects. She is also to train a party of women undergraduates who have come to the Verulam site for their first experience of excavation work.[22]

Despite the ease with which she dealt with the press, Verney Wheeler did not enjoy being the focus of their articles. While lecturing came easily to her, she was shy in the camera's eye. She was also a very private person emotionally, the last person to enjoy the drama of the press. Her interviews, like her letters, are charming, funny, and professionally full of good sense; but it is rare for her to reveal her own feelings in them.[23] The personal reticence in both sources is not surprising. Apart from making sense in a woman of Tessa's character, it was one of the two courses she could take in dealing with the ongoing pressure of Rik's philandering. Both the evidence and her personality show us that the alternative course—to complain or unburden herself in writing to their friends—would have been anathema to her. The valiant character so often commented on by her

---

[21] *Daily Mail*, 9 August 1930. The overseas edition of the paper ran the same article under the headline 'Women Work As Excavators'.

[22] *Sheffield Independent*, 25 August 1930. The same article appeared in the *Birmingham Evening Dispatch* of 21 August 1930.

[23] Fox (1936: 107).

contemporaries is as evident here as in her professional work, but it also reminds us that Tessa was not without personal pride. She was always a surprisingly tough woman, as Cyril Fox wrote in his obituary of her for the *Museums Journal*.

> A capable woman of affairs, a very hard worker, she retained the dainty airs and graces, and, if need be, the weapons of woman.

Verney Wheeler's opinion of photography is preserved in the Verulamium Museum, where a letter from one of the Wheelers' old students, Margaret E. Wood, survives in the odds-and-ends archive of the site's ephemera. She had become an expert on medieval buildings, and was another successful Wheeler product. It is dated 15 August 1960.

> As you know Mrs Wheeler was very averse to being photographed. I expect you already have the 1931 excavation group with her looking down [. . .] I have no print in my album of the one with Sir Mortimer in it, otherwise I would send it to you. What a wonderful woman she was [*sic*] I shall never forget her.[24]

Unfortunately it is no longer clear which photographs Wood was sending with the letter. In most of the posed photographs of Verney Wheeler she looks almost pained. The best she can usually summon is a wry expression that is rather telling; the Lydney site photographs are typical. There are only a few examples of Verney Wheeler really smiling for the camera—most charmingly in the photograph included in the chapter on Verulamium. This is in complete contrast to Wheeler, a man never more comfortable than in front of any kind of camera, and naturally most photogenic.

If Verney Wheeler disliked the process of the press, why did she allow herself to feature so heavily in the articles about Verulamium? Probably the answer is simply that she was there, and subverted her own preferences for the dig's good. With Wheeler dashing in and out, but Verney Wheeler always present and easily found, it is no wonder that pressmen ended up working more with her. Verney Wheeler might have hated being photographed, but she interviewed extremely well. Her clear mind lent itself well to the task of bringing the past into an easily understandable form, and reporters delighted in the

---

[24] Margaret E. Wood to 'Mr Anthony', 15 August 1960. Wheeler correspondence, folder 1, VMA.

way she used objects to illustrate the past. If the Wheelers are allowed
to play to type, *he* was excellent for a colourful view of the military
condition of southern Roman Britain, and *she* could be counted on
for the lively description of the development of the town that would
attract their 'Sunday Supplement' readers.

No discussion of the Wheelers' joint press persona would be
complete without the 1930 article 'Master Michael's Wonderful
Holiday.' The tone is sensational, but worth it for the immediacy of
the personalities it describes. Verney Wheeler generally gave much
more than two sentences to the men and women of the press; perhaps
this reporter made the wine cellar look particularly attractive.

> If I ever become an archaeologist I should like to pursue my calling in
> the company of Dr Mortimer Wheeler, who is very fortunate in
> his excavations; Mrs Mortimer Wheeler, who plunges into Roman
> entrenchments wearing Russian boots and smoking Russian cigarettes,
> and their son Michael, who has been archaeologising [*sic*] since he was
> five—and as he is now fourteen he knows everything!
>
> They are digging at Verulamium [. . .]This was an ancient British
> settlement. Then it became a Roman settlement. Now it is a Mortimer
> Wheeler settlement [. . .]
>
> 'Caesar came here [a typical Rik exaggeration-bordering-on-
> fabrication],' said Dr Wheeler as we [. . .] came to a spot where a
> Roman wineshop stood—its cellar has just been excavated, beside a
> dwelling house with remains of excellent drains, and another, a superior
> suburban Roman's house with decorated floor [. . .] Mrs Wheeler gave
> me two sentences and broke off with a far-away look in her eyes. She
> vanished into the Roman cellar. Michael was deputed to guide me, and
> what that boy knows!²⁵

Behind the silliness of the *Daily Express* piece, a regular method in the
Wheelers' self-presentation is discernible. In this article, as in many
others, the site's historical credentials are established by familiar
classical references to Tacitus and the Twelve Caesars. The reporter's
attention is then drawn to the 'superior suburban Roman's home', a
familiar advertising phrase for the reading audience. Another article
even describes Verulamium as a Roman 'garden city', echoing the
recent fad for green-belt developments outside London. The emphasis on the excellent Roman drains occasionally makes articles begin to

---

²⁵ *Daily Express*, 23 September 1930. Michael said later that he got it in the neck
when he returned to Rugby after the holidays; all of his classmates had read the article.

sound like estate agent's ads, and this is not unintentional. The Wheelers wanted people to see the Romans of the past as similar to themselves, with tiled floors, central heating, excellent drains, and easy proximity to London. And if some attractive young ladies appeared enthusiastically cleaning those tiled floors in the photographs, then so much the better.

The Wheeler's version of archaeology began to creep into other media outlets, as well—most particularly as a plot device in E. F. Benson's *Lucia's Progress* (1935), published as the Wheelers got fully under way at Maiden Castle. It was a successful entry in his very popular series of 'Mapp and Lucia' novels, focusing on the intellectual and social pretensions of the magnificently monstrous titular ladies in a small country town. *Lucia's Progress* betrays its author's early training as a classical archaeologist; by 1935 Benson had been living off the proceeds of his prolific writing career for decades, but he was obviously still aware of new developments in the field. He also appreciated that his middle-class readership might appreciate a satirical look at the intellectual pretensions of recreational historians.

His readers were familiar enough with the vocabulary and process of archaeology to get the joke, whether from reading newspaper articles, watching newsreels, or listening to lectures in person or on the radio. This long quotation features a number of key words the Wheelers had popularized, a misguided attempt at stratigraphic dating, the use of site reports and guidebooks, and even a supposed hypocaust. Thanks to the Wheelers, archaeology was popular enough to be satirized.

> Lucia carried her tile reverently into the house, and beckoned to Georgie.
>
> 'That square-tiled opening confirms all I conjectured about the lines of foundation in the cellar,' she said. 'Those wonderful Romans used to have furnaces underneath the floors of their houses and their temples—I've been reading about it—and the hot air was conveyed in tiled flues through the walls to heat them. Undoubtedly this was a hot-air flue and not a drain at all [...]Without doubt, Georgie, a Roman villa stood here or perhaps a temple. I should be inclined to say a temple. On the top of the hill, you know: just where they always put temples.'
>
> [...] She searched in vain in her books from the London Library for any mention of Tilling having once been a Roman town, but its absence made the discovery more important, as likely to prove a new chapter in the history of Roman Britain. Eagerly she turned over the pages: there were illustrations of pottery which fortified her conviction that her fragments were of Roman origin: there was a picture of a Roman tile

as used in hot-air flues which was positively identical with her speci-men. Then what could S.P. stand for? She ploughed through a list of inscriptions found in the South of England and suddenly gave a great crow of delight. There was one headed S.P.Q.R., which being inter-preted meant *Senatus Populusque Romanus*, 'the Senate and the People of Rome.' Her instinct had been right: a private villa would never have borne those imperial letters; they were reserved for state-erected build-ings, such as temples. [. . .] It said so in her book.

[. . .] all day she supervised the excavations in her garden. To the great indignation of her gardener, she hired two unemployed labourers at very high wages in view of the importance of their work, and set them to dig a trench [. . .] so that she must again strike the line of the hot-air flue [. . .] the soil was rich in relics, it abounded in pieces of pottery of the same type as those she had decided were Roman, and there were many pretty fragments of iridescent, oxidised glass, and a few bones [. . .]

'It's most important, Georgie,' she said, 'as you will readily under-stand, to keep note of the levels at which objects are discovered. Those in Tray D come from four feet down in the corner of the asparagus bed: that is the lowest level we have reached at present, and they, of course, are the earliest.'

'Oh, and look at Tray A,' said Georgie. 'All those pieces of clay tobacco pipes. I didn't know the Romans smoked. Did they?'

Lucia gave a slightly superior laugh.

'*Caro*, of course they didn't,' she said. 'Tray A: yes, I thought so. Tray A is from a much higher level, let me see, yes, a foot below the surface of the ground. We may put it down therefore as being subsequent to Queen Elizabeth when tobacco was introduced. At a guess I should say those pipes were Cromwellian. A Cromwellian look, I fancy. I am rather inclined to take a complete tile from the continuation of the air flue which I laid bare this morning, and see if it is marked in full S.P.Q.R.[. . .] To-morrow I expect my trench to get down to floor level. There may be a tessellated pavement like that found at Richborough [. . .] and if it goes under the garden-room, I shall have to underpin it, I think they call it. Fancy all this having come out of a smell of gas! [. . .][26]

To return to a real lady of much greater archaeological knowledge and infinitely less pretence: at Maiden Castle, Verney Wheeler is not as visible in either photographs or printed interviews. This does not

---

[26] Benson (1935).

mean she had less of a role with reporters; but it was a changing one. She was beginning to assert her own preferences as a worker.

> For the first two seasons the Wheelers themselves conducted weekly meetings with the press, and reporters blessed Tessa for her simple clarity in exposition. After her death the briefings were handed over to Margot Eates.[27]

There were no interviews with Verney Wheeler 'in her tent' in Dorset as at Verulamium. Much more personal attention was given to Wheeler. He was personally present on the Maiden Castle dig to an unusual extent, probably because it was not within easily commutable distance of London and thus forced longer sustained activity. After Verney Wheeler's death, her husband reassigned the responsibility of the minutiae of press management to Margot Eates with seemingly little regret, though he continued to be very much the public face of the dig.

There is an unknown story here, one apparent only from its results: at some moment between Verulamium and Maiden Castle, Tessa must have spoken with Rik and made it clear she disliked the press-work and expected him to take some of it on. It is a very rare, fleeting glimpse of the power she could wield in their otherwise harmonious professional relationship. It also reminds us that their partnership was not harmonious merely because he proposed and she disposed. The marital division of labour went both ways.

---

[27] Hawkes (1982: 166).

10

Maiden Castle, Dorset (1934–1937)

It is irresistibly tempting to open this chapter with the classic Thomas Hardy description of Maiden Castle (Fig. 16), from his 1885 story 'A Tryst at An Ancient Earthwork.' Generations of archaeologists (including the Wheelers) have failed to find words as evocative as those of Dorset's great novelist.

> The profile of the whole stupendous ruin, as seen at a distance of a mile eastward, is cleanly cut as that of a marble inlay. It is varied with protuberances, which from hereabouts have the animal aspect of warts, wens, knuckles, and hips. It may indeed be likened to an enormous many-limbed organism of an antediluvian time—partaking of the cephalopod in shape—lying lifeless, and covered with a thin green cloth, which hides its substance, while revealing its contour. This dull green mantle of herbage stretches down towards the levels, where the ploughs have essayed for centuries to creep up near and yet nearer to the base of the castle, but have always stopped short before reaching it. The furrows of these environing attempts show themselves distinctly, bending to the incline as they trench upon it; mounting in steeper curves, till the steepness baffles them, and their parallel threads show like the striae of waves pausing on the curl. The peculiar place of which these are some of the features is 'Mai-Dun,' 'The Castle of the Great Hill,' said to be the Dunium of Ptolemy, the capital of the Durotriges, which eventually came into Roman occupation, and was finally deserted on their withdrawal from the island.[1]

---

[1] Hardy (1885). While Wheeler quoted this description approvingly several times in connection with Maiden Castle, its more recent excavator Niall Sharples finds it powerful but physically inaccurate. He prefers the analogy of a 'sleeping giant'. Sharples (1991: 12).

Figure 16. Maiden Castle.

The story's narrator is at the 'stupendous ruin' to help an intrepid antiquarian make an illegal midnight excavation of a Roman grave at its summit. His description of the eager scrabbling of 'a professed and well-known antiquary with capital letters at the tail of his name' remains, with *Lucia's Progress*, a classic literary account of amateur archaeology.

Wheeler said bluntly in retrospect that when funding problems and the building of a major new road began to turn him away from Verulamium in 1934, he began looking for a project that was *not* Roman, or at the very least *less* Roman. He 'suffered from a satiety of Roman things.' His focus on the British tribesmen of Verulamium reflected a growing disinterest in 'high' Roman culture, about which he is characteristically blistering in his autobiography.

> The mechanical, predictable quality of Roman craftsmanship, the advertised *humanitas* of Roman civilisation, which lay always so near to brutality and corruption, fatigued and disgusted me so that my [*sic*] Verulamium report fell short in some parts of its record, and J. N. L. Myres very properly rapped me over the knuckles for it.[2]

[2] Wheeler (1955: 102).

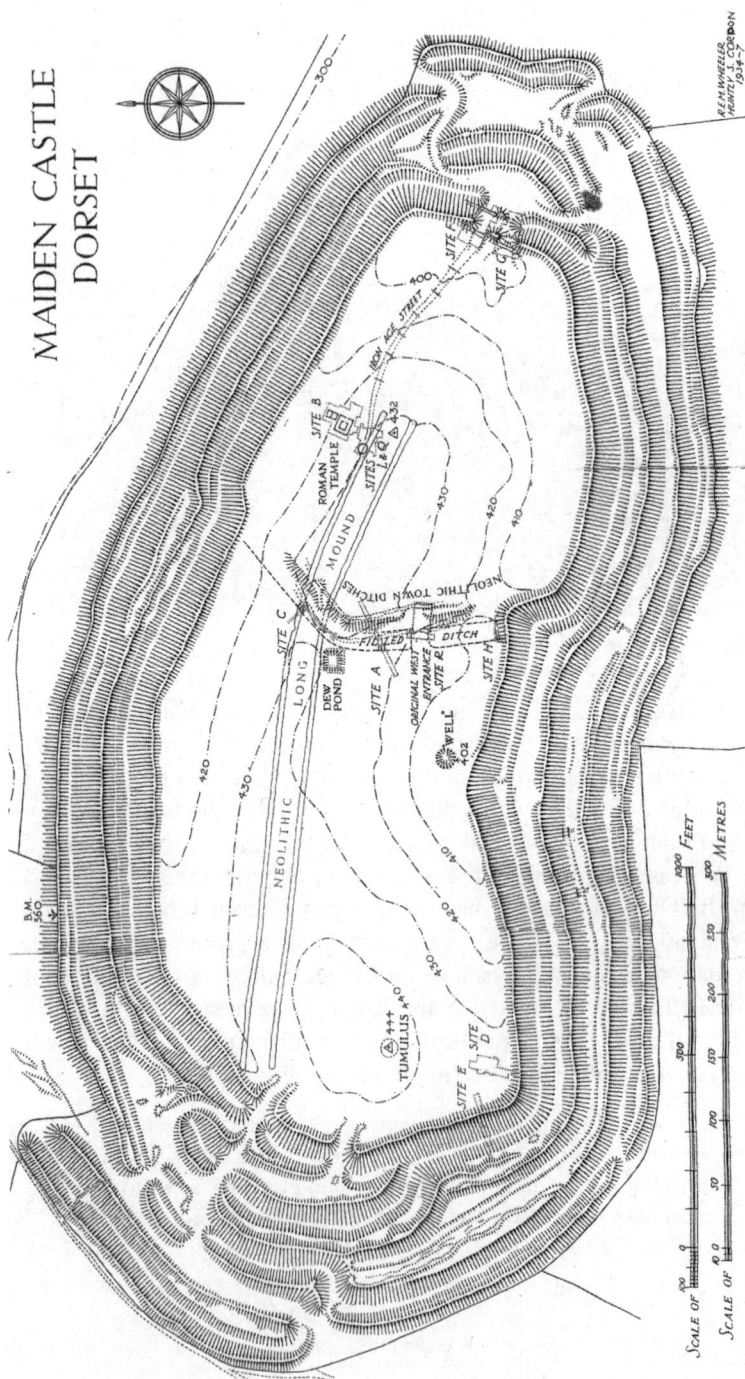

Figure 17. Plan of the Wheeler excavations.

Verney Wheeler's feelings are less clear. As the solidly productive Wheeler partnership became more and more of a brand, it increasingly hid her as an individual—or perhaps this is a false impression arising from her absence in the archives of the London Museum. For whatever reason, she retreats a little. As Wheeler strides across the windy landscape of Maiden Castle with visitors, modern eyes strain sometimes to see her in the background directing student work (Fig. 17).

Prior archaeological work on the site had been done by the secretive antiquarian of Hardy's story, who was based on a real FSA named Edward Cunnington; the piece is thought to be a fictionalized account of a real 'raid' he and Hardy made together.[3] The local poet Reverend William Barnes was also involved in the investigations, which focused on Maiden Castle's potential as a Roman site. Cunnington partly excavated a 'villa' and its associated small finds, and performed numerous site surveys via field walking. The villa was actually the small temple of the Wheelers' 'Site B', which Verney Wheeler did a particularly fine job excavating.

From these sources Cunnington deduced that the invading Roman forces had settled on the earthwork, an idea not without its contemporary critics. He was not an easy man to deal with; Hardy perfectly captured the contrarian spirit that powers many archaeologists and antiquarians.

> I ask, What if it [Maiden Castle] is Roman? A great deal, according to him. That it proves all the world to be wrong in this great argument, and himself alone to be right! Can I wait while he digs further?[4]

Cunnington's results remained primarily in manuscript form, though Barnes referred to them extensively in an address to the Royal Archaeological Institute on the site in 1865, and again in an on-site talk for the British Archaeological Association in 1871. Both accounts were published by the respective Institute's house journal.[5] Wheeler was thus a little disingenuous when he wrote that he went to Maiden Castle to get a break from the Romans; it was certain that there was at least one Roman structure on the hill, and it was known

---

[3] Sharples (1991: 12). See also the more extensive discussion of Cunnington in Wheeler (1943: 6–8).

[4] Hardy (1885).

[5] *Archaeologia* 22 (1865), 353; and *Journal of the British Archaeological Association* 18 (1872), 99–102.

to produce classical finds of the type Verney Wheeler loved best—coins and mosaics. The attraction lay in the chance to work back through to the period previous to the Roman settlement. At Lydney Park, the Wheelers had worked forward past the Roman period, and at Verulamium they had begun to work backwards towards the Belgian *oppidum*. Now, they would begin an excavation for the first time where the primary object was not Rome, but its predecessors.

Cunnington was associated with the local Dorset Natural History and Archaeological Society, or the Dorset Field Club as it was known in his day. Hardy was also an active member of the group, reading papers before it on occasion and using it as a historical resource for his Wessex novels.[6] As was usual, the Dorset group maintained mutually beneficial links with the Society of Antiquarians in London via men like Cunnington, dual members of both societies. This association continued through the nineteenth century to the present day. As at Verulamium, Burlington House was the first stop on the way to exhaustive excavation.

Examining the Maiden Castle minutes in some detail reveals how much of an Antiquaries (and Wheelers) production the dig was from the start. While the local Dorset society provided vital links with local workers, and more importantly the expert local knowledge of men like the Wheelers' co-director Charles Drew, it could not compete equally in terms of organization or financing with the London association. Sensibly, it does not seem to have wanted to.

As early as 15 January 1930, the Society's President appears in the Research Council minutes telling that body that he wishes them to consider two prehistoric sites before any other projects: Chysauster in Cornwall, and Maiden Castle in Dorset.[7] The meeting goes on to consider issues arising from the first fact-finding mission sent to St Albans. Maiden Castle is consequently shelved for a few years, but on 7 April 1933 it reappears. Charles Peers urges a special sub-committee of the Research Committee to limit the Society to engaging in only one major excavation of two or more years at a time, while running several smaller and (crucially) cheaper ones simultaneously. The latter are not to last longer than one month, and unlike the longer excavations, must be designed to answer one specific question about a site.[8] Maiden Castle is given as a specific example of the type of long-term site he has in mind, and it is therefore not surprising that on 8 December of the same year, the following minutes were noted.

---

[6] The Dorset County Museum preserves its links to Hardy, and has maintained a reconstruction of the author's Max Gate study since 1936.

[7] Research Council minutes, 15 January 1930, SALA.

[8] Research Council minutes, 7 April 1933, SALA.

The Committee then proceeded to consider the question of the excavation of Maiden Castle. The President reported that an organizing committee had been appointed which had done a certain amount of preliminary work and that it was advisable that this committee should be formally constituted a sub-committee to the Research Committee.

Whereupon it was resolved:

To recommend to Council that the Organizing Committee consisting of: The President, the Earl of Ilchester, Lt. Col. Drew (Secretary Treasurer), and Messrs. Bushe-Fox, Crawford, Cyril Fox, St George Gray, Keiller, Leeds, V.L. Oliver, C.S. Prideux, Davies Pryce, Mortimer Wheeler, Mrs Wheeler, Captain Pitt-Rivers—be appointed a sub-committee of the Research Committee to organize the excavations at Maiden Castle.[9]

This group's last set of informal minutes, neatly kept by Charles Drew, are read to the assembly and pasted in to the Committee's own book. Drew reads them a general memorandum on Maiden Castle, and Wheeler gives a review of the five main 'problems to be solved.' This is simply a list of five sub-sites: the cross-bank at the entrance, the cross-bank at its junction with the inner rampart, the Roman buildings in the east section observed by Cunnington, the entrance proper, and the pit-dwelling area near the modern dewpond at the site's centre. The Chairman (Peers) suggests £1,200 is a good estimate of the money needed, and promises a substantial grant from the Society. The Dorset Natural History and Archaeological Society wants to help, but can promise nothing financially until the New Year. Drew and Wheeler agree to draft a public appeal, the conservative St George Gray offers to approach the Western Gazette for publicity (a sign of how much the Wheelers had normalized this), and Alexander Keiller, that dashing playboy-pioneer, offers to have new aerial photographs taken for study and sale. In a side note, the Committee also plans to approach the Prince of Wales (the future Edward VIII) for permission, as the site belongs to him via the Duchy of Cornwall. He was willing enough, provided any disturbed tenants were compensated and permission also obtained from the Office of Works. He also originally asked to receive all finds made, but in the end these quite properly made their way to the Dorset County Museum instead. Perhaps the prince could not think of a use for that many prehistoric sling stones.

---

[9] Research Council minutes, 8 December 1933, SALA.

The minutes continue more or less tediously until 4 April 1935, when Keiller contests the selling of potsherds, tesserae, and other small bulk finds as souvenirs to visitors. The matter is left to the Directors of the site to decide—the Wheelers and Colonel Drew, that is. As it was no doubt originally their idea, the practice continues and proves moderately profitable. More important is what follows:

> Resolved: To recommend to Council that, when the [Research] Committee is reappointed after the Anniversary, Mrs Wheeler should be added to it.

She was added, and became the Committee's first female member. Just as Caerleon gained her entrance to the Society, and Lydney to its publications and papers lists, Maiden Castle got her a place on what was arguably its most influential body—the one that determined funding.

Disappointingly, Verney Wheeler remains a silent presence here; she is not mentioned in the minutes as commenting to the group. This is puzzling. She co-presented interim reports on the site to the Society alongside Drew and her husband; as an expert on the subject, why would she remain invisible in meetings? Did she simply let the men take the lead? While this seems strange from a modern perspective, it would not be surprising. The few women present in the Society at this time rarely sign blue papers or nominate candidates for election; they are also often silent in meetings unless specifically asked to speak (for example in the presentation of a paper).[10] Burlington House was still very much a male enclave, and even the emancipated women who desegregated it must have felt intimidated at times.

Colonel Charles Drew, the man who became the Wheelers' co-director, was the mind behind the site's adoption by the Society of Antiquaries. Field Secretary of the Dorset Natural History and Archaeological Society from 1929, and FSA from that date as well, he was known in both groups as an unusually gentle and kind man, devoted to his county and home town. One proof often given of his sweet nature was his enduring friendship with both Wheeler and Keiller.[11] He provided a good foil to Rik's more aggressive style, and as co-Director was invaluable to both Wheelers. Unlike Davies Pryce,

---

[10] Verney Wheeler signs six blue papers during her eight years of membership, and four of these are honorary (meaning they are likely to be passed no matter what). Blue papers 1928–1936, SALA.

[11] Piggott (1958: 25).

he was an excavator himself, and as he lived in the area year-round the Wheelers could depend on him to a much greater extent as an active colleague, both in and out of the digging season.[12]

OPENING CUTS: ANOTHER HILL-TOP ROMAN TEMPLE

The work at Maiden Castle began on 24 July 1934. The Wheelers were not present, and a small party of workman under Drew made the opening cuts. Their foreman was a young and precociously experienced Somerset man, William Wedlake (Fig. 18), who had been steadily amassing experience as a paid digger in his own county and was in growing demand. Acquiring him for Maiden Castle was a minor coup on Drew's part, and proof of his excellent regional connections.

Wedlake left formal education at 12. Before that, he had been at an excellent village school where he acquired a neat round hand and a pleasant written manner. He had a facility for prose, and his writings have fortunately been preserved in the Somerset County Records Office. These include three valuable sources for Maiden Castle: his voluminous unpublished memoir, a patchy diary kept in a series of little memo books, and an extensive correspondence from and about Maiden Castle, mainly with his great friend and archaeological mentor, Prior Ethelbert Horne. A diary entry for Tuesday, 24 July 1934 is typical.[13] His technical use of the Latin word *vallum* should be noted; he was already using the language of the more intellectual group he wished to be part of.

> Arrived at the Castle at 9 AM where I met the SIX men [the initial team of labourers] [...] and took their cards. Col Drew + Mr [Bernard] Sturdy arrived later about 9:30 AM.
> We first went to the supposed original eastern entrance of the Castle. Here we sat down + Col Drew gave the men a short discription [*sic*] of the place + told them the object of the present excavations. We then

---

[12] *Proceedings of the Dorset Natural History and Archaeological Society* 78 (1957), 10–17.

[13] In his later memoirs, Wedlake remembered it as June, but his diary of the summer shows the later date.

Figure 18. William Wedlake (left, with shovel) and Charles Drew in 1934.

erected the bell tent + marked out the 1st Cutting which is 9.5 ft × 10 ft. This cutting cuts through the vallum and bottom of the supposed original bank [...]The greater part of the turf was stripped from this cutting, + a good deal of fencing around this area was also done. Some pottery was also found in the post holes [...] Col Drew was away for the afternoon but came back in the evening + we went for a walk around the Eastern half of the camp.[14]

The Wheelers arrived from London a few days later on the 30th of the month (a Monday). They brought luck with them.

Dr Wheeler + Mrs Wheeler + party of 5. 4 Students of Archaeology. Continued tracing Roman Building. 6 more men this morning. Bronze

[14] Box 127: 2004.77/18, DCMA.

figures with Bull. 7 coins morning. 3 coins afternoon, one of Diocletian [. . .] cutting continued at Site A.[15]

By Wednesday, we hear: 'Keeping my own section today. Mrs Wheeler very helpful.' A week later, and he marks that she is away for the day. Barring the first mention, there has been no word yet of Rik Wheeler, but in Wedlake's unpublished memoirs he writes that he was immediately struck by the 'Keeper's' character.

It was clear from the start that the tall slim athletic figure, known as the 'Keeper' (Dr Wheeler) had taken over his command. His firm but kindly and jocular manner soon gained respect from both the workmen, volunteers and the staff, but life was not without its 'ups and downs' at times. On such occasions the quiet, friendly, petite Mrs Tessa Verny [*sic*] Wheeler in her inimitable manner soon had us working happily together.[16]

The nature of an excavation being what it is, the first material the excavators dealt with at Maiden Castle was far later than the prehistoric period the site is rightly best known for. The little Roman temple and house on the top of the castle, dating from its final phase of occupation, was designated Site B and proved a rich source of small finds, including the curious bronze figure of a bull topped with human busts that Wedlake had noted on the day of the Wheelers' arrival (Fig. 19) and many interesting coins. It also served as an excellent training ground for their first batch of students, who were more likely to be familiar with Roman materials and buildings already. They could get their eyes in archaeologically without too much worry, before proceeding to the more important prehistoric phase that formed the primary interest of the excavation.

The temple complex (for despite its small size it can be so described) was also of a type that would especially appeal to Verney Wheeler, given her work on similar small temples at Lydney and Verulamium, and her particular knowledge of Roman coins. The last hands-on archaeological excavating she did in her life was, in this first year in Dorset, one of the periods she liked best. After 1934, she began to delegate more and more. This was partly because of the enormous size of the site and partly because the earthworks became, even more than Verulamium, a giant training camp.

[15] Box 127: 2004.77/18, DCMA.
[16] Wedlake autobiography, p. 184. DD/SAS/G 1818/1/1/3, SCRO.

Figure 19. The votive bull with busts found in the Roman temple. Verney Wheeler was quoted in the *Dorset City Chronicle* of 13 August 1934 referring to the strange statuette as 'the most beautiful small find that it has ever been her luck to be associated with'.

Her role was less that of the practical excavator and more of the overseeing teacher, though she never completely stopped digging (Fig. 20).

The temple represents the last and briefest period of Maiden Castle's occupation, and has thus been rather passed over in discussion despite its interesting implications about the interplay of Roman and native British religions. Apart from that, it carries enough interest on both the technical and personal fronts to make it the first level of investigation thematically as well as chronologically. As usual the notebook relating to the site follows the familiar format of text faced

Figure 20. Verney Wheeler (far right) on site at Maiden Castle in 1934, overseeing the excavation of the Roman temple (detail).

by plans and drawings, but there is an intriguing difference. Instead of Verney Wheeler's confident site notes and fine freehand planning, there are a number of hands and names identifying different workers. The work is of wide-ranging quality. Many of the plans and drawings are pasted in, with the author's name at the page's top, and occasionally Verney Wheeler's hand appears crisply annotating an inaccurate or incomplete piece. At the front, she has written out a list of reminders for herself. This is a new kind of plan notebook: one that synchronizes the separate work of at least nine students into one volume, with each piece 'graded' by Verney Wheeler. While the teaching notebooks of Verulamium prefigured this method, here she openly marked up student work from the outset of the excavation.

What is p 24, 26, 32.
John must describe purpose of any trench made; no trench is cut without one.

Put F
p 33. not 'plotted'
p 38 Always relate strata to structure.
George. Why go to p. 42 when 18–20 are pt. B?
p. 14 who dug it?
Is drawing 'checked.
Pit H surely under W wall of ambulatory
note Pit J. is p. 12 pit in N. ambulatory.
are all pits on sketch plan? for reference?[17]

On the book's first few pages, she keeps a running list of which that quoted above is representative, and an ongoing sketch plan of the temple, much smudged and amended. It is not hard to see how the temple was excavated. Verney Wheeler assigned small trenches in this very small area to one or two students, and they directed its uncovering by Wedlake and his team of workmen. Their job at this stage was still more one of management than of personal physical labour. This changed as the Maiden Castle excavations went on, and indeed it became notorious for its gangs of trouser-clad digging girls. But hired labour was never entirely dispensed with, and there was always a division between those who dug for love (middle- and upper-class students, of both genders) and those who dug for money (lower-class men). Wedlake was one of the few workers who managed to do both at once, and it sometimes made his position socially murky.

The students filled notebooks of their own with information as their trench is cleared, and gave the results to Verney Wheeler. Probably she took their plans back to the Antelope Hotel in Dorchester, which was her base in the area, and in the evenings either copied or pasted them into her master notebook. She then annotated and corrected the work as necessary. The next day the students were given feedback as they worked; Verney Wheeler preferred to demonstrate a technique herself when explaining it, rather than lecture on it academically. The list in the front of the book already quoted must be her reminders of what to discuss with her students.

'John'—who the volunteer book reveals as John K. Adams of Oxford —found it especially hard going.[18] His admittedly poor sketch

[17] Box 58: 1939.55.28.1.58/2, frontispiece, DCMA.
[18] Box 64: 1939.55.28.1.64/4, DCMA.

plan of a trench along the east Roman wall is labelled '?Drain cut' at its top in Verney Wheeler's hand. She enlarged on his problems opposite the section: 'Wrong. This section has no location, no orientation.' It also had no measurements, though he left a place for them.[19] Later on she added: 'immediately N + W of S.W. corner of priest's house.' It is clear she was still doing a great deal of the technical work herself, but also that her role is changing more and more into that of a teacher, demonstrating techniques rather than practising them. All first-hand accounts of her site management describe her gentle patience in demonstration and correction, but her crisp criticism of her students' planning reminds us of the no-nonsense tone she sometimes adopted in letters to Nash-Williams. Verney Wheeler was kind, and undoubtedly soft-hearted, but those qualities enhanced her professionalism rather than dictating to it. She could not compromise the quality of a dig.

Verney Wheeler worked with about ten or twelve students besides the unfortunate John Adams. A few of the other young volunteers whose work appears in the Site B notebook went on to impressive careers. Besides Wedlake, two names that leap out are 'Seton-Williams' and 'Mr Wu'. These two are Veronica Seton-Williams of UCL, last seen at University College, and C. D. Wu of the Courtauld Institute, who went on to a distinguished archaeological career in his native China. Seton-Williams's future career lay in the Middle East, though she always remembered its beginnings as Maiden Castle. The Wheeler influence was beginning to extend internationally.

Both Wu and Seton-Williams showed their talent early on, producing excellent work and requiring relatively little correction: Seton-Williams became a site supervisor in later seasons and was much depended on. Advanced students were occasionally asked to come back to Verney Wheeler's rooms at the Antelope in Dorchester in the evening for special tuition; Beatrice de Cardi remembers learning how to clean and wrap a horse skull in this way.[20] Huntley Gordon, a Verulamium veteran who planned the Maiden Castle earthworks with Michael Wheeler, stayed at the Antelope himself and thus had the peculiar enjoyment of watching the Wheelers plan the day's work over breakfast.[21]

[19] Box 58: 1939.55.28.1.58/2, p. 32, DCMA.
[20] Interview with Beatrice de Cardi, 14 November 2006.
[21] Hawkes (1982: 165).

Both Wheeler and Verney Wheeler had a tremendous generosity of spirit in their approach to teaching. They used it to raise their university students up to an equal level with themselves, and make them colleagues rather than subordinates. To go on a Wheeler dig was to receive the best practical education in archaeology available at the time, because students were taught to think and plan as well as dig and measure.

The published plans of the temple were signed, as were all the plans in the report, by Wheeler. One focused on the underlying pre-Roman pits rather than the temple itself, and the other was a simplified plan of the Roman levels only. When the two are put side by side with Verney Wheeler's master notebook plan, the way in which Wheeler broke down the rough on-site synthesis she made as the temple was being stripped into its component periods can be seen. It is an appealing symbol of their work together—Verney Wheeler as the provider of the raw information that Wheeler digested into a universally understandable form.

LIFE ON THE DIG

Over a hundred people eventually worked on Maiden Castle—workmen, students, young professional archaeologists, and an incredibly varied group of international volunteers. Wheeler spent the rest of his life running into them in all sorts of odd places, usually in his professional capacity. The beginnings of a teaching environment were in place at Verulamium, but Maiden Castle produced far more international-class archaeologists than its predecessor. Why was it so successful as a teaching excavation, and what did it mean to those workers?

Most of the hundred merely passed through briefly, contributed what they could, and moved on with an increased appreciation of archaeology and the Dorset landscape. But archaeologists with later careers as far apart as Somerset and Syria first put their hands into the earth at Maiden Castle, learning basic methods of excavation and recording that they would take across the world.

Veronica Seton-Williams and William Wedlake were at Maiden Castle from its first season, and both went on to make excellent careers in archaeology. As they also wrote detailed autobiographies,

Figure 21. M. V. Seton-Williams (known as 'Bloss' on the dig) in 1936.

they provide unusually clear explanations of what Maiden Castle meant to them.

Two more different backgrounds could hardly be imagined. Seton-Williams (Fig. 21), the Australian girl who moved to London on the strength of the Wheelers' name in the 1930s, found herself sharing a tent on the earthworks itself with Rachel Clay (a Verulamium alumna) within months of leaving Australia. Most of the students stayed in bed and breakfast rooms found for them by Drew and Verney Wheeler, but Clay and Seton-Williams preferred the adventure of camping.

> The great fort [. . .] was a wonderful place to start one's archaeology [. . .] I had never worked so hard physically before but I found I liked picking and shovelling as long as it was dry. Indeed we could not work when it was wet for fear of messing up the stratification.
>
> The actual direction of the work was initially under the supervision of Mrs Tessa Wheeler with Dr Wheeler in charge of the overall strategy, while the day-to-day arrangements and the liaison with the local society [the Archaeological Society . . .] and the accounts were looked after by Lieutenant-Colonel C. O. Drew [. . .] A vast concourse of students came here from Britain and other parts of the world to take their field training [. . .]We employed a lot of local Dorset labour, mostly men

who were unemployed for various reasons. I remember best the foreman Bill Wedlake, who came from Somerset and who had a splendid
rich Somerset accent; he had already spent many years excavating in
that county [. . .] I worked for three seasons at Maiden Castle starting
as a student in 1934 knowing nothing and for the next two years was in
charge of one of the areas as a Field Supervisor.[22]

At the end of that first summer, Seton-Williams escaped to hike in
Cornwall, but was soon tracked down and recalled by the Wheelers.
They were desperate for help in the final hectic weeks of the year's work
in Dorset. As a UCL archaeology student, she then spent a good deal of
her winter mending the Maiden Castle finds in odd corners of the
Museum of London. In a pleasant crossing of paths, Seton-Williams's
other mentor, Margaret Murray (now near retirement), was also
tempted to Maiden Castle in 1934 as a prestigious visitor-volunteer
(Fig. 22).

Figure 22. Margaret Murray (centre, white hat with black ribbon, coat with
dark fur collar) visiting the Maiden Castle finds table. Note the board with
photographs and text for visitors in the background, and the on-site sale of
photographs, postcards, and offprints.

[22] Seton-Williams (1988: 21–2).

By the summer of 1935, Seton-Williams returned to Maiden Castle 'as a fully-fledged site manager earning the princely sum of £3 a week', directing Bill Wedlake and his gang of labourers. It was a happy and profitable summer. When the Sussex archaeologist Dr Cecil Curwen asked the Wheelers for a few students to work on a rescue dig in Brighton, they sent Seton-Williams along with her fellow Maiden Castle alumni Lesley MacNair Scott, Margaret Drower, and Bernard Sturdy. Wheeler students, recommended by their tough training, were starting to be in demand. While in Brighton, Seton-Williams heard that she had been selected to work in Sinai with Flinders Petrie—something closer to her favourite Egyptology at last. Both Verney Wheeler and Murray had pushed to send their protégée to the Middle East.[23]

Passing over Sinai, a period of tremendous professional and personal importance to Seton-Williams, seems superficially absurd; but in this context it matters mainly as an example of the long reach and influence the Wheelers were exerting in the world of British archaeology. When Seton-Williams came back to England in 1936, Tessa Wheeler was dead. As a result Wheeler needed her badly at Maiden Castle as a site supervisor. She went to him somewhat reluctantly, full of memories of Verney Wheeler, and found the site had lost its magic.[24]

William Wedlake's story is somewhat different, so different that it appears in this chapter rather than the one dealing with the Institute of Archaeology. Only six years older than Seton-Williams, he grew up on a farm in the small village of Camerton in Somerset and left school at twelve. He was interested in antiquities, and began to make a living locally as a digger and foreman. Here his articulate intelligence and ability quickly brought him into more and more demand regionally, though he was still considered very much a servant by his employers. Regrettably, some of the archaeologists he worked with emphasized that a little more than was necessary; it is not hard to imagine that his increasingly high level of self-education would make strict traditionalists uncomfortable.

The Wheelers were cut of different cloth. Wedlake was brought on to the Maiden Castle dig in its first days, and he made it his priority until the dig was over. Interestingly, he was the Wheelers' second

[23] Ibid. 34.   [24] Ibid. 55–6.

choice for foreman in 1934, though after that always their first. They had wanted William Young, but he was already engaged at Avebury with their rival Alexander Keiller. There was a fair amount of competition between the two men over the 1930s, as Maiden Castle coincided with the important work at Avebury. The pay was very good—at least one shilling and three pence per hour—and his prior employer, Wheeler's minor rival St George Gray, hoped pettishly it would not make him 'spoiled'.[25]

In the event, all it made him was an archaeologist. His mentor Father Horne encouraged him constantly to stay on as long as he could, going so far as to help get Wedlake out of conflicting prior contracts. The unselfish prior was even ready to sacrifice his own pet archaeological projects in Wedlake's (and the Wheelers') interests.

> Stay as long as they will keep you at Maiden Castle, as you will learn (+ earn) far more there than you would with me [at one of Horne's digs].[26]

Both Wheelers took to Wedlake, though he was always more Wheeler's protégé than Verney Wheeler's. For Wedlake, their respect and willingness to teach him as much as their university students allowed him to make an interesting move in the site photographs: from the posed photographs of flat-capped 'diggers' at the opening of the excavations, to the much more informal photographs of the 'staff' by the end. They asked him to perform excavations unaided, left him in sole charge when they were away, paid for him to attend relevant lectures and events in London, and most importantly, asked him for regular interim reports on his work that allowed him to practise writing as an archaeologist.

Wedlake was conscious of his chance to 'move up'. He made a point of signing the visitor's log, in which volunteer (unpaid) workers were recorded, and lived in a tent on site with Bernard Sturdy rather than lodging with the workmen. He and Sturdy became lifelong friends as a result of the shared adventure of camping on the earthworks, though they did successfully petition in later seasons to be allowed to sleep in the finds shed with the dig kittens. Like Seton-Williams, Wedlake went on to a successful and highly respected career. His work (independent

---

[25] Ethelbert Horne to William J. Wedlake, 8 July 1934. Box 127: 2004.77/1, DCMA.
[26] Ethelbert Horne to William J. Wedlake, 20 September 1934. Box 127: 2004.77/1, DCMA.

of the Wheelers) was mainly accomplished in the Bath and Camerton area of his birth. Wedlake's autobiography makes interesting reading today. He was a little 'apprehensive' of joining the Dorset dig, but rose to the challenge and never regretted it. His chatty chapter on Maiden Castle captures the camaraderie of the dig, and the childish pranks and silliness with which the student staff (whom Wedlake is always careful to retrospectively identify himself with) alleviated the occasional boredom of the dig. If the camp was an archaeological classroom, it was one with a high proportion of class clowns. Poems, plays, dinners, late-night rabbit poaching, and trips to local pubs enlivened every summer. Most charming was a play written and produced by the dig staff and put on by them for the citizens of Dorchester: 'Maiden Castle, the City with a History'. Wedlake loved amateur dramatics and threw himself into this one, playing Neolithic Man alongside Charles Drew's two young daughters in what may have been the world's first and only pantomime mammoth.

The Wheelers were also characters in 'Maiden Castle', played by members of the wrong gender in the best farcical tradition. The students had planned to perform on the Castle itself, but heavy rain and wind drove actors and audience down to a packed hall in Dorchester. There student-actors representing the people of each level of occupation followed each other on stage, to be sealed with a blanket and labelled by a Greek chorus-line of diggers with buckets and brushes, singing 'Pass that shovel, pass that pail, muddle all the labels and you'll end in hell.' By the time Gilbert Carruthers came on as Early Iron Age 'C', a considerable number of occupation levels had accumulated, with Wedlake on the bottom. Carruthers was supposed to light a campfire, which he had mocked up by hiding a primus stove in a pile of wood. Unfortunately he lit more than the stove.

> [T]he primus burst into flames which reached the ceiling and caught fire to the stage curtains. From my position lying on the stage I was relieved to see Dr Wheeler, who was in a front row seat, leap onto the stage and tear down the burning curtains. With assistance, the fire was put out and the play continued [. . .] we never discovered with what fuel Gilbert had primed his primus, but I suspect that it was petrol. The local paper recorded the event [. . .] with no mention of the fire incident.[27]

---

[27] Wedlake autobiography, pp. 195–6. DD/SAS/G 1818/1/1/3, SCRO.

Plays, poems, dinners, skittles competitions, and nights out at pubs in Dorchester were all much in evidence during the summer excavations, often with teams organized into diggers versus staff. Wedlake had a motorbike which proved invaluable for victory laps, one of which he took with Verney Wheeler on pillion.[28]

With so many young people in such a casual and lively atmosphere, there was naturally a certain amount of romance. The deep pits couples worked in proved a particular temptation to unarchaeological diversions. However, Verney Wheeler always had an eye on events, and in the same way that she would unobtrusively move a poor excavator to the 'chicken run' zone of the dig where they could scrape harmlessly, she would move an amorous young man to a different section before he could really manage to distract himself— or anyone else.[29]

KITTENS AND OYSTER SHELLS: AN ENDLESS STREAM OF FINDS

One of the greatest problems Maiden Castle presented was an embarrassment of riches. From the discovery of a mutilated burial in the first few days, through the much-argued-over skeletons of the 'war cemetery' at the dig's end, finds and features came forth in such quantity that there seemed a very real possibility that the excavators would be overwhelmed. The London Museum acted as a clearing-house for the archiving and conservation of finds, and the clearest indication of the Wheelers', and especially Verney Wheeler's, importance to the dig is the long trail of finds that went to London to be cleaned, catalogued, and eventually dispatched all the way back to the County Museum in Dorchester. Verney Wheeler's supervision of the process during her museum months in London was worth the cost and difficulties of haulage. She also had valuable term-time access to the large pool of free, semi-trained labour represented by the new UCL archaeology students.

Wedlake and Drew kept both Wheelers apprised of local situations, but Verney Wheeler corresponded more with the former. She always addressed him as Wedlake in writing. For Verney Wheeler,

---

[28] Hawkes (1982: 165).   [29] Ibid. 166–9.

addressing someone by their last name could be a sign of respect—
when she refers to 'Seton-Williams' and 'Miss Glasby', the context
leaves no doubt which woman she thinks the better archaeologist.
Her nickname of 'Old Lad' for V. E. Nash-Williams shows a similarly
boyish Edwardian slang. In Wedlake's case, though, it might reflect
his subordinate status on the dig—he was a hired man, not a social
equal. Wheeler called him Will from the beginning, the diminutive
pointing up Wedlake's dependent position. The older man was also
not above scheduling Wedlake's working summer for him. Though
this may seems a little high-handed, or even proprietary, in retrospect
his advice was always excellent and Wedlake appreciated it greatly.[30]

Verney Wheeler's letters to Wedlake cover a wide variety of subjects; as usual she was required to deal with a wide variety of trivial
details about the dig at long distance during the winter. This included
updates on the welfare of a pair of kittens that had spent the summer
in the finds shed as general pets, and been taken back to the
London Museum with the rest of the finds in the fall. The inanimate
small finds were even more demanding. Verney Wheeler wrote a little
despairingly on the subject to Wedlake on 16 November 1935, the last
letter of hers he preserved. In the first two sentences, Verney Wheeler
disposes of the extra excavation photographs very thoughtfully.

> Will you accept and distribute any or none of these prints as you think
> best? They are only Cookie's [M. B. Cookson's] rough pulls, they don't
> do the negatives justice therefore; but they are 'spare'—so I thought
> some of the men might like them [. . .] We have indexed 600 small
> finds so far (a lot of them rubbish it's true, from the Museum point of
> view) and haven't even touched Site F.[31]

Some of the 'rubbish' was got rid of almost instantly, labelled attrac-
tively and then sold as souvenirs to the many visitors the site drew. The
practice had begun in a minor way at Verulamium, where Roman
oyster shells were sold for a penny. Those interested in tracing economic fluctuations may like to know that surplus stock drove the price
of shells down to a half-penny at Maiden Castle. Wheeler marketed
the strategy heavily in the Maiden Castle report, in a section of the

---

[30] See e.g. R.E.M. Wheeler to William J. Wedlake, 14 March 1939. Box 127:
2004.77/1, DCMA.
[31] TVW to William J. Wedlake, 16 November 1935. Box 127: 2004.77/1, DCMA.

introduction titled 'Finance'. Ultimately it has never caught on, but his suggestion of an on-site gift shop has its modern adherents. It echoes Verney Wheeler's advice to Nash-Williams at Caerleon, when she suggests he keep offprints of her shorter excavation report in the dig shed for a quick sale to tourists.[32]

> [A] well-stocked post-card stall is as popular as it is profitable. Picture post-cards of the site can be produced at a cost of little more than a halfpenny each and will sell readily at twopence each. Interim reports of the work, produced at fourpence each, will sell at one shilling each. (Approximately 64,000 postcards and 16,000 interim reports were sold at Maiden Castle.) And trivial oddments such as beach-pebble sling-stones, fragments of Roman tile, Roman oyster-shells, scraps of surface-pottery, all marked in Indian ink with the name of the site, sell readily for a few pence each, and, under proper control, are an entirely justifiable source of income.[33]

It is not clear how much bulk material was sold off in this way, or what quality it was. One of the great arguments against this type of sale is that it is impossible to be sure what material will be of use to researchers of the future, whose priorities and technology cannot be anticipated. At least the bulk materials were thoroughly documented before they were sold. Any member of a small county museum service may be excused a sneaking sympathy for any system by which the seemingly endless number of archaeological deposits marked 'Bulk Roman tile—10 kg' might be somewhat reduced.

Finds judged good enough for a trip to London were eventually returned to Dorset. Although there were some initial plans for building a museum on the site itself (like the one in progress at Verulamium), it was eventually decided to integrate the site's results into the excellent Dorset County Museum in Dorchester, under the auspices of the Dorset Natural History and Archaeological Society. As Drew was the Museum's Director and the Society's Field Secretary, as well as the dig's co-director, this was triply appropriate.[34] The solution

---

[32] TVW to V. E. Nash-Williams, 19 June 1929. Caerleon site archive, NMWA. The 1928 report was for a long time reprinted as the Office of Works general guide to Caerleon.

[33] Wheeler (1943: 3).

[34] The archives of the Dorset Natural History and Archaeological Society (DCMA) are still held by the Dorset County Museum, and are some of the most complete and easily studied that I have engaged with. The former Museum Curator, Mr Peter Woodward, is mentioned more fully in the acknowledgements, but it is a pleasure

also allowed Maiden Castle to be maintained solely as an atmospheric earthworks, without the additional roads and construction a museum would have entailed.

Letters between the Wheelers and Wedlake also dealt with ongoing minor winter work on the site: the filling-in of finished trenches and occasionally some work on specific sites. Both Wheelers encouraged Wedlake to take on increasing responsibility at these times, asking him to write them formal reports on various pieces of work and showing him they valued his judgement as a colleague as well as an employee. The Wheelers also made an effort to bring him to London for their annual Maiden Castle work-in-progress reports at the Society of Antiquaries.

'IT SEEMS IMPOSSIBLE THAT MAIDEN CASTLE CAN GO ON WITHOUT HER . . .'[35]

In the midst of the bustle of preparation for the 1936 summer season, only six weeks after giving the annual Maiden Castle interim report to the Society of Antiquaries with Wheeler and Drew, Verney Wheeler died. It was wholly unexpected. She had gone into a nursing home for a minor operation on her toe, waiting until Wheeler was travelling in the Middle East and not telling him about it before he went. She considered the operation very small beer, and like many people wanted to keep her medical procedures private until they were over. The details surrounding her death are looked at in the next chapter, and the impact it had on the lives and careers of those closest to her considered. At the moment, the narrative must press on with Maiden Castle. It is enough to know that she developed abdominal pains in the nursing home, and was sent from there to the National Temperance Hospital in Bloomsbury. In a grim coincidence, it was only a few streets from her first home with Rik at 16 Taviton Square. Appendicitis was wrongly diagnosed, but she appeared to be recovering well

to thank him and his museum again here for their hospitality, and for his own insights into the role of Charles D. Drew and the Dorset County Museum in the Maiden Castle dig. It is hoped that he will soon commit his own thoughts and theories about this interesting man to paper.

[35] Charles Drew to William J. Wedlake, 5 May 1936. Box 127: 2004.77/1, DCMA.

from the exploratory operation it engendered when she died of a pulmonary embolism early on the morning of 15 April. Her son had visited her the night before with a college friend. Her husband was in the Middle East with another woman, visiting archaeological sites.[36]

Verney Wheeler's teaching and guidance set the tone of the excavation at Maiden Castle from the start, and yet when she dies there is little trace of it in the site archive. Only a few letters in the Wedlake archive bear witness to her death, usually with sympathy for Wheeler and concern for his work. His dependence on his wife was well known, and more than one of his colleagues was a little apprehensive about what direction he might take without her.

> Dr Wheeler spoke very sadly of his loss, and said how much he would have to depend on you now.[37]

When Prior Horne wrote these words to Wedlake in May 1936, he could not have realized how much Verney Wheeler's death would force her husband to depend on others. Deprived of his first, best partner, he assigned her tasks to many others—in particular to Wedlake, the archaeologist Molly Cotton, Veronica Seton-Williams, and Colonel Drew. They, especially Drew, took on the minutiae of daily management and the detailed overseeing of the general work, but no one person could take her place, or fill as many, varied roles as gracefully as she had.

For Wheeler, no one person could replace Verney Wheeler, with whom he had worked for so long in intellectual harmony. But considered coldly, her death was by no means the total disaster for him, or for the larger cause of British archaeology, that it would have been even five years earlier. Verney Wheeler was always a teacher, and at Maiden Castle she was in the peak of her powers. By the time she died she was able to delegate tasks to any number of trained assistants—men and women she could trust to do a job properly because she had taught them how herself. She was still invaluable, but for more than her ability to lift mosaics or identify layers. At Maiden Castle, she was truly a leader. Nowhere is this

---

[36] Hawkes (1982: 137–8).
[37] Ethelbert Horne to William J. Wedlake, 20 May 1936. Box 127: 2004.77/1, DCMA.

better proved than in the late site notebooks, where one finds none of the mistakes that so irritated her in the early days of Site B. The dig kept the same efficient, high-quality section notes she had taught them even after her death. Verney Wheeler never rendered herself unnecessary or redundant—her experience and personality are still sadly missed years later. But on a technical level, she would have been proud to see her students graduate into independence after her death (Fig. 23).

They missed her badly. The two last years on Maiden Castle were not happy ones. It was hard even for Molly Alwyn Cotton, who had worked closely with both Wheelers and was fond of both, to take her friend's place and maintain the level of intuitive control by which the dead woman had managed both Rik and a dig. Veronica Seton-Williams also tried to help, though for a little while her love for Tessa made it difficult for her and Wheeler to work together easily.

Before we left Acre [where Seton-Williams was working with John Garstang] news came of the death of Mrs Wheeler. This was totally

Figure 23. The eastern entrance of Maiden Castle under excavation in 1936, photographed by M. B. Cookson.

unexpected and a great loss to me as she had always advised and helped
me in my archaeological career, and I had a deep affection for her as a
person. She had been unsparing of herself in her archaeological work,
an excellent organiser and was very good with people [. . .] On my
return to England I went back to excavate with Wheeler at Maiden
Castle. The death of his wife had made things very difficult for him, and
Molly Cotton and I had quite a time organising things so that they
worked smoothly.

I became one of his site supervisors on trench H [. . .] But for me by
1936 the magic of the great hill had gone: Mrs Wheeler was dead. Rik
Wheeler was in many ways a perfectionist with drive and ambition but
no patience with the minutiae of the day-to-day running of things. He
was a difficult man to work with [. . .] he said to me 'I can see what
I wish to achieve but when I fall short of this I tend to lash out at the
nearest person.'[38]

Wheeler had more or less discreetly continued his pursuit of other
women throughout Verney Wheeler's life. Increasingly, those women
were their students. While she was aware of and tortured by it, neither
allowed this part of his personality to take too much precedence over
their archaeological work. Now that she was gone, he let himself go
sexually. It could not go unnoticed by either the women he romanced
or the ones who disapproved. Those who were attracted to Wheeler
must have felt the time had come to finally secure the primary place
in his affections, and those who loved Verney Wheeler never forgave
him for what they saw as his emotional contribution to her early
death. To add to the difficulties, it was on Maiden Castle that Wheeler
met and simultaneously pursued his next two wives. His second,
Mavis de Vere Cole, was one of Augustus John's mistress-models
and visited Maiden Castle with the artist in 1937. The pair married in
early 1939. She was a charming, voracious, adorable woman and, as
Wheeler found, quite uncontrollable. The marriage did not last long,
though they remained friends long after its dissolution. His third wife
was Margaret (Kim) Collingridge, one of the students who became a
site supervisor at Maiden Castle. This marriage was also a failure,
though Kim's devout Catholicism prevented another divorce.[39]

[38] Seton-Williams (1988: 54–6).
[39] Hawkes (1982: 139).

WAS IT A SUCCESS?

The dig went on, but while Verney Wheeler's death could not halt it, growing international conflicts could and did. The publication did not appear until 1945, by which time Wheeler was already leading a squadron of field gunners. He had enlisted as soon as possible on the declaration of war, and enjoyed himself tremendously in the desert.[40]

The report was enormous and beautifully illustrated, issued by the Society of Antiquaries despite paper shortages. Its technical details have stood up to rigorous modern research, but the same cannot be said for Wheeler's synthesis. His problems at Verulamium recurred here in a greater magnitude, for example in his discussion of the so-called 'war cemetery' that emerged in the last part of the dig—a cemetery he interpreted as reflecting the violent taking of the earthworks by the Roman forces of AD 43. Niall Sharples has outlined the problems with Wheeler's interpretation clearly and without heat. The bodies he sees as hastily bundled into graves were in fact placed fairly carefully. The thick layer of charcoal at the entrance, which to Wheeler means the burning of homes, indicates the presence of iron working to Sharples. Given Wheeler's general predilection for eventful explanations, and the general European political situation as he wrote the report, it is not hard to see how he could violently magnify events. And in retrospect, the Roman occupation of Maiden Castle represents the shortest part of its history. While we need not believe everything Rik Wheeler writes, his mistakes should not blind us to his far more numerous successes. One cannot but wonder if he would have gone so far if Verney Wheeler had co-authored the report with him. The answer is yes, if Verulamium is any guide.

More importantly, while the Wheeler method emerged for the first time at Lydney Park, Maiden Castle was and is the point most identified with its real establishment as a school of thought. It was the report that most perfectly embodied all that the Wheelers stood for as archaeologists: technical rigour and a full presentation of materials unearthed, as well as a literary discussion of their meaning calculated to appeal to a larger audience.

---

[40] See Wheeler (1955: ch. 9) for a full account.

Maiden Castle had its critics, though the Second World War delayed their discussion. Chief among them was W. F. Grimes, who wrote a critical review of it in 1945 after taking over Wheeler's job as Keeper of the London Museum. He was not impressed with the selection of digging spots, and felt that Wheeler had deliberately chosen spots reflecting brief but highly coloured and violent parts of the earthwork's history, rather than digging for daily life in the long term settlements.[41] Selective excavation became a major criticism of Wheeler—and two of its most energetic opponents were his former students, J. N. L. Myres and C. F. C. Hawkes. Myres and Wheeler were still grappling over Verulamium when Hawkes lectured critically on selective excavation at the newly opened Institute of Archaeology.[42] Whether Hawkes was affected by Verney Wheeler's death in the way he phrased his criticism is open to debate, but for Myres it remained a small but steady personal flame. Despite all this, as always we must judge the 1930s excavations to have been a success. The problems of Wheeler's interpretation are minor compared to the extent of the work achieved, and the degree to which it was witnessed and taken part in by the public.

Verney Wheeler died halfway through the progress of the Maiden Castle dig. The report was published under Wheeler's name alone, though naturally she provided substantial input before her death and co-authored the first three interim reports presented to the Society of Antiquaries. Were Verney Wheeler and Wheeler growing closer or further apart professionally at this point? Did she fade out in the light of his increasing glamour, or quietly create a separate and less obvious path for herself, one that allowed her to retain their powerful partnership, but also to increase the self-respect and intellectual satisfaction her work brought her?

This question is in many ways the key to Tessa Wheeler. A person—especially a woman—who is denied an outlet for his or her emotions will force them into a new channel. Tessa and Rik's marriage might be solid at bottom, but it had been from its crowded first days in military camps a source of emotional, financial, and even physical insecurity in her life. Other Edwardian women might have turned to a religion or a cause or their children to give them a driving

---

[41] See Jacquetta Hawkes' notes from her interview of W. F. Grimes. JHA.

[42] Hawkes (1982: 176). See also Christopher Hawkes's review of the report: Hawkes (1944).

purpose. Tessa, intellectual, intelligent, interested in the world, turned instead to archaeology and found in it a fulfilment her husband could not give her—though ironically he provided the means. As their marriage aged, it brought her less and less emotional happiness, but more and more professional interest. The importance of this to her character was such that had she lived, Rik's later work would probably still have been the Wheelers' work, and it would have been much the better for her rigorous involvement.

This chapter should close with another literary passage: Wheeler's dedication on the frontispiece of the enormous Maiden Castle report.

TO THE MEMORY OF TESSA VERNEY WHEELER.
I could wish that this book were a worthier memorial to the name which I have written here above.[43]

---

[43] Wheeler (1943: frontispiece).

11

The Legacies of the Dead

In April 1936, the Wheelers were at high tide. The Institute was finally off the ground, almost ready to move into its new quarters in St John's Lodge, and with an eager young crowd of students waiting to take possession. The Museum of London was popular with casual visitors and increasingly well respected in the more rarefied curatorial world. Both Wheelers sat on influential committees at the Society of Antiquaries and elsewhere; and in early April they presented, along with Charles Drew, their third interim report on Maiden Castle at Burlington House. Wheeler's written reports on the dig were being published in the *Antiquaries Journal* on a yearly basis.

Wheeler and Verney Wheeler's influence was extending up and down the professional and academic ladder. They had never been more powerful, or more active, in the small, widely influential world of British archaeology. Their personal life was equally busy. Rik's serial infidelities had increased in number as he aged, and his predatory habits become more marked on digs. Not for nothing was it said that the best way to get promoted on a Wheeler dig was to be an attractive blonde. The pro-Tessa/pro-Rik division observers often noticed among workers (and in their circle of close friends and colleagues) was a natural outgrowth of the situation.

The effect on Tessa's health was not negligible. She suffered from bad migraines, and even blackouts, as early as the excavations at Caerleon. While her declining health was partly due to the long, unrelenting working hours, the emotional stress she suffered played a role in her growing inability to recover quickly or completely. One of the more obvious physical results was a painful duodenal ulcer, a common, unromantic gastric response to anxiety. After her death, friends expressed astonishment that her small frame had held up as long as it had.[1]

Rik's affairs with young women working for them may not have affected his work, but they often made his wife's working environment very difficult. Still, their professional partnership as the Wheelers remained intact. Rik's girlfriends were always pretty and usually intelligent, but none had Tessa's depth of knowledge or archaeological instinct. It is also doubtful that any could anticipate Rik's own intellect with the same degree of accuracy (and vice versa). As a partner, she was irreplaceable. She and he had been students together, matured together, done their first professional work together. Their minds had developed in response to one another.

With the receipt of the Petrie Collection, the Institute had perforce become a focus for Near Eastern research. As its physical establishment grew nearer to a reality, Rik decided it was necessary that he have 'something more than paper-knowledge of the Near Eastern field'. He had never visited that region, although British archaeologists had been active there from the earliest days of the discipline and were at the time particularly powerful. He writes in *Still Digging* that Tessa did not accompany him because of the lack of funds.[2] This was no doubt true, but his trip was in pursuit of a woman as well as antiquity. For six weeks he travelled, criticized, noted, and loved with his usual vigour. At the Gare du Nord in Paris, he acquired his first English newspaper since setting out, and opened it to Tessa's obituary.[3]

Molly Aylmer Cotton, who took Tessa's place to some extent at Maiden Castle, was 'perhaps the most fully mature human being in the Wheelers' archaeological circle'.[4] She had overlapped with Rik's travels slightly, meeting him unexpectedly in Jerusalem with his current girlfriend. Realizing that the timing of his return journey meant he might not learn of his wife's death before arriving back in London, she met every French boat train for two days and nights so that he might be spared the shock as much as possible. It was a kindness he never forgot.[5]

Tessa had taken advantage of his absence to schedule a small foot operation—nothing requiring major surgery, but something she wished to take care of while he was away. The procedure was so minor that it

---

[1] Hawkes (1982: 137).   [2] Wheeler (1955: 110).   [3] Ibid. 61–2.
[4] Hawkes (1982: 135).   [5] Wheeler (1955: 62).

did not even interrupt her composition of an article for the *Numismatic Chronicle* on the Verulamium theatre coins.[6] It was her last article, prepared for publication though not substantially changed or added to after her death by B. H. St J. O'Neill at Wheeler's request.

The operation was performed in a nursing home rather than a more formal medical setting, and something—what, is still unclear— went wrong.[7] Tessa developed severe abdominal pains. The doctors diagnosed appendicitis and she was transferred to the National Temperance Hospital on the Hampstead Road. It was not the best medical facility in London, but it was quite adequate. Oddly enough, it was within a short walk of both St John's Lodge, which she had just earmarked for the Institute, and 16 Taviton Street, where she, Rik, and Michael had first lived together as a young family.

In 1936 a diagnosis of appendicitis was confirmed by surgical examination of the organ itself. Tessa was duly operated on—and her appendix found to be perfectly healthy. Her health seemed to improve briefly after the pointless operation, and she felt quite out of danger. Michael Wheeler, by that point an Oxford undergraduate, came to see her in the hospital on 14 April with a college friend, and they had a cheerful evening. He went back to 108 Park Street, where his parents were then living, to stay for the night.

At two a.m., the phone rang. The doctors at the National Temperance Hospital thought he ought to return as quickly as possible; Michael feared the worst. When he arrived at the hospital, his mother had been dead for two hours. A post mortem confirmed that her death was the result of the unnecessary surgery and the resulting infection and pneumonia.[8] Tessa was weak and run down, in no condition to fight off fresh illness.

Among her friends, the immediate assumption was that she had died from a broken heart—that Rik had killed her with his philandering.[9] This sentimental view is rightly refuted by Hawkes and others close to both Wheelers, not just one. Tessa had been a woman in the midst of at least three major and interesting professional projects, any one of which provided more than enough incentive to live. She was beloved

[6] T. Verney Wheeler (1937).
[7] Medical records from this period have been destroyed; the information given here was obtained from Verney Wheeler's death certificate.
[8] Hawkes (1982: 137–8).
[9] See ibid. 137–9 for a contemporary's account of her last days and death.

by her friends, and had just spent a typically enjoyable evening with her loving son. She was not at a first-rate hospital when she died—and had just suffered an unnecessary, major operation, at a time when an appendectomy was still a dangerous undertaking. Against all this evidence can be weighed the infidelities of her much-loved husband, who had caused her an inexcusable amount of personal grief and yet quite failed to kill her over the past ten years. It does not seem likely she would break under the strain at this point.

THE EFFECT ON RIK WHEELER

The most moving passages of *Still Digging*—in some ways the only passages of real human emotion—are those in which Rik describes learning of Tessa's death. For thematic reasons, he chose to place it early in his life, just after his memories of the battle of Passchendaele in 1917. Both were under the sub-heading 'Standards of Misery'. Passchendaele, for Rik, represented the absolute 'nadir of physical misery'. Learning of Tessa's death represented the peak of mental misery, and marked the end of his ability to feel a certain kind of love. Such devotion as he could give died with her.

> Of neither episode need I, nor indeed could I, say much. But I have been acutely aware of the significance of both from the moment of their happening [. . .]The shock [of Tessa's death] passed away, leaving the subtly impaired facilities of a first 'stroke'.[10]

Wheeler, with his typical black humour, viewed both experiences as gifts of sorts; nothing could ever hurt him as these two events had, and thus he was to some extent insulated from the suffering of life from then on.

The memoir returns to Tessa's death at the appropriate chronological point as well. It is the only point in the book where he allows Tessa to speak directly to the reader, quoting rather than interpreting her.

> I remember turning back as I went down the stairs of our little Park Street flat, and can still hear the words which followed me in her quiet

---

[10] Wheeler (1955: 59).

voice: 'Good-bye—and remember, you are very precious'. That was the last time I saw her.[11]

Rik's war service had left him 'oppressed with the brevity of life', but he also lacked any strong spiritual views to comfort him; for him, the dead were gone forever.[12] He famously scoffed at the idea of the dead being disturbed by archaeology.

> They have been dead a long time [. . .] and they were going to be dead a long time [. . .] they're still dead [. . .]We do no harm to these poor chaps. When I'm dead you can dig me up ten times for all I care [. . .] I won't haunt you—much.[13]

On the other hand, he was also a man of enormous animal high spirits, and by the resumption of the Maiden Castle work he had also resumed his womanizing. He was primarily in pursuit of Mavis de Vere Cole, the artist's model and amiable good-time girl who briefly became his second wife. At the same time, he wrote a sad letter to J. N. L. Myres—whether before or after the disaster of the Verulamium report is not clear.

> [E]very sign of the book [the Verulamium report] reopens a wound which isn't much likely to heal [. . .] Anyway there it is. I'm rather old and tired tonight, my dear Nowell, and you've helped me. Oh bless you. Rik.[14]

He was right; the wound never healed. No other woman could be all that Tessa was to him, emotionally and intellectually. Mavis was lovely, but as sexually rapacious and amoral as Rik himself; their marriage was an enjoyable disaster and the two parted friends.[15] His third wife, Kim Collingridge, was, despite her Maiden Castle training, not the archaeologist Verney Wheeler had been. She lacked the innovating, improving instinct that made Verney Wheeler special as a professional, and was simply not interested enough in archaeology to subordinate her whole life to it—even if it came as a condition of her marriage. More importantly, she lacked the toughness needed to create her own professional identity alongside, rather than in

---

[11] Ibid. 110.   [12] Ibid. 63.   [13] Bahn (1984: 128).

[14] R. E. M. Wheeler to J. N. L. Myres, 23 June or July 1936. J. N. L. Myres Papers, Bodleian Library, Oxford.

[15] Owen (1974: 89–116).

opposition to, Wheeler's.[16] It is rather a shock to meet Kim towards the end of *Still Digging*, when she makes a momentary cameo; if the page is skipped, it is possible to finish the book imagining Rik Wheeler as a pure-hearted widower, forever chastely devoted to the memory of his wife.[17] And perhaps this impression is not wholly inaccurate, if we (generously) consider his intellectual, emotional devotion rather than his sexual fidelity.

Even in the 1930s, there were those who wondered why Tessa never divorced Rik, or vice versa. The simplest answer is probably the correct one in both cases. Tessa was a very loving and devoted woman, and Rik had loved her deeply in the past—perhaps more deeply, or more truly, than anyone else in his life. More importantly, one aspect of their marriage had only ever grown stronger through the years: the intellectual. Whatever happened elsewhere in their lives, they were always able to meet on a professional plane at a level no one else could provide, and this contact of the minds gave their work together its strength and their relationship its permanency.

Professionally, Verney Wheeler's death reveals for a moment the true extent of her labours. Molly Cotton, Veronica Seton-Williams, and Charles Peers all had to step in to replace her at Maiden Castle—three people as the equivalent of one small woman. While Wheeler never wrote an official obituary for Verney Wheeler, he included a memorial of sorts in *Archaeology from the Earth*: a militaristic description of the ideal 'Deputy Director'.[18] It is the most complete recognition he made of the role she played in their excavations, though it still leaves out her innovations in objects management and technique. Those have a place under other thematic headings in the volume.[19]

It is the most complete description extant of their professional relationship. When Wheeler speaks of the 'Director' he is speaking of himself, and when he describes the perfect deputy director, he is thinking of Verney Wheeler. Particularly of note is his use of the female pronoun in the second sentence of the passage quoted. It is the only job

---

[16] As may be judged by Wheeler's autobiography, in which Verney Wheeler plays a large role and Kim is barely mentioned. When she is, it is not in an archaeological or professional context. Wheeler (1955: 207).

[17] Ibid.

[18] His description of the ideal director is certainly a self-portrait. Wheeler (1954: 130–37).

[19] See e.g. ibid. ch. 13, 'The Pottery Shed'. He especially acknowledges Molly Cotton's help at the beginning of this chapter.

description in the chapter in which he makes that distinction, and suggests the possibility of the job being ordinarily done by a woman.[20]

> While the director is the operational leader of the expedition, the deputy director is primarily in charge of the administration. He (or she) deals with the well-being and pay of the various grades of staff, and is personally responsible for the smooth workings of the machine. He should also be a trained field-archaeologist, in close touch with the director and able in emergency to represent him, but is not officially responsible for the scientific aspects of the work. If he is a specialist in some relevant branch of archaeology, so much the better.
>
> The following are amongst his duties: (a) Billeting or housing [...] (b) Equipment [...] (c) Accounts [...] (d) Supplies [...] (e) Hospital [first aid ...][21]

Wheeler saw the director (himself) as the general, in openly military terms. His account of the director's duties runs to several pages of qualitative (rather than purely practical) description. It is *very* thinly veiled autobiography. The deputy director must be able to take on any physical task the dig requires. The director, while well versed in the practicalities, should make the synthesis of the site and its report his priority.

> [Unlike photography, draftsmanship, linguistics ...] the qualities which *cannot* be delegated [by the director] are the instant understanding of structural and stratigraphic problems, the quick and accurate correlation of the various groups of evidence as they appear, the reasoned appreciation [...] of the immediate need of the work as it proceeds [...] the capacity for undelayed but well-founded decision, and the ability to ensure even progress in all the various departments and sub-departments of the enterprise. To these qualities must be added a clear anticipation of the need of the ultimate report, and the capacity to present that report in clear, concise, and intelligible form. In other words and in brief, a precise and trained mind and an informed and informing imagination are the qualities of the director of an archaeological expedition [...] First and foremost, the director must be a free agent, free from administrative detail. His primary and constant duty is to circulate from site to site and from workshop to workshop.[22]

Archaeology from the Earth, that seminal textbook of twentieth-century practical archaeology, would be entirely different if Verney

---

[20] Ibid. 137.   [21] Ibid. 137–8.   [22] Ibid. 134–5.

Wheeler had not been Wheeler's deputy director during the first twenty years of his career. In the description of how small finds should be organized and cared for, her detailed mind surfaces again years after her death.[23] Indeed, when he wants to explain the difficult specialist task of removing and conserving a Roman mosaic, he simply cites and then reprints Verney Wheeler's 1933 article on the subject for the *Museums Journal*. He never found another deputy director, or even group of co-deputy directors, who lived up to the ideal Tessa had left him with: someone who was his intellectual equal, but still willing and able to take on the tedious day-to-day running and recording of an excavation's work that he disliked. In these circumstances it is not surprising that Verney Wheeler developed the objects recording techniques that form the most applicable portion of the Wheeler method today, or that she is remembered today as the better field archaeologist.[24] She simply got more practice.

After Tessa's death, Rik had to cut down on his commitments. It was no longer possible for him to race from project to project the way he liked to race from site to site within an excavation; he had no partner whom he could unquestioningly trust to work steadily and at his own exacting standards in his absence. Of all the 'what ifs?' in this story, the most interesting is the most unanswerable. What if the *Wheelers* had been sent to India after 1945?

VERNEY WHEELER'S LEGACY

There are two major reasons archaeologists are remembered after their careers (and usually lives) are over. These play into the creation of hero-predecessors touched upon already, and may be called the locational and the methodological. We remember Evans 'of Knossos' and Woolley 'of Ur', but Mortimer Wheeler and Tessa Verney Wheeler of 'the Wheeler Method'. It is interesting that Wheeler, with all his charisma and personal force, never became firmly associated with one site in this way, even in his Indian work. Perhaps his

---

[23] Ibid. ch. 9 .

[24] Not least by their Verulamium student Kathleen Kenyon. See Chapter 7, and below.

various projects were *too* varied—any one of them could have and did define the careers of less strenuous men.

This emphasis on methodology comes as an anticlimax to the more usual and robust image of the virile archaeologist striding out across a dig's landscape. But it was the sound methodology of the Wheelers, and their insistence on teaching those methods, that opened up archaeology to generations of new students, helping them to learn an entirely new skill in a systematic and effective way. One could truthfully say 'the Wheelers *of Verulamium*', or Wales, or Maiden Castle, or Lydney Park, and they are occasionally so identified. However, what matters about the Wheelers in the larger history of archaeology remains the Method they engendered, and for which their name remains the clearest shorthand.

When pondering this frequent locational identification of archaeologists, it is helpful to consider the work of Joseph MacGillivray. He has written brilliantly and provocatively about the role of what he refers to as relative or creative archaeology, particularly in *Minotaur*, his 2000 biography of that supremely creative archaeologist Arthur Evans. MacGillivray's view is, in brief, that there is no such thing as absolute archaeological or historical truth, merely a 'succession of [. . .] relative histories that satisfy a set of changing [social] requirements for a while'. He believes that archaeologists must not just admit, but embrace, the inevitability that they will actively and creatively interpret what they find through the lenses of their own experience and reasonable mental requirements. Like most liberation ideologies, his proposal walks a knife-edge between a necessary recognition of the realities of life and an unprofitable escape into anarchy. But to ignore it would ensure the withering and death of its subject.

REMEMBERING VERNEY WHEELER

Tessa Verney Wheeler's claim to remembrance is threefold.

Technique

Verney Wheeler's focus on the small-scale, technical aspects of excavations can be seen on every dig where she was a participant.

Given this, it is unsurprising that the Wheeler Method's emphasis on accurate and reproducible methodologies for objects recording and analysis can be laid at Verney Wheeler's door. The object context sheets she developed almost as she taught them to her students are still a familiar and essential feature of today's digs. Modern researchers examining Wheeler sites prove the value of her detailed attention to stratigraphy, objects, and context. It is, ironically, possible to reassess and even correct published Wheeler and Verney Wheeler site reports, via the evidence so carefully collated by the pair.[25]

Teaching

Verney Wheeler's effect on the students she trained was considerable; it may be judged by the support and muted passion her memory elicited years after her death. The combination of personal warmth and innovative technique was a very potent one. J. N. L. Myres always remained quietly devoted to her. She stayed with him when visiting Oxford in 1930, and the charming letter she wrote to her 'dearest Child' has been quoted already.[26] From Kathleen Kenyon comes the remarkable personal tribute, which Kenyon would only acknowledge privately, that Verney Wheeler was the source of 'what she had learned of dig management and field technique, notably the detailed control of stratigraphy and pottery recording'.[27] Aileen Fox was grateful to her as a trailblazer; Veronica Seton-Williams dedicated her autobiography to her former teacher and remained, like Myres, a little in love with her throughout her life.

The emotional and intellectual impacts of Verney Wheeler were closely allied, unsurprisingly considering the parental style of management she and Wheeler practised. It is unnecessary to separate the two fully. But it must be acknowledged that the methods Verney Wheeler inculcated in her students, and which they went on to pass down to theirs, existed independently of her personal charms. Those charms aided the transmission of ideas, but the qualities of the lectures themselves are what matters. Her intellectual DNA continues to unfold in the present day, and its features may be traced in both

[25] For examples, see Segontium, or Lydney Park.
[26] M. V. Taylor to J. N. L. Myres, 18 October 1930. J. N. L. Myres papers, Bodleian Library.
[27] Moorey (1992: 96).

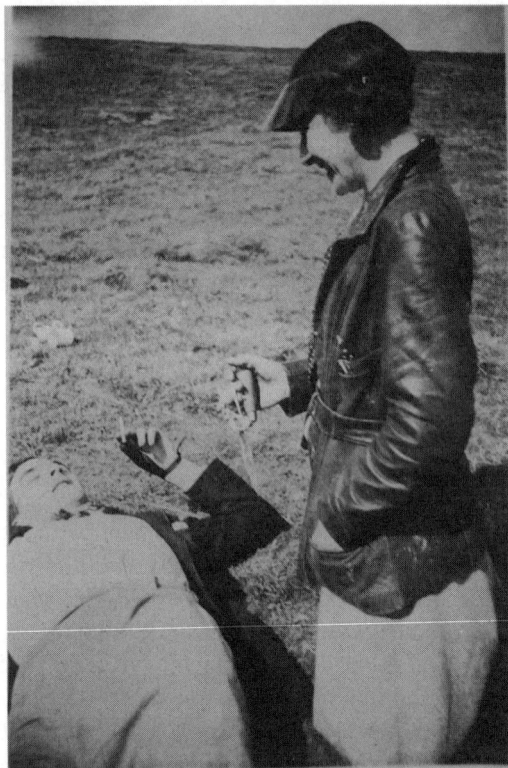

Figure 24. Verney Wheeler in an unguarded shot with a young friend.

modern excavation methods and the Institute of Archaeology at UCL. She was the heir of the women who preceded her, and the progenitrix of the women and men who have been quoted throughout this work (Fig. 24).

Public work

University students were not the only people to benefit from Verney Wheeler's teaching. In her public work, especially her museum lecturing and her work encouraging the public to visit active digs, she seems to have agreed with her husband wholeheartedly: that explaining one's work to the public, either in person or via the media, was essential. There was the ever-present need to raise money and justify funds already received; the almost moral duty to explain to the public where their money went; and the value to the archaeologist of having to break down and defend his ideas explicably. In many ways, she was a promoter or press officer in the modern sense: she made good use of the media, but they came to her for information rather than the other way around. The best practical examples of this in Verney Wheeler's life are the London Museum and Verulamium, but it is a theme going back to her earliest days lecturing to the Geological Association in Cardiff. On her death at Maiden Castle, Wheeler was forced to formally assign someone to deal exclusively with the press for the first time. This was Margot Eates, who also took over two other Verney Wheeler jobs: touring visitors and introducing new recruits to the site.[28]

VERNEY WHEELER AND WOMEN IN ARCHAEOLOGY

Tessa Verney Wheeler is a transitional figure, forming a vital bridge between women like Hilda Petrie, Gertrude Evans, and Margaret Murray—who had to be invisible or gender-rebels to work in archaeology—and women like Veronica Seton-Williams, who could obtain degrees and jobs in a way at least similar to that of their male friends. It is important to remember how fast progress was, and how these 'generations' of women actually often overlapped by only a few years: Seton-Williams worked in the field with both Hilda Petrie and Verney Wheeler.

Verney Wheeler still made an unobtrusive point of wearing skirt suits to dig, and acted the part of the nurturing and maternal homemaker as well as the trained archaeologist. Her skirt was often noticed in prints by newspaper writers, who juxtaposed and tacitly compared it to the more gamine outfits of her young female students. But she had another example for them as well: when she published, it was under her own name. If she appeared on a title page with her husband, it was because they collaborated on the volume, not because she required his name to give her professional validation.

---

[28] Hawkes (1982: 166).

Figure 25. Verney Wheeler overseeing gridded excavations at Maiden Castle's Site B.

The Wheelers' mother/father approach to leadership is also worthy of greater attention. Most important is the idea that a feminine approach to academic and practical teaching may in fact sometimes work *better* than a traditional masculine approach, or at the very least provide it with a necessary balance (Fig. 25). Verney Wheeler's emphasis on training students to work as a well-organized team, positive reinforcement, and even her nurturing pastoral care are all aspects of the Wheeler legacy that have had as much of a long-term impact on archaeological teaching as her husband's more old fashioned, top-down military discipline. And, like his disciplinary tactics, her nurturing came from outside the field and continues to be applicable within and without it.

Along with Dorothy Garrod and Gertrude Caton-Thompson, Verney Wheeler represents a new generation, one more closely related to Margaret Murray than to Hilda Petrie. Like Murray, the younger woman made an active point of reaching out intellectually, encouraging students to see archaeology as a normal subject for a woman to study and work in. This is Verney Wheeler's great role within the feminist revolution that changed Western society for good and for the better in the twentieth century: she made it normal and even matter-of-fact for a woman to dig, publish, and have an academic life in archaeology, as well as showing that a married woman could still be an intellectual one. That last lesson is sadly still a very necessary one, for men and women of all professions.

The Wheelers should not have completely separate identities as archaeologists; they cannot be viewed in total isolation from one another. They worked closely enough together that their result belonged to both parties, though fortunately it is sometimes possible to determine, as this study does, who did what from the archival evidence. It must be re-stated and remembered that even if Verney Wheeler entered archaeology because of her husband, her work as an archaeologist was valuable independently of this. We cannot give continuing credit for her work to the factor that began her engagement with it, or dismiss her professional career because it did not begin in a way familiar to modern eyes.

WHO WAS TESSA VERNEY WHEELER?

Verney Wheeler is valued today because she represents an early, excellent woman archaeologist, because she was part of a remarkable team, and because she was a vital factor in her great husband's work. Which aspect is most important depends on the angle of consideration. In the context of her age, she was a classic partner-wife, helping her husband achieve far more than any one man could, because he was part of a well-functioning team. Her contemporary visibility on that team reminds us that she was more than his helper—she was his equal. It is again a reflection of the times she moved in, when women were gaining more and more academic and practical legitimacy in all subjects (though true equality was still far away).

To turn the argument around, Verney Wheeler must also be acknowledged as an individual, not just as an early archaeologist, but as one whose teaching and practical technique were superior to the majority of her contemporary colleagues. That statement does not exclude her husband, who often depended on her to take on both roles in their excavations.

It is traditional to end a biography with a subject's death, but Verney Wheeler has been associated long enough with suffering and sudden loss. It is more interesting, and more in keeping with her spirit, to close with a more cheerful moment: a final consideration of Verney Wheeler and her elusive character, beginning with a simple proposal of an alternate history.[29] This means effectively projects her truncated career forward in time, attempting to determine from its real-world trajectory where it might have gone had it not been cut short.

What if Rik Wheeler had died in 1936, and Tessa Verney Wheeler had lived? Would their positions in the history of archaeology be reversed—would he be the footnote, and she the revered elder? The answer can only be yes: Tessa Verney Wheeler would have gone on in archaeology. By 1936 she was independently published and well known within her field. Maiden Castle would have been dedicated to a different Wheeler, and this book would not exist in its present form, because there would already be general biographies and books on Verney Wheeler; perhaps even an autobiography. If this work did exist, it would be about some specific aspect of Verney Wheeler's career as the first major woman to teach and develop Romano-British archaeology. More probably, this book would be about her young husband, who died tragically and whose legacy she always tried to uphold in her own long career, and would make a conscious effort throughout to bring him out of the shadow of his brilliant wife.

It is unlikely that Verney Wheeler would have agitated to be sent abroad as her husband did after the Second World War. Her career would have stayed in Britain, and in the Roman and prehistoric period she found so rewarding. Given her objects orientation and meticulous eye for conservation and discussion, she would probably have remained based at the London Museum—though it is hard to imagine her completely leaving the field, or teaching, both of which she also enjoyed and excelled in.

In the past pages, Verney Wheeler has been approached via the road she would have found most comfortable: her archaeological work. While this book's primary purpose has been to explore her professional career and determine her larger contribution to the discipline of archaeology, it is hoped that (like her students, and the writer) the reader has also felt something of the charm of Tessa Wheeler's personality, of the resilient and radiant little woman

---

[29] The validity of counterfactual history as a technique for considering the past has been well defended and demonstrated, most readably in Gaddis (2002: 100–102).

whose memory was treasured, very privately and protectively, by so many people.

She was a funny, quick, charming woman, always a little shy but also always loving and maternal. The rare, 100-watt grin captured in a few photographs gives some hint of why her smile was always remembered, and spoken of as illuminating. She was more than the stereotype of a 'woman wronged': her devotion to her husband despite his philandering reflected a fully human love that found a way to have an enduring, working relationship despite infidelity. Their intellectual marriage was deeper and more complete the day she died than the day they married, and any attempt to categorize her as a mere Patient Griselda is deflected by the broad, unguarded smile of the candid photographs and the snapping wit of her letters. The words chosen to describe her by her friends after she died are absolutely accurate: 'valiant', 'courageous', 'ardent'. As far as a life can be judged from the outside, she was mainly happy: in her husband, her son, her students, and, most importantly, in her work.

A typewritten poem was found in R. E. M. Wheeler's papers after his death. It is signed 'J.C.R.', but the author has never been identified beyond those initials. Its subject, though, is instantly familiar.

> 'T.V.W.'
> Rememb'ring you we will remember love,
> Laughter and kindliness, not for the few
> but free to all. The sunshine from above
> That flooded Verulamium's fields and grove,
> Was no more generous to us than you.
> Now, in high fellowship among your peers,
> And all our bitter offering of tears
> But blurs the gracious courage of your years.
> Not grief but gratitude must be your due,
> For, not content with giving us so much
> You still transmute the fabric of the mind
> And make us momently your debtors, who,
> Heirs to that heritage you leave behind,
> Remember love when we remember you.

APPENDIX 1

Timeline of Main Events
in Tessa Verney Wheeler's Life

1893   Tessa Verney born in Johannesburg, South Africa, to Annie
            Kilburn and (?) Dr John Verney.

1899?   Annie Kilburn returns to England with Tessa, enters into
            common-law marriage with Theophilus Morgan Davis. They
            live at 225 Lewisham High Road, London. Tessa attends the
            Addey and Stanhope School in south-east London.

1911   Tessa matriculates at University College London to read History.
            Studies (in succession) Latin and Roman History, English,
            French, English History, History, and Italian. Is formally
            courted by John or George Mowlem Burt.

1912   Meets R. E. M. Wheeler (REMW), probably when both serve on
            the University College Literary Society Committee, Rik as one of
            the Vice-Presidents and Tessa as the sole Secretary and Treasurer.
            Passes Intermediate Arts Exams.

1913   Tessa and REMW become engaged.

1914   Marries REMW after he is appointed a Junior Investigator for the
            Royal Commission on Historical Monuments. Leaves UCL just
            before taking final exams. REMW volunteers for the University of
            London Officer's Training Corps, before being sent to the Royal
            Field Artillery for most of the War. He and Tessa Verney Wheeler
            (TVW) live with his family at Herne Hill in London.

1915   TVW gives birth to Michael Wheeler (only child of the marriage).

1915–17   TVW is first female assistant surveyor of Income Tax for duration
            of war. TVW and REMW move around various army camps in
            England and Scotland until he is sent to France in 1917.

1919   REMW returns home after demobilisation and the family move to
            16 Taviton Street, London. He resumes his post at the Royal
            Commission on Historical Monuments.

1920   REMW accepts a position as Keeper of Archaeology at the
            National Museum of Wales. They move to Cardiff.

1921   Summer excavations begin at the Roman fort of Segontium at
            Caernarvon. TVW's first direct exposure to archaeology.

1922   The Segontium excavation is concluded. REMW publishes the
            first version of what will become his first book, *Segontium and the
            Roman Occupation of Wales* (1924).

1924   REMW appointed Director of the National Museum of Wales. Summer excavations begin at the Brecon Gaer in the Brecon Beacons. TVW plays an increasingly large role in site recording and finances. Assisted by C. F. C. Hawkes and J. N. L. Myres, then of New College, Oxford. Myres and TVW form a lasting friendship and she begins to help him in his professional career. Becomes first woman president of the Archaeological Section of the Cardiff Naturalists' Society. Lectures throughout Cardiff.

1925   Summer excavations at the Brecon Gaer are concluded.

1926   REMW accepts a post as Keeper of the London Museum, and leaves Wales. TVW remains behind to finish current archaeological projects, travelling to London on weekends. TVW begins to excavate the amphitheatre of the Roman fort Isca at Caerleon, working almost completely independently. REMW publishes *The Roman Fort Near Brecon*.

1927   Excavations at Caerleon are concluded. TVW hands the site off to V. E. Nash-Williams upon leaving, beginning an extensive correspondence between the two. Joins REMW in London. TVW and REMW run the London Museum together, with separate offices in the museum building. She begins extensive lecturing throughout London and area. Joins committee of the British School of Archaeology in Egypt. Discussion of a London Institute of Archaeology begins.

1928   TVW publishes for the first time, with 'The Caerleon Amphitheatre: A Summary' appearing in the June volume of *Archaeologia Cambrensis*. REMW and TVW co-publish *The Roman Amphitheatre at Caerleon, Monmouthshire*. The Wheelers begin to excavate Lydney Park, Gloucestershire. TVW appointed part-time lecturer by the London Society. Becomes Fellow of the Society of Antiquaries of London and is soon appointed to its Council. Takes over regular gallery and school lectures at the Museum of London. Lectures extensively in London and throughout the surrounding regions over the next eight years.

1929   The excavations at Lydney Park are concluded.

1930   The Wheelers begin to excavate at Verulamium (St Albans).

1931   Museum of London votes TVW yearly salary of £190 for her lecturing work.

1932   REMW and TVW co-publish *Report on the Excavation of the Prehistoric, Roman, and Post-Roman site in Lydney Park, Gloucestershire*.

1933   The excavations at Verulamium are concluded.

1934   Excavations begin at Maiden Castle in Dorset. The Institute of Archaeology is founded on paper, though as yet there is no physical institution. REMW is its first Honorary Director.

1935   Appointed Chairman of the British School of Archaeology in Egypt's Executive Committee. Appointed to Research Committee of the Society of Antiquaries.

1936   REMW and TVW co-publish *Verulamium: A Belgic and Two Roman Cities* (Oxford). The lease of St John's Lodge, Regent's Park, is concluded for the Institute of Archaeology. TVW dies at the National Temperance Hospital after a minor operation goes wrong.

1937   St John's Lodge opens as the Institute of Archaeology. It is dedicated to TVW. The excavations at Maiden Castle are concluded.

1943   REMW publishes *Maiden Castle, Dorset*.

APPENDIX 2

Tessa Verney Wheeler: An Ongoing Bibliography

By T. Verney Wheeler

1928. 'The Caerleon Amphitheatre: A Summary, *Archaeologia Cambrensis* (June), 1–32.

1929. 'Pipe-Burial', *Antiquaries Journal* 9.

1930. 'The Preliminary Excavations of Verulamium, 1930', *Transactions of the St. Albans and Hertfordshire Architectural and Archaeological Society 1930*.

1931. 'Summary of the Verulamium Excavations, 1931', *Transactions of the St. Albans and Hertfordshire Architectural and Archaeological Society 1931*.

1933. 'Experiment in Removing a Fragment of a Roman Pavement', *Museums Journal* 33, 104–6.

1934a. 'Gold Rings from London', *Antiquaries Journal* 14, 430–31.

1934b. 'Recherches à Salone, Tome II' (book review), *Journal of Roman Studies* 24, 100–1.

1935. 'Gold Ring from London [note]', *Antiquaries Journal* 15, 79.

1937. 'A Hoard of Radiate Coins from the Verulamium Theatre', *Numismatic Chronicle* XVII, 211–28.

By R. E. M. Wheeler and T. Verney Wheeler

1928. *The Roman Amphitheatre at Caerleon, Monmouthshire* (London).

1932a. *Report on the Excavation of the Prehistoric, Roman, and Post-Roman site in Lydney Park, Gloucestershire* (Oxford).

1932b. 'Summary of the Verulamium Excavations, 1932', *Transactions of the St. Albans and Hertfordshire Architectural and Archaeological Society 1932*.

1936. *Verulamium: A Belgic and Two Roman Cities* (Oxford).

1952. *The Roman Amphitheatre, Caerleon* (London).

Bibliography

Adams, H. F., Bradburn, E., and Boon, George C., 1965. 'Coal from the Legionary Fortress of Caerleon, Monmouthshire', *Geological Magazine* 102.6, 469–73.

Adamson, David, 1999. 'The Intellectual and the National Movement in Wales', in Fevre and Thompson (1999: ch. 3).

Allen, J. R. L., 2003. 'The Building Stone at the Roman Religious Complex, Lydney Park, Gloucestershire: Character and Fate', *Archaeological Journal* 160, 229–33.

Annan, Lord, 1991. 'Introduction', in Harte and North (1991).

Anon., 1995. *The Romans in Breconshire and Radnorshire: A Field Guide* (Borth).

Arwill-Nordbladh, Elisabeth, 1998. 'Archaeology, Gender, and Emancipation: The Paradox of Hanna Rydh', in Díaz-Andreu and Sørensen (1998: 155–74).

Bahn, Paul G., 1984. 'Do Not Disturb? Archaeology and the Rights of the Dead', *Oxford Journal of Archaeology* 3.1, 127–39.

——(ed.), 1996. *The Cambridge Illustrated History of Archaeology* (Cambridge).

Bathurst, W. H., 1879. *Roman antiquities at Lydney Park, Gloucestershire. Being a posthumous work of the Rev. William Hiley Bathurst, M. A. With notes by C. W. King* (London).

Beaumont, Caitriona, 2001. 'The Women's Movement: Politics and Citizenship, 1918–1950s', in Zweiniger-Bargielowska (2001: 262–77).

Beddoe, Deirdre, 1988. 'Women between the Wars', in Herbert and Jones (1988).

Bell, Gertrude, 1894. *Persian Pictures* (London).

Benson, E. F., 1935. *Lucia's Progress* (London).

Bentley, Michael (ed.), 1997. *Contexts for the Writing of History* (London).

Berg, Maxine, 1996. *A Woman in History: Eileen Power, 1889–1940* (Cambridge).

Bledisloe, Lord, 1929. 'The Antiquities of Lydney, Gloucestershire, England', *Transactions of the Bristol and Gloucestershire Archaeological Society* 51.

Boon, George C., 1962. 'The Roman Sword from Caernarvon-Segontium', *Bulletin of the Board of Celtic Studies* 19, 85–9.

——1966. 'Gilt Glass Beads from Caerleon and Elsewhere', *Bulletin of the Board of Celtic Studies* 22.1, 104–9.

——1972. *Isca: The Roman Legionary Fortress at Caerleon, Mon.* (Cardiff).

—— 1976. 'Segontium Fifty Years On, I: A Roman Stave of Larch-Wood and Other Unpublished Finds Mainly of Organic Materials, Together with a Note on Late Barracks', *Archaeologia Cambrensis* 124 (1975), 52–67.

—— 1977a. 'Segontium Fifty Years On, II: The Coins', *Archaeologia Cambrensis* 125 (1976), 40–79.

—— 1977b. 'Sir Mortimer Wheeler, 1890–1976 (President, 1931–1932)', *Archaeologia Cambrensis* 125 (1976), 172–3.

—— 1987. *The Legionary Fortress Of Caerleon-Isca* (Caerleon).

Bosanquet, R. C., and King, Frank (with appendix by George C. Boon), 1963. 'Excavations at Caerleon, 1909', *Monmouthshire Antiquary* 1.3.

Braybon, Gail, 1981. *Women Workers in the First World War* (London).

—— and Summerfield, Penny, 1987. *Out of the Cage: Women's Experiences in Two World Wars* (London).

Brewer, Richard J., 1987. *Caerleon-Isca: The Roman Legionary Museum* (Cardiff).

Bruley, Sue, 1999. *Women in Britain Since 1900* (London).

Byrne, Stephen, 1965. *The Changing Face of Lewisham* (Lewisham).

Carr, Lydia, 2007. 'Tessa Verney Wheeler, Archaeologist: An Introductory Note', *Bulletin of the Association for Roman Archaeology* 18, 7–10.

—— 2008a. 'Joining the Ladies: Women and the Society of Antiquaries', *Current Archaeology* 216, 40–44.

—— 2008b. 'Research-in-Progress Statement: Tessa Verney Wheeler, Women and Archaeology Before World War II', *Bulletin of the History of Archaeology* (May).

Casey, P. J., 1975. 'Excavations Outside the North-East Gate of Segontium, 1971', *Archaeologia Cambrensis* 123 (1974), 54–77.

—— and Davies, J. L., with Evans, J., 1993. *Excavations at Segontium (Carnarfon) Roman Fort, 1975–1979*. CBA [Council for British Archaeology] Research Report 90 (Bootham).

—— and Hoffman, B., 1999. 'Roman Temple Excavations, Lydney Park, Gloucestershire, 1980–1981', *Antiquaries Journal* 79, 81–143.

Castle, Kathryn, 1996. *Britannia's Children: Reading Colonialism through Children's Books and Magazines* (Manchester).

Caton-Thompson, Gertrude, 1983. *Mixed Memoirs* (Gateshead).

Champion, Sara, 1998. 'Women in British Archaeology: Visible and Invisible', in Díaz-Andreu and Sørensen (1998: 175–97).

Champion, Tim, 1996. 'Three Nations or One? Britain and the National Use of the Past', in Díaz-Andreu and Champion (1996a: 119–45).

Christie (Mallowan), Agatha, 1946. *Come, Tell Me How You Live* (London).

Christie, Agatha, 1977. *Agatha Christie: An Autobiography* (Glasgow).

Claessen, Cheryl (ed.), 1992a. *Exploring Gender Through Archaeology: Selected Papers from the 1991 Boone Conference* (Madison, WI).

260 Bibliography

——(tr. and ed.), 1992b. 'Workshop 3: Teaching and Seeing Gender', in Claassen (1992a: 137–53).

——(ed.), 1994. *Women in Archaeology* (Philadelphia).

——1996. 'Equity Issues for Women in Archaeology' (book review), *American Antiquity* 61.2, 421–2.

Cohen, Getzel M., and Joukowsky, Martha Sharp (eds), 2004. *Breaking Ground: Pioneering Women Archaeologists* (Ann Arbor, Mich.).

Collingwood, R. G., 1939. *An Autobiography* (Oxford).

Collinson, Patrick, 2004. 'Pollard, Albert Frederick (1869–1948)', in *Oxford Dictionary of National Biography* (Oxford).

Conkey, Margaret W., and Spector, Janet D., 1998. 'Archaeology and the Study of Gender', in Hays-Gilpin and Whitley (1998: 11–45).

Corder, P., 1938. *The Verulamium Museum and its Collections* (St Albans).

Crawford, O. G. S., 1955. *Said and Done: The Autobiography of an Archaeologist* (London).

Cunliffe, Barry, 1984. *Roman Bath Discovered* (London).

——2002. 'Antiquity and Britain', *Antiquity* 76.294, 1112–15.

Daniel, Glyn, 1981. *A Short History of Archaeology* (London).

——1986. *Some Small Harvest: The Memoirs of Glyn Daniel* (London).

——and Chippindale, Christopher (eds), 1958. *The Pastmasters: Eleven Modern Pioneers of Archaeology* (London).

Daunton, Martin, 2002. *Just Taxes* (London).

Davies, Charlotte Aull, 1989. *Welsh Nationalism in the Twentieth Century* (London).

Dever, William G., 2004. 'Kathleen Kenyon: 1906–1978', in Cohen and Joukowsky (2004: 525–53).

Dews, N., 1884. *The History of Deptford* (London).

Díaz-Andreu, Margarita, 1998. 'Spanish Women in a Changing World: Strategies in the Search for Self-Fulfilment through Antiquities', in Díaz-Andreu and Sørensen (1998: 125–45).

——2005. 'Gender identity', in Díaz-Andreu et al. (2005: 13–42).

——and Champion, Tim (eds), 1996a. *Nationalism and Archaeology in Europe* (London).

——— 1996b. 'Nationalism and Archaeology in Europe: An Introduction', in Díaz-Andreu and Champion (1996a: 1–23).

——and Lucy, Sam, 2005. 'Introduction', in Díaz-Andreu et al. (2005: 1–12).

——— Babic, Stasa, and Edwards, David N. (eds), 2005. *The Archaeology of Identity: Approaches to Gender, Age, Status, Ethnicity and Religion* (London).

——and Sørensen, Marie Louise Stig (eds), 1998. *Excavating Women: A History of Women in European Archaeology* (London).

Dickens, A. G., 1966. 'Introduction', in Pollard (1966).

Drower, Margaret S., 1985. *Flinders Petrie: A Life in Archaeology* (London).

—— 2004a. 'Hilda Mary Isobel Petrie, née Urlin, 1987–1956', accessed at: http://www.brown.edu/Research/Breaking.

—— 2004b. 'Margaret Alice Murray: 1863–1963', in Cohen and Joukowsky (2004: 109–41).

Dyhouse, Carol, 2001. 'Education', in Zweiniger-Bargielowska (2001: 119–33).

Elsner, Jas, and Rutherford, Ian, 2005. *Pilgrimage in Graeco-Roman and Early Christian Antiquity: Seeing the Gods* (Oxford).

Evans, D. R., and Metcalf, V. M., 1992. *Roman Gates Caerleon: The 'Roman Gates' Site in the Fortress of the Second Augustan Legion at Caerleon, Gwent. The Excavations of the Roman Buildings and Evidence for Early Medieval Activity* (Oxford).

Evans, Edith, 2000. *The Caerleon Canabae: Excavations in the Civil Settlement 1984–90.* Britannia Monograph Series No. 16 (Swansea).

Evans, Joan, 1956. *A History of the Society of Antiquaries* (Oxford).

Farrar, R. A. H., 1957. 'Charles Douglas Drew: An Appreciation', *Proceedings of the Dorset Natural History and Archaeological Society* 78, 10–17.

Fevre, Ralph, and Thompson, Andrew (eds), 1999. *Nation, Identity and Social Theory: Perspectives from Wales* (Cardiff).

Fotou, Vasso, and Brown, Ann, 2004. 'Harriet Boyd Hawes: 1871–1945', in Cohen and Joukowsky (2004: 198–273).

Fox, Aileen, 1941. *The Roman Legionary Fortress at Caerleon in Monmouthshire: Report on the Excavations Carried Out in Myrtle Cottage Orchard in 1939* (Cardiff).

—— 2000. *Aileen: A Pioneering Archaeologist* (Leominster).

Fox, Cyril, 1936. 'Tessa Verney Wheeler, F.S.A.', *Museums Journal* 36, 107.

Frere , Sheppard, 1972. *Verulamium Excavations I* (London).

—— 1983. *Verulamium Excavations II* (London).

—— 1984. *Verulamium Excavations III* (Oxford).

Gaddis, John Lewis, 2002. *The Landscape of History: How Historians Map the Past* (Oxford).

Gero, Joan, 1985. 'Socio-politics of Archaeology and the Woman-at-Home Ideology', *American Antiquity* 50, 342–50.

—— 1988. 'Gender Bias in Archaeology: Here, Then, and Now', in Rosser (1988: 33–43).

—— and Conkey, Margaret W. (eds), 1991. *Engendering Archaeology: Women and Prehistory* (Oxford).

Gilchrist, Roberta, 1998. 'Women's Archaeology? Political Feminism, Gender Theory, and Historical Revision', in Hays-Gilpin and Whitley (1998: 47–56).

Giles, Judy, 1995. *Women, Identity and Private Life in Britain, 1900–50* (New York).

Gill, David, 2004. 'Grimes, William Francis (1905–1988)', in *Oxford Dictionary of National Biography* (Oxford).

Greep, S. J. (ed.), 1993. *Roman Towns: The Wheeler Inheritance. A Review of 50 Years' Research* (York).

Grimes, W. F., 1945. 'Maiden Castle' (book review), *Antiquity* 19.73, 6–10.

Hall, Lesley A., 2001. 'Sexuality', in Zweiniger-Bargielowska (2001: 51–85).

——2004. 'Stopes, Marie Charlotte Carmichael (1880–1958)', in *Oxford Dictionary of National Biography* (Oxford).

Hall, R., 1977. *Marie Stopes: A Biography* (London).

Hammerton, A. James, 1979. *Emigrant Gentlewomen: Genteel Poverty and Female Emigration, 1830–1914* (London).

Hardy, Thomas, 1885. 'Ancient Earthworks and What Two Enthusiastic Scientists Found Therein', *Detroit Post*, 15 March.

Harris, J., 1993. *Private Lives, Public Spirit: A Social History of Britain* (Oxford).

Harte, Negley, and North, John, 1991. *The World of University College London, 1828–1990* (London).

Hawkes, Christopher, 1930. *The Roman Legionary Fortress at Caerleon in Monmouthshire: Report on the Excavations Carried out in the Eastern Corner in 1929* (Cardiff).

——1932. 'Report on the excavation of the prehistoric, Roman, and Post-Roman site in Lydney Park, Gloucestershire' (book review), *Antiquity* 6.24, 488–90.

——1944. 'Maiden Castle, Dorset' (book review), *Journal of Roman Studies* 34, 155–7.

——1958. 'Christopher Hawkes', in Daniel and Chippindale (1958: 46–60).

——1982. 'Archaeological Retrospect no. 3', *Antiquity* 56.217, 93–101.

Hawkes, Jacquetta, 1982. *Adventurer in Archaeology: The Biography of Sir Mortimer Wheeler* (New York).

Hays-Gilpin, Kelley, and Whitley, David S., 1998a. 'Introduction: Gendering the Past', in Hays-Gilpin and Whitley (1998b: 4–10).

——— (eds), 1998b. *Reader in Gender Archaeology* (London).

Hayter, A. G. K., 1921. 'Excavations at Segontium, 1920', *Archaeologia Cambrensis* (June), 1–36.

Henig, Martin, 1984. *Religion in Roman Britain* (London).

——1985. *The Art of Roman Britain* (London).

Herbert, Trevor, and Jones, Gareth Elwyn (eds), 1988. *Wales Between the Wars* (Cardiff).

Holton, Sandra Stanley, 2001. 'The Women's Movement, Politics and Citizenship from the Late Nineteenth Century Until 1918', in Zweiniger-Bargielowska (2001: 247–61).

Hopkins, Deian, 1988. 'Social Reactions to Economic Change', in Herbert and Jones (1988).

Hudson, Keith, 1981. *A Social History of Archaeology: The British Experience* (London).

Hufton, Olwen, 1997. 'Women, Gender, and the *Fin de Siècle*', in Bentley (1997: 929–40).

Jaff, Fay, 1963. *They Came To South Africa* (London).

Janssen, Rosalind, 1992. *The First Hundred Years: Egyptology at University College London, 1892–1992* (London).

——and Janssen, Jac, 1996. *Getting Old in Ancient Egypt* (London).

Jones, Helen, 2001. 'Health and Reproduction', in Zweiniger-Bargielowska (2001: 86–101).

Jorgensen, Lise Bender, 1998. 'The State of Denmark: Lis Jacobsen and Other Women in and around Archaeology', in Díaz-Andreu and Sørensen (1998: 214–34).

Kehoe, Alice, 1992. 'The Muted Class: Unshackling Tradition', in Claassen (1992: 23–32).

Kenyon, Frederic, 1936. 'Anniversary Address', *Antiquaries Journal* 16, 250–9.

Kenyon, Kathleen, 1934. 'The Roman Theatre at Verulamium, St. Albans', *Archaeologia* 84, 213–61.

——1961. *Beginning in Archaeology* (London).

Kilbride-Jones, Howard, 1990. 'The Experience of Knowing Childe and Wheeler', *Archaeology Ireland* 4.3 (Bray, Ireland), 18–20.

Kilburn, Peter, 2008. 'The Kilburn Family of Witton le Wear, Bishop Auckland and Canada'. Unpublished genealogical manuscript.

Knight, J. K., 2003. *Caerleon Roman Fortress* (Cardiff).

Lamberg-Karlovsky, C. C., 1976. 'Robert Eric Mortimer Wheeler', *Journal of Field Archaeology* 3, 472–4.

Lane, Margaret, 1968. *The Tale of Beatrix Potter: A Biography* (London).

Lee, John Edward, 1862. *Isca Silurum; or, an Illustrated Catalogue of the Museum of Antiquities at Caerleon* (London).

——1868. *Supplement to Isca Silurum; or an Illustrated Catalogue of the Museum of Antiquities at Caerleon* (Newport).

Light, Alison, 2007. *Mrs Woolf and the Servants* (London).

London Museum, 1972. *Guide to the London Museum* (London).

Lowther, Anthony W. G., 1935. *The Roman Theatre at Verulamium (St. Albans): A Reconstruction* (London).

MacGillivray, Joseph Alexander, 2000. *Minotaur: Sir Arthur Evans and the Archaeology of the Minoan Myth* (London).

Magee, Gary B., and Thompson, Andrew S., 2010. *Empire and Globalisation: Networks of People, Goods and Capital in the British World, c.1850–1914* (Cambridge).

Mallowan, M. E. L., 1977. *Mallowan's Memoirs* (London).

Mattingly, Harold B., 1971. 'The Verulamium (1960) Hoard of "Barbarous Radiates"', *Britannia* 2, 196–9.

McIntosh, Jane, 2004. 'Wheeler, Tessa Verney (1893–1936)', in *Oxford Dictionary of National Biography* (Oxford).

McKenzie, K., 2005. *Scandal in the Colonies: 1820–1850* (Melbourne).

Meredith, M., 2007. *Diamonds, Gold, and War: The British, the Boers, and the Making of South Africa* (London).

Moore, Donald, 1975. *Caerleon: Fortress of the Legion* (Cardiff).

Moore, Doris Langley, 1966. *E. Nesbit: A Biography* (Philadephia).

Moorey, P. R. S., 1992. 'British Women in Near Eastern Archaeology: Kathleen Kenyon and the Pioneers', *Palestine Exploration Quarterly* 124, 91–100

Morgan, Prys, 1975. *Iolo Morganwg* (Cardiff).

Moss, Michael, 1997. 'Archives, the Historian, and the Future', in Bentley (1997: 960–73).

Murray, Lynda J., 2004. 'Keiller, Alexander (1889–1955)', in *Oxford Dictionary of National Biography* (Oxford).

Murray, Margaret, 1904. *The Osireion at Abydos* (London).

—— 1963. *My First Hundred Years* (London).

Myres, J. N. L., 1938. 'Verulamium: A Belgic and Two Roman Cities' (book review), *Antiquity* 12.45, 16–25.

Nash-Williams, V. E., 1927. 'Note on the Roman Name of Caerleon', *Archaeologia Cambrensis* (December), 378–9.

—— 1930. *The Roman Legionary Fortress at Caerleon in Monmouthshire: Report on the excavations carried out in Jenkins's Field in 1926* (Cardiff).

—— 1931. 'The Roman Legionary Fortress at Caerleon in Monmouthshire: Report on the Excavations Carried out in the Prysg Field in 1927–29', *Archaeologia Cambrensis* 1931, 99–157.

—— 1932. 'The Roman Legionary Fortress at Caerleon in Monmouthshire: Report on the Excavations Carried out in the Prysg Field in 1927–29, Part II: The Finds', *Archaeologia Cambrensis* 1932, 48–104.

—— 1933. *The Roman Legionary Fortress at Caerleon in Monmouthshire: Report on the Excavations Carried out in the Prysg Field in 1927–29, Part III: The Finds of Pottery, Together with Notes on the Plant and Animal Remains* (Cardiff).

—— (with a preface by Cyril Fox), 1946. *The Roman Legionary Fortress at Caerleon, Monmouthshire* (Cardiff).

—— 1951. 'Note on the Site of the Roman Legionary Fortress at Caerleon, Monmouthshire', *Bulletin of the Board of Celtic Studies* 14.2, 176–7.

—— and Nash-Williams, A. H., 1935. *Catalogue of the Roman Inscribed and Sculptured Stones Found at Caerleon, Monmouthshire* (Cardiff).

National Museum of Wales, 1926. *Annual Report 1925–1926* (Cardiff).

—— 1957. *National Museum of Wales Jubilee: 1907–1957* (Cardiff).

—— 1977. *National Museum of Wales 1927-77* (Cardiff).

Neale, J. E., 1949. 'Albert Frederick Pollard', *English Historical Review* 64.251, 198-205.

Nesbit, Edith, 1899. *The Story of the Treasure-Seekers* (Cambridge).

—— 1909. *Harding's Luck* (London).

Niblett, R., 2000. *Roman Verulamium* (St Albans).

—— 2001. *Verulamium: The Roman City of St. Albans* (Stroud).

—— and Thompson, I., 2005. *Alban's Buried Towns: An Assessment of St. Albans' Archaeology up to AD 1600* (Oxford).

Oram, Alison, 1996. *Women Teachers and Feminist Politics, 1900-1939* (Manchester).

Owen, Roderic (with Tristan de Vere Cole), 1974. *Beautiful and Beloved: The Life of Mavis de Vere Cole* (London).

Pearsall, R., 1973: *Edwardian Life and Leisure* (Newton Abbot).

Peers, Charles, 1936. 'Obituary Notice: Mrs. Mortimer Wheeler', *Antiquaries Journal* 16, 327-8.

Petrie, William Flinders, 1931. *Seventy Years in Archaeology* (London).

Piggott, Stuart, 1958. 'Stuart Piggott', in Daniel and Chippindale (1958: 20-33).

—— 1977. 'Robert Eric Mortimer Wheeler, 10 September 1890-22 July 1976', *Biographical Memoirs of Fellows of the Royal Society* 23, 623-42.

Pollard, A. F., 1907. *Factors in Modern History* (London).

—— 1966. *Wolsey: Church and State in Sixteenth-Century England* (New York).

Port, M. H., 2004. 'Burt family (*per. c.*1830-1964)', in *Oxford Dictionary of National Biography* (Oxford).

Prag, Kay, 1992. 'Kathleen Kenyon and Archaeology in the Holy Land', *Palestine Exploration Quarterly* 124, 109-23.

Ralegh Redford, C. A., 1947. *The Roman Fort of Segontium, Caernarvonshire* (London).

Read, Joan, 1992. *Lewisham Local History*, vol. 1 (Lewisham, London).

Renfrew, Colin, and Bahn, Paul, 2000. *Archaeology: Theories, Methods and Practice* (London).

Richmond, I. A., 1960. 'Roman Britain, 1910-1960', *Journal of Roman Studies* 50, 173-91.

Robinson, Annabel, 2002. *The Life and Work of Jane Ellen Harrison* (Oxford).

Roman Legionary Museum, 1987. *Souvenir Program to Celebrate the Opening of the Roman Legionary Museum: Isca: Roman Festival and Victorian Far, Caerleon, Gwent, Saturday, 13 June, 1987* (Caerleon).

Root, Margaret Cool, 2004. 'Introduction. Women of the Field: Defining the Gendered Experience', in Cohen and Joukowsky (2004: 1-33).

Rose, J., 1986. *The Edwardian Temperament 1895-1919* (Athens, OH).

Rosser, Sue (ed.), 1988. *Feminism within the Science and Health Care Professions:. Overcoming Resistance* (New York).

Sanders, Ronald H., and Gill, David W. J., 2004. 'Theresa B. Goell, 1901–1985', in Cohen and Joukowsky (2004: 482–524).

Scott, Joan Wallach, 1999. *Gender and the Politics of History* (New York).

Seton-Williams, M. V., 1988. *The Road to El-Aguzein* (London).

Sharples, Niall M., 1991. *English Heritage Book of Maiden Castle* (London).

Sheppard, Francis, 1991. *The Treasury of London's Past: An Historical Account of the Museum of London and its Predecessors, the Guildhall Museums and the London Museum* (London).

Shorter, Edward, 1977. *The Making of the Modern Family* (New York).

Simpson, Grace, 1962. 'Caerleon and the Roman Forts in Wales in the Second Century A.D.: Part I—Caerleon and Northern Wales', *Archaeologia Cambrensis* 111, 103–66.

Smith, David, 1988. 'Wales between the Wars', in Herbert and Jones (1988).

Smith, P. J., 2004. 'A Splendid Idiosyncrasy: Prehistory at Cambridge, 1915–50', D.Phil thesis, University of Cambridge.

Sørensen, Marie Louise Stig, 1998. 'Rescue and Recovery: On Historiographies of Female Archaeologists', in Díaz-Andreu and Sørensen (1998: 31–60).

Stone, S., 1965. *The Changing Face of Lewisham* (London).

Sutherland, Gillian, 1990. 'The Plainest Principles of Justice: The University of London and the Higher Education of Women', in Thompson (1990a: ch. 2).

Sweely, Tracy, 1994. 'Male Hunting Camp or Female Processing Station: An Evolution within a Discipline', in Claassen (1994: 173–81).

Szreter, Simon, and Fisher, Kate, 2010. *Sex Before The Sexual Revolution: Intimate Life in England 1918–1963* (London).

Taylor, M. V., 1938. 'Verulamium: A Belgic and Two Roman Cities' (book review), *Journal of Roman Studies* 28, 107–8.

Taylor, D., 1968. *The Godless Students of Gower Street* (London).

Thomas, Dennis, 1988. 'Economic Decline', in Herbert and Jones (1988).

Thompson, F. M. L. (ed.), 1990a. *The University of London and the World of Learning, 1836–1986* (London).

—— 1990b. 'The Humanities', in Thompson (1990a: ch. 3).

Thompson, P., 1975. *The Edwardians: The Remaking of British Society* (London).

Todd, Malcolm, 1984. 'The Early Roman Phase at Maiden Castle', *Britannia* 15, 254–5.

Tolkien, J. R. R., 1995. *The Letters of J. R. R. Tolkien* (New York).

Various, 1920. *How to Observe in Archaeology* (London).

Verney Wheeler, T., 1928. 'The Caerleon Amphitheatre: A Summary', *Archaeologia Cambrensis* (June), 1–32.

—— 1929. 'Pipe-Burial', *Antiquaries Journal* 9.

—— 1930. 'The Preliminary Excavations of Verulamium, 1930', *Transactions of the St. Albans and Hertfordshire Architectural and Archaeological Society 1930.*

—— 1931. 'Summary of the Verulamium Excavations, 1931', *Transactions of the St. Albans and Hertfordshire Architectural and Archaeological Society 1931.*

—— 1933. 'Experiment in Removing a Fragment of a Roman Pavement', *Museums Journal* 33, 104–6.

—— 1934a. 'Gold Rings from London', *Antiquaries Journal* 14, 430–1.

—— 1934b. 'Recherches à Salone, Tome II' (book review), *Journal of Roman Studies* 24, 100–1.

—— 1935. 'Gold Ring from London [note]', *Antiquaries Journal* 15, 79.

—— 1937. 'A Hoard of Radiate Coins from the Verulamium Theatre', *Numismatic Chronicle* 17, 211–28.

Webb, Sidney, 1904. *London Education* (London).

—— 1907. 'London Secondary Schools: Work of the L.C.C.', *Educational Times* (March), 132.

Webster, Diana Bonakis, 1991. *Hawkeseye: The Early Life of Christopher Hawkes* (Stroud).

Wedlake, William. Unpublished and undated manuscript autobiography. Somerset and Taunton County Records Office.

Wheeler, R. E. M., 1921. 'Segontium Excavations, 1921', *Archaeologia Cambrensis* (December), 170–204.

—— 1922a. *Roman and Native in Wales: An Imperial Frontier Problem* (London).

—— 1922b. 'Segontium Excavations, 1922: Part One', *Archaeologia Cambrensis* (December), 258–326.

—— 1923. 'Segontium Excavations, 1922: Part Two', *Archaeologia Cambrensis* (June), 1–27.

—— 1924. *Segontium and the Roman Occupation of Wales* (London).

—— 1925. *Prehistoric and Roman Wales* (Oxford).

—— 1926. *The Roman Fort Near Brecon* (London).

—— 1929a. 'A Roman Pipe-Burial from Caerleon, Monmouthshire', *Antiquaries Journal* 9.1, 1–7.

—— 1932a. 'A Prehistoric Metropolis: The First Verulamium', *Antiquity* 6.22, 133–47.

—— 1932b. 'Wales and Archaeology', *Proceedings of the British Academy* 15, 1–11.

—— 1935. 'The Excavation of Maiden Castle, Dorset: First Interim Report', *Antiquaries Journal* 15, 265–75.

—— 1936. 'The Excavation of Maiden Castle, Dorset: Second Interim Report', *Antiquaries Journal* 16, 265–83.

—— 1937a. 'The Excavation of Maiden Castle, Dorset: Third Interim Report', *Antiquaries Journal* 17, 261–82.

—— 1937b. *Twenty-Five Years of the London Museum: An Album of Photographs Illustrating the Range of the Collections* (London).

—— 1943. *Maiden Castle, Dorset* (Oxford).

—— 1954. *Archaeology from the Earth* (Oxford).

—— 1955. *Still Digging* (London).

—— 1957. *Roman Archaeology in Wales: A Tribute to V. E. Nash-Williams* (London).

—— 1966. *Alms for Oblivion: An Antiquary's Scrapbook* (London).

—— and Verney Wheeler, T., 1928. *The Roman Amphitheatre at Caerleon, Monmouthshire* (London).

—— —— 1932a. *Report on the Excavation of the Prehistoric, Roman, and Post-Roman Site in Lydney Park, Gloucestershire* (Oxford).

—— —— 1932b. 'Summary of the Verulamium Excavations, 1932', *Transactions of the St. Albans and Hertfordshire Architectural and Archaeological Society 1932*.

—— —— 1936. *Verulamium: A Belgic and Two Roman Cities* (Oxford).

—— —— 1952. *The Roman Amphitheatre, Caerleon* (London).

Wilkes, John, 1992. 'Kathleen Kenyon in Roman Britain', *Palestine Exploration Quarterly* 124, 101–8.

Williams, Charlotte, 1999. 'Passports to Wales? Race, Nation, and Identity', in Fevre and Thompson (1999: ch. 4).

Wills, W. H., and Barrett, R. J., 1905. *The Anglo-African Who's Who and Biographical Sketchbook* (London).

Woodall, J. Ned, and Perricone, Philip J., 1981. 'The Archaeologist as Cowboy: The Consequence of Professional Stereotype', *Journal of Field Archaeology* 8, 506–9.

Woolf, Virginia, 1929. *A Room of One's Own* (London).

Woolley, Leonard, 1953. *Spadework: Adventures in Archaeology* (London).

Wright, R. P., 1985. 'A Revised Restoration of the Inscription on the Mosaic Pavement Found in the Temple at Lydney Park, Gloucestershire', *Britannia* 16, 248–9.

Zienkiewicz, J. David, 1986. *The Legionary Fortress Baths at Caerleon*, II: *The Finds* (Cardiff).

Zweiniger-Bargielowska, Ina (ed.), 2001. *Women in Twentieth-Century Britain* (Harlow).

Archives

Addey and Stanhope School minutes, 1908–1911 (ASSM).

Cadw archives (CADW). Plas Carew, Parc Nantgarw, Wales.

Archives of the Dorset Natural History and Archaeological Society at the Dorset County Museum (DCMA). Dorset County Museum, Dorchester.

General Register Office, London.

C. F. C. Hawkes papers. Bodleian Library, University of Oxford.
Jacquetta Hawkes archives (JHA). J. B. Priestley Library, University of Bradford.
Local History and Archives Centre, Lewisham Library, London.
Lydney Park Museum archives. Lydney Park, Gloucestershire.
National Museum of Wales archives (NMWA). National Museum of Wales, Cardiff.
Society of Antiquaries of London archives (SALA). Society of Antiquaries, London.
UCL Records Office archives (UCLA). University College London.
Verulamium excavation archives (VMA). Verulamium Museum, St Albans.
William Wedlake archive. Somerset County Records Office (SCRO), Taunton, Somerset.
Museum of London archives (MOLA). London Museum, London.
J. N. L. Myres papers, Bodleian Library, University of Oxford.
Wheeler family papers (WFP). Access provided by Carol Wheeler Pettman.

Interviews

All interviews were conducted and recorded by the author. By request, only sources who were contacted and then agreed to an interview have been listed here.

Beatrice de Cardi: 14 November 2006, London.
Cecil Davies: 1 December 2006, Caerleon, Gwent.
Margaret Drower: 19 January 2007, London.
Carol Wheeler Pettman: 10 January 2007, Bramley, Hampshire.

Index